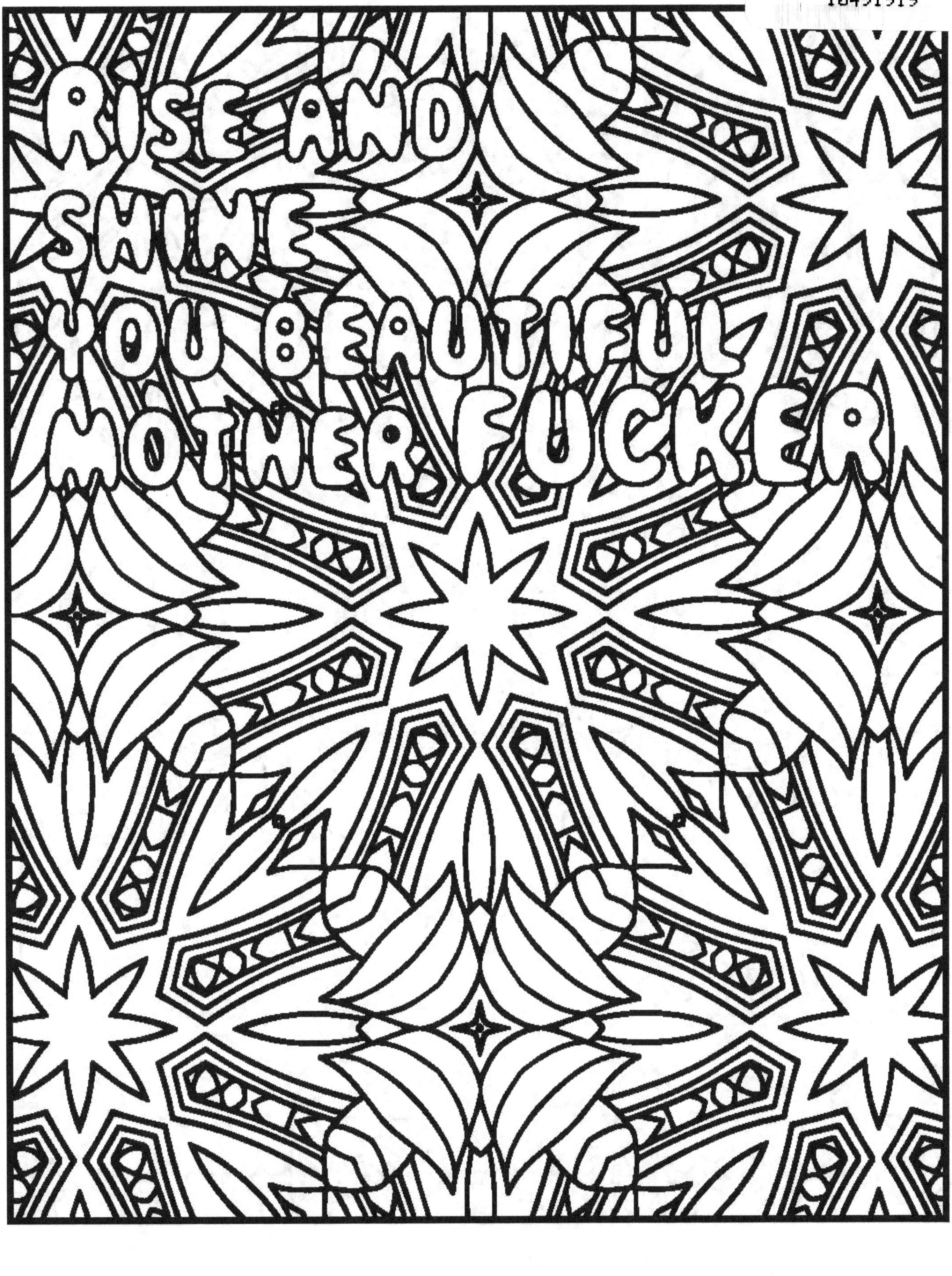
RISE AND
SHINE
YOU BEAUTIFUL
MOTHER FUCKER

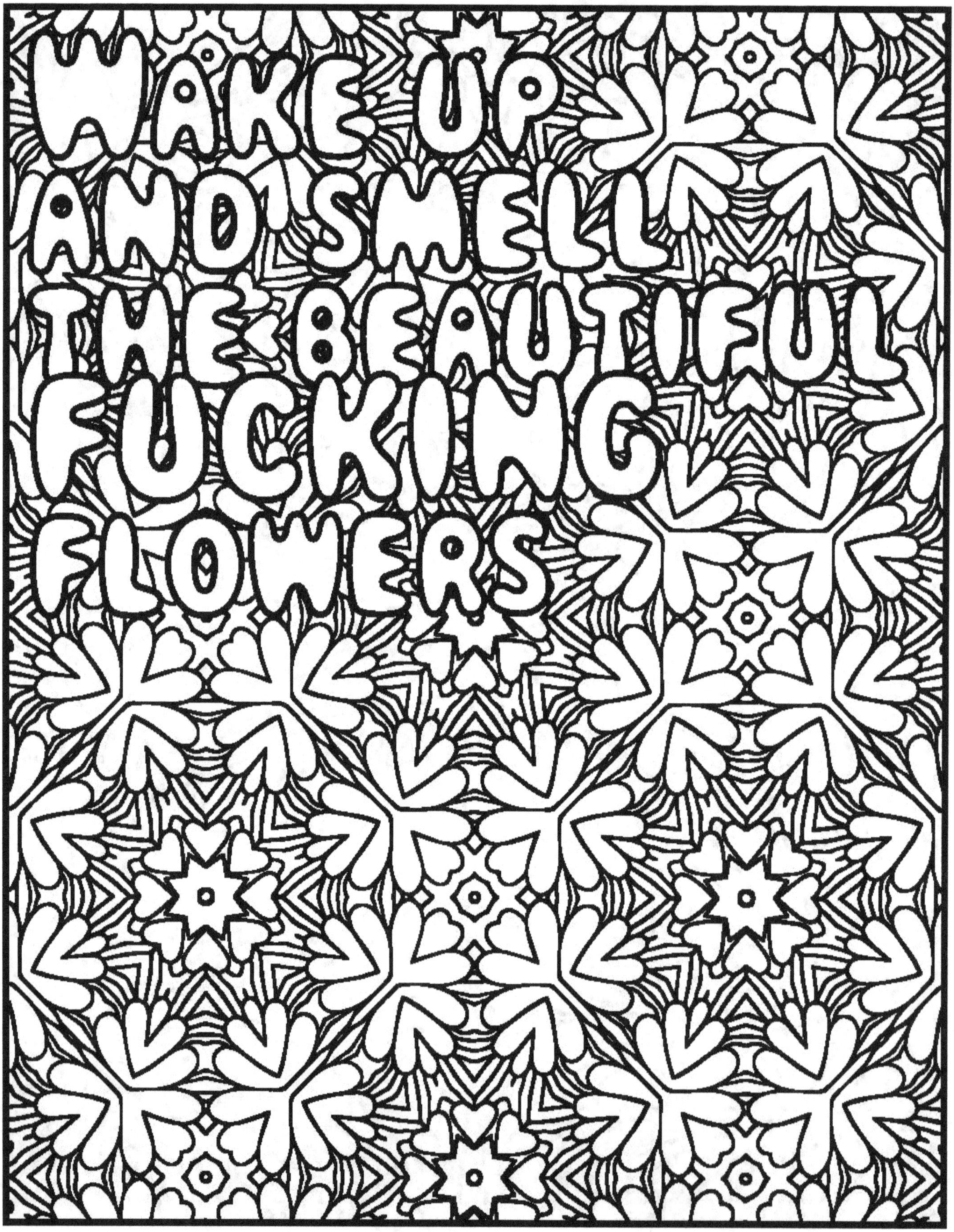
WAKE UP
AND SMELL
THE BEAUTIFUL
FUCKING
FLOWERS

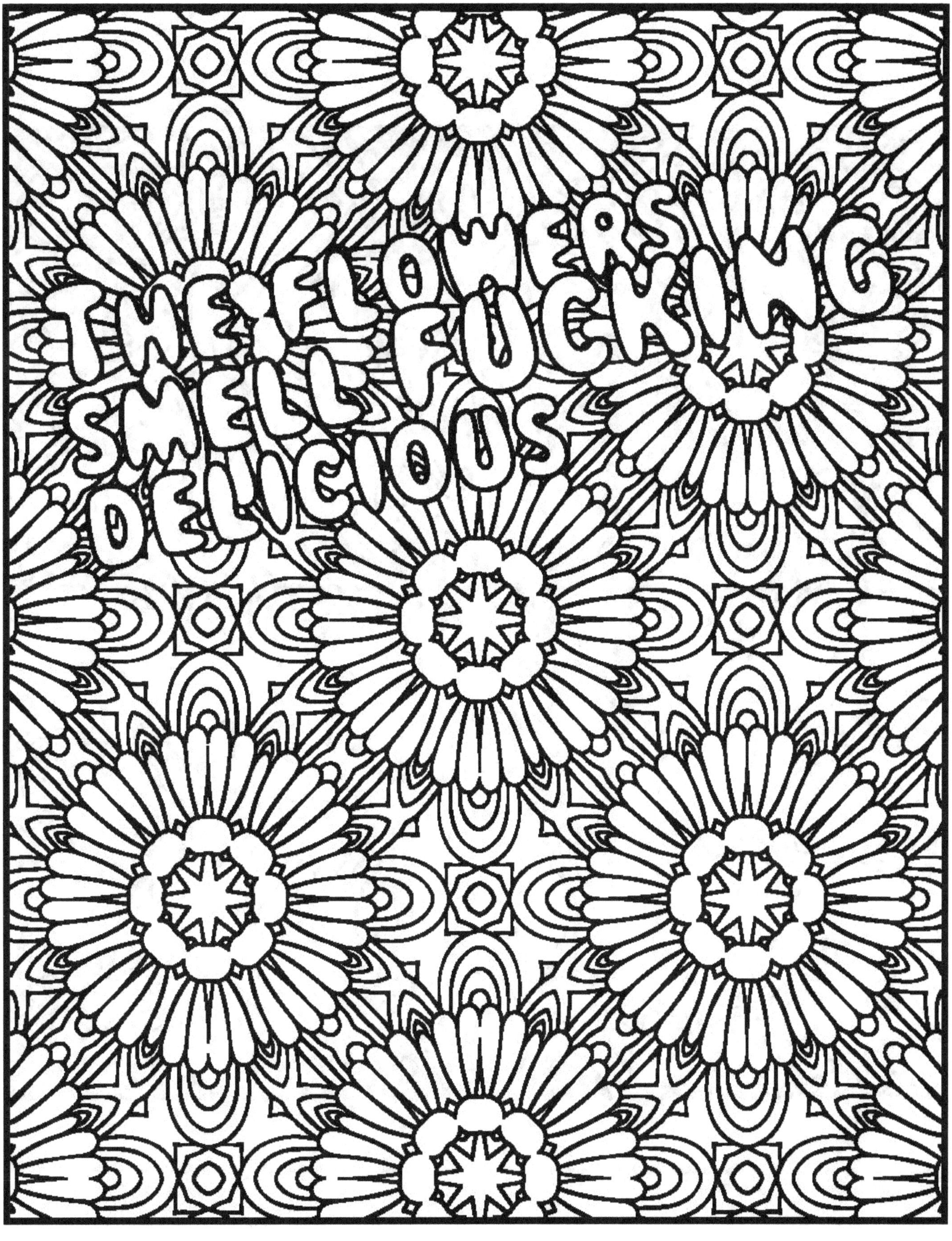
THE FLOWERS
SMELL FUCKING
DELICIOUS

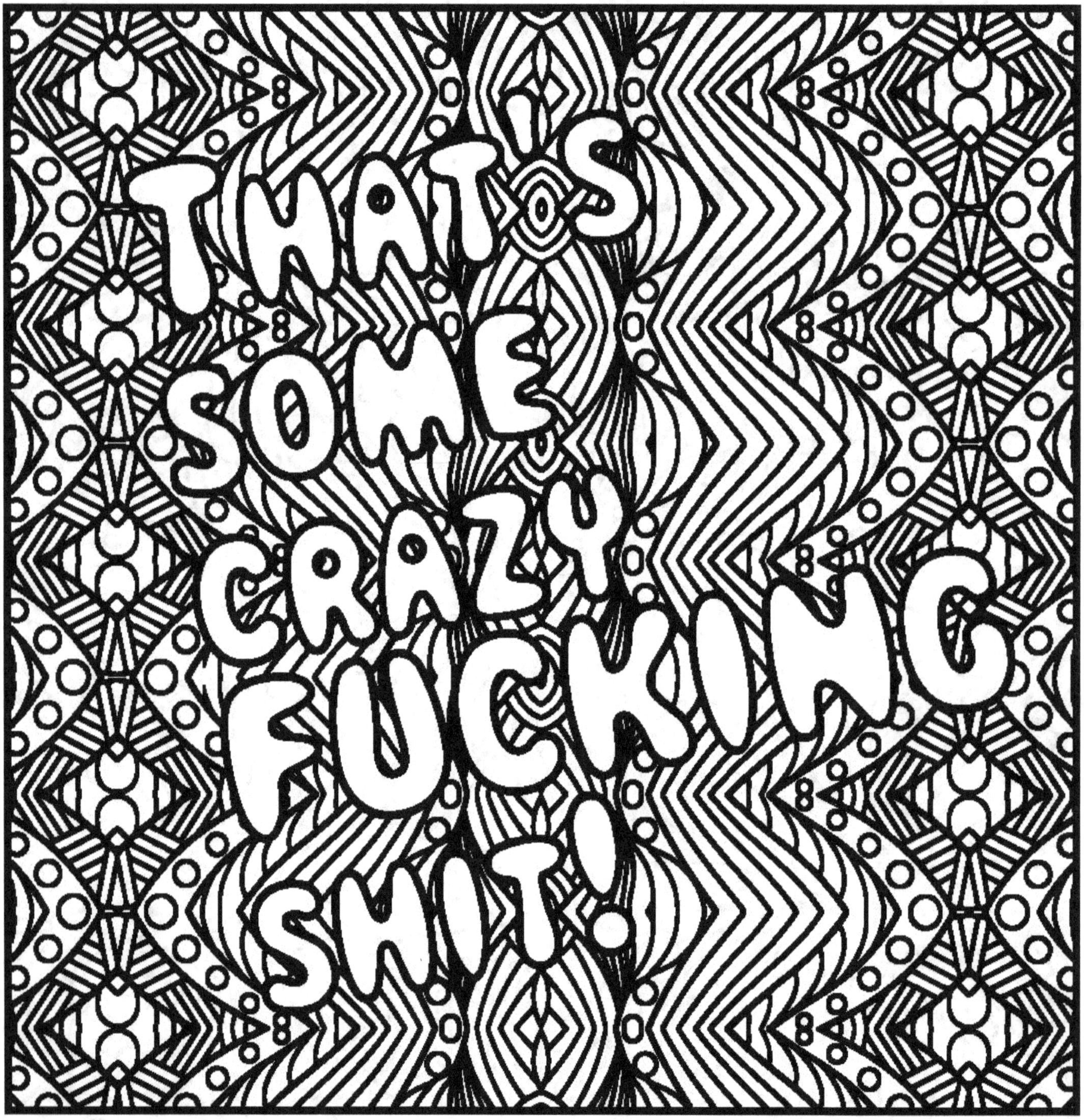
THAT'S
SOME
CRAZY
FUCKING
SHIT!

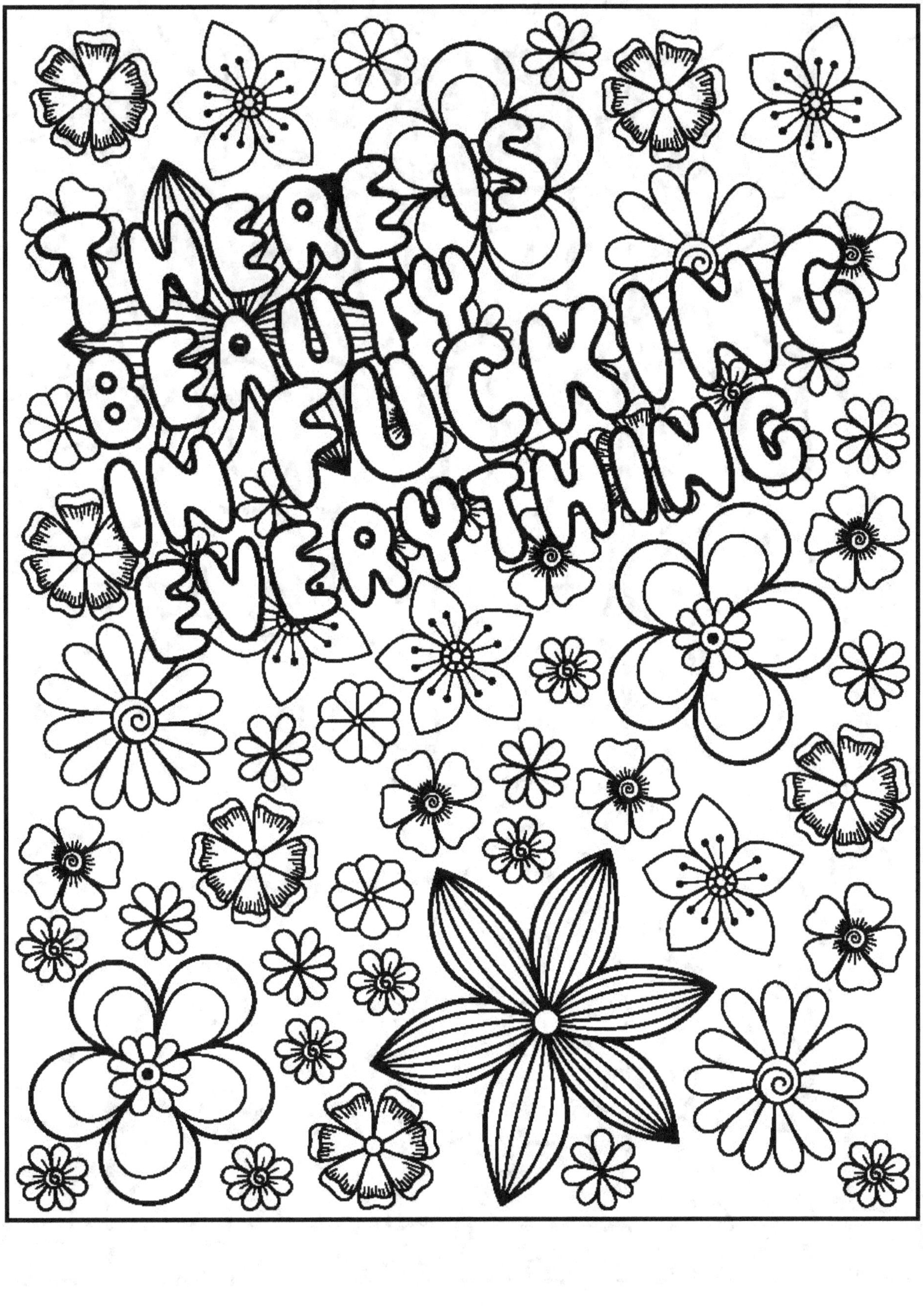
THERE IS
BEAUTY
IN FUCKING
EVERYTHING

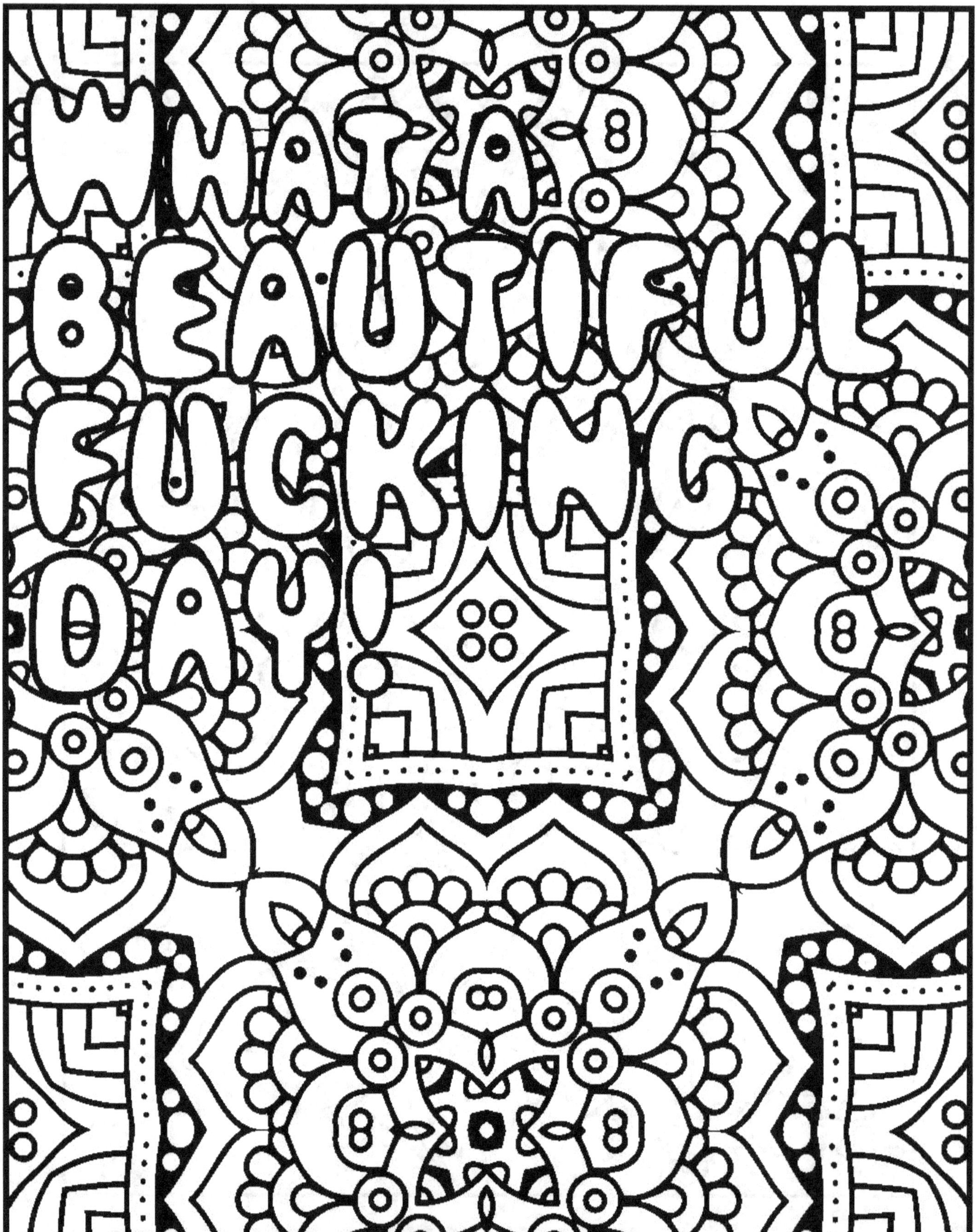
WHAT A
BEAUTIFUL
FUCKING
DAY!

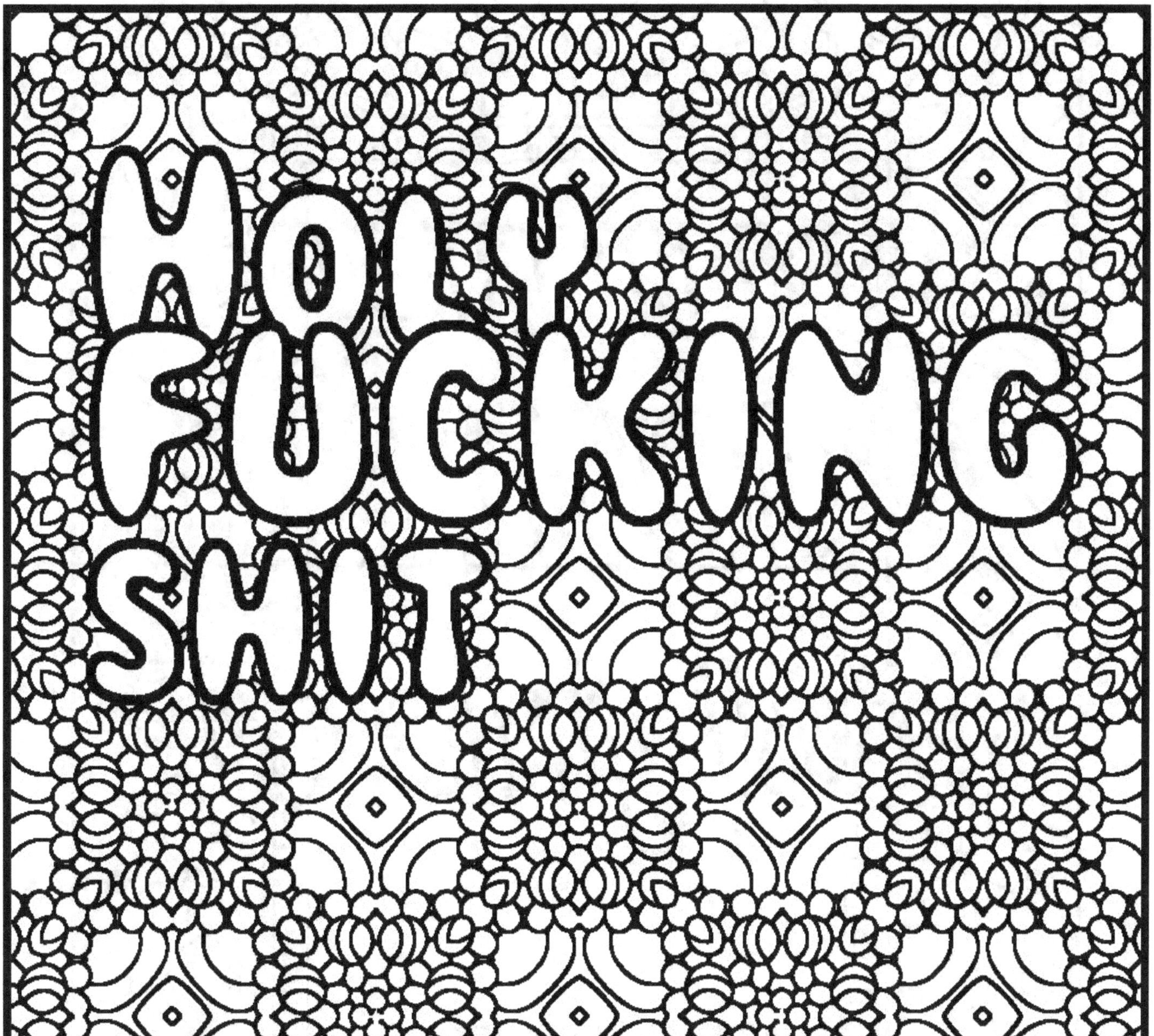
HOLY
FUCKING
SHIT

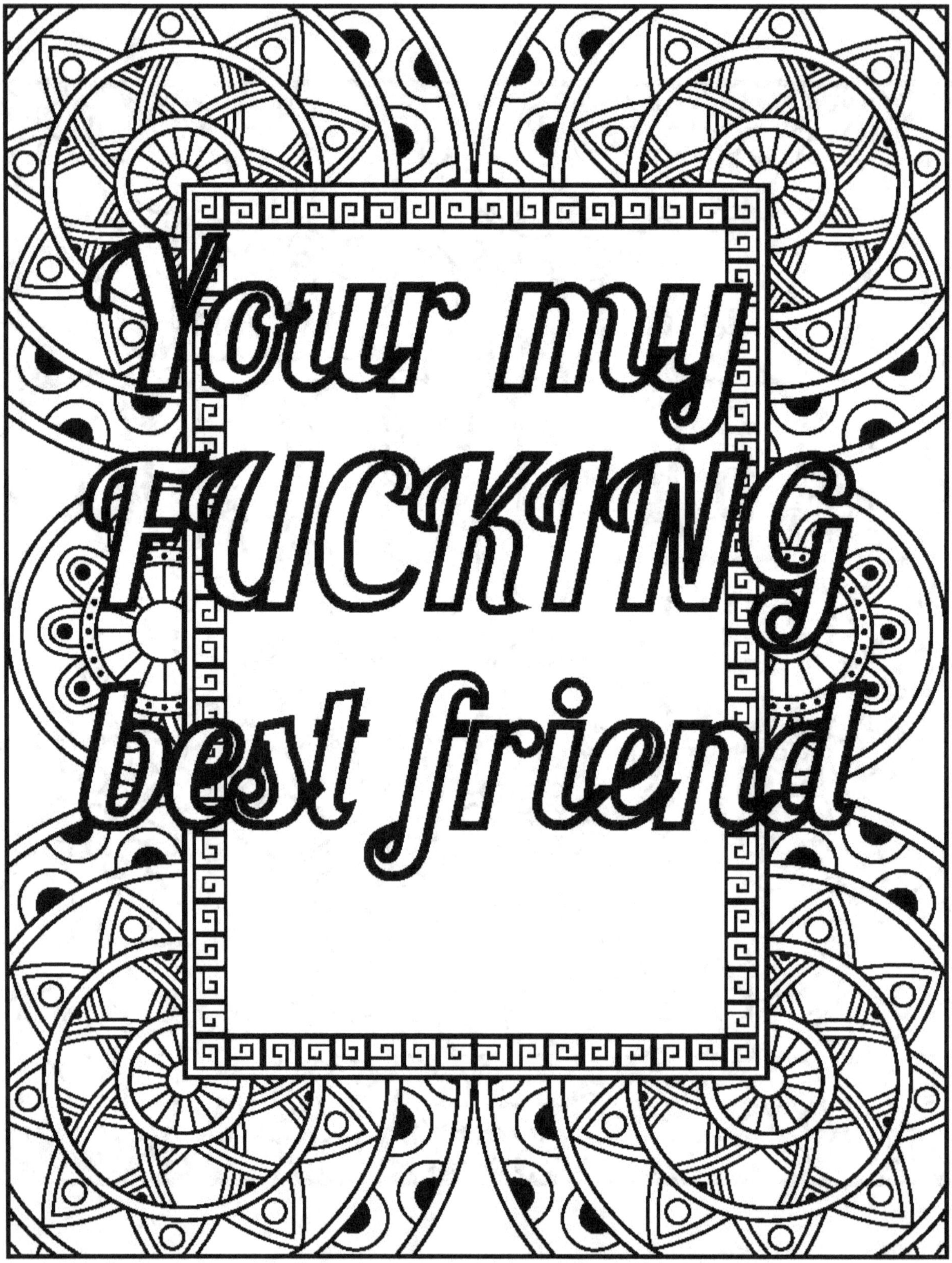
Your my
FUCKING
best friend

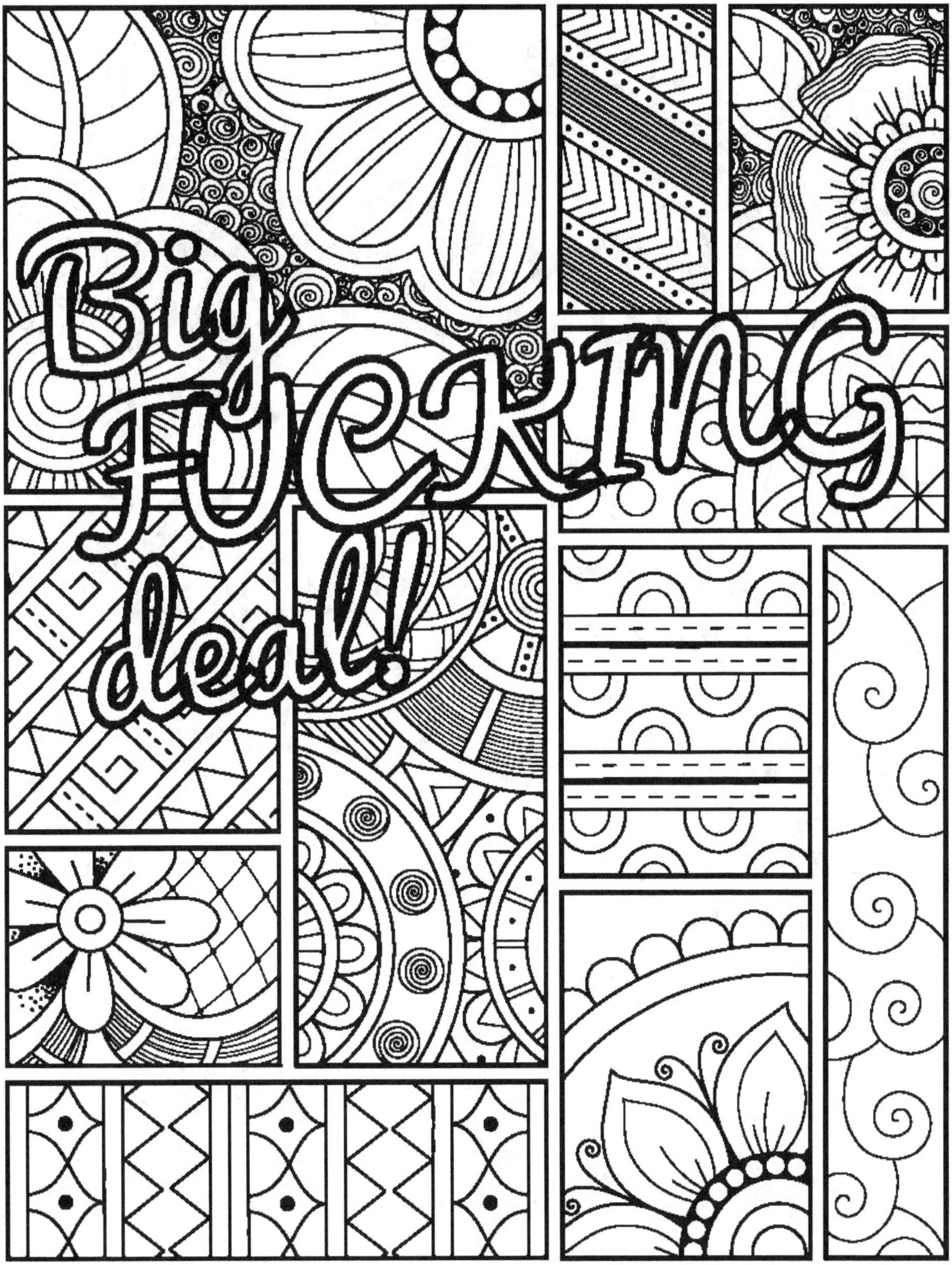
Big
FUCKING
deal!

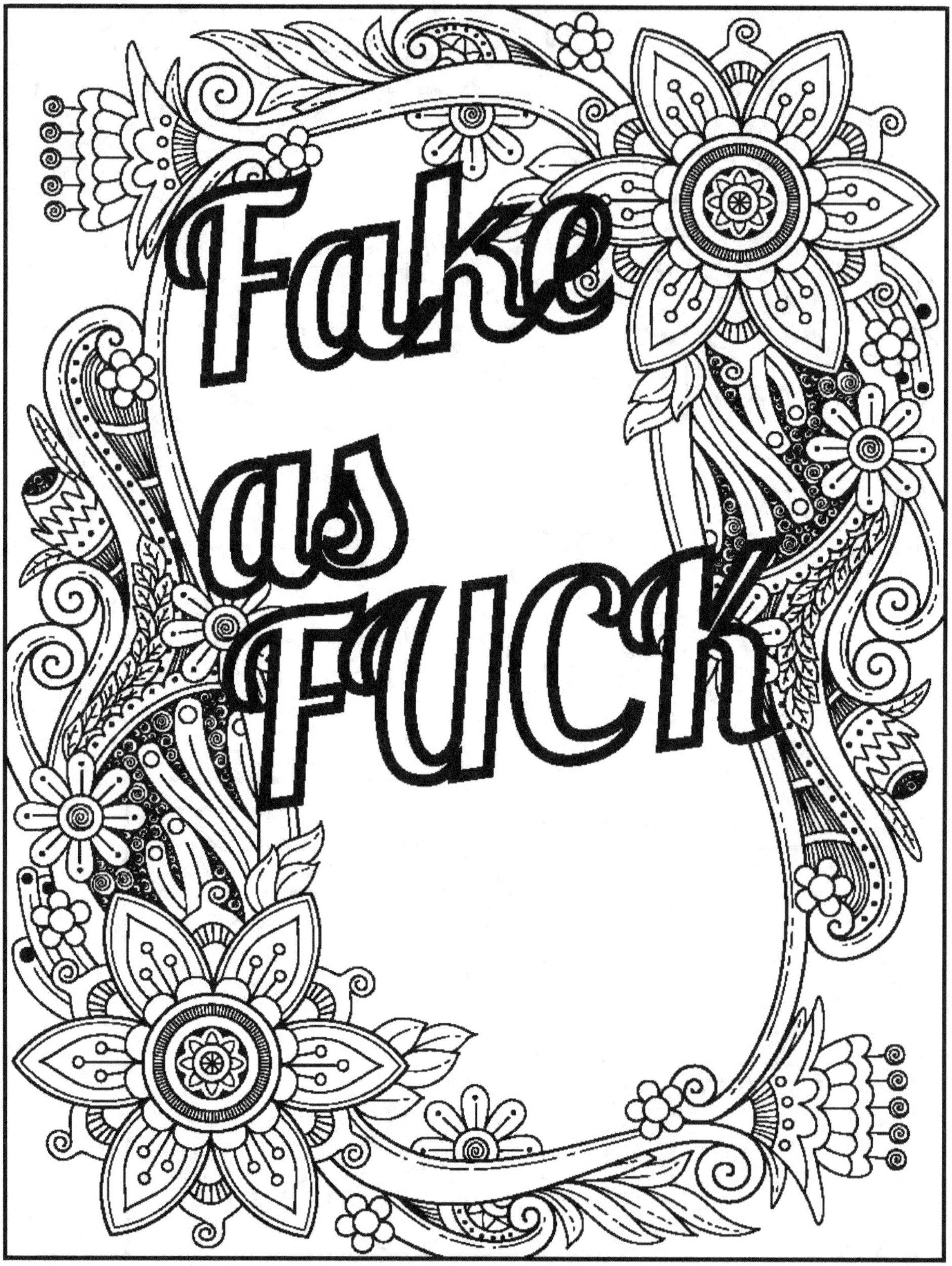
Fake
as
FUCK

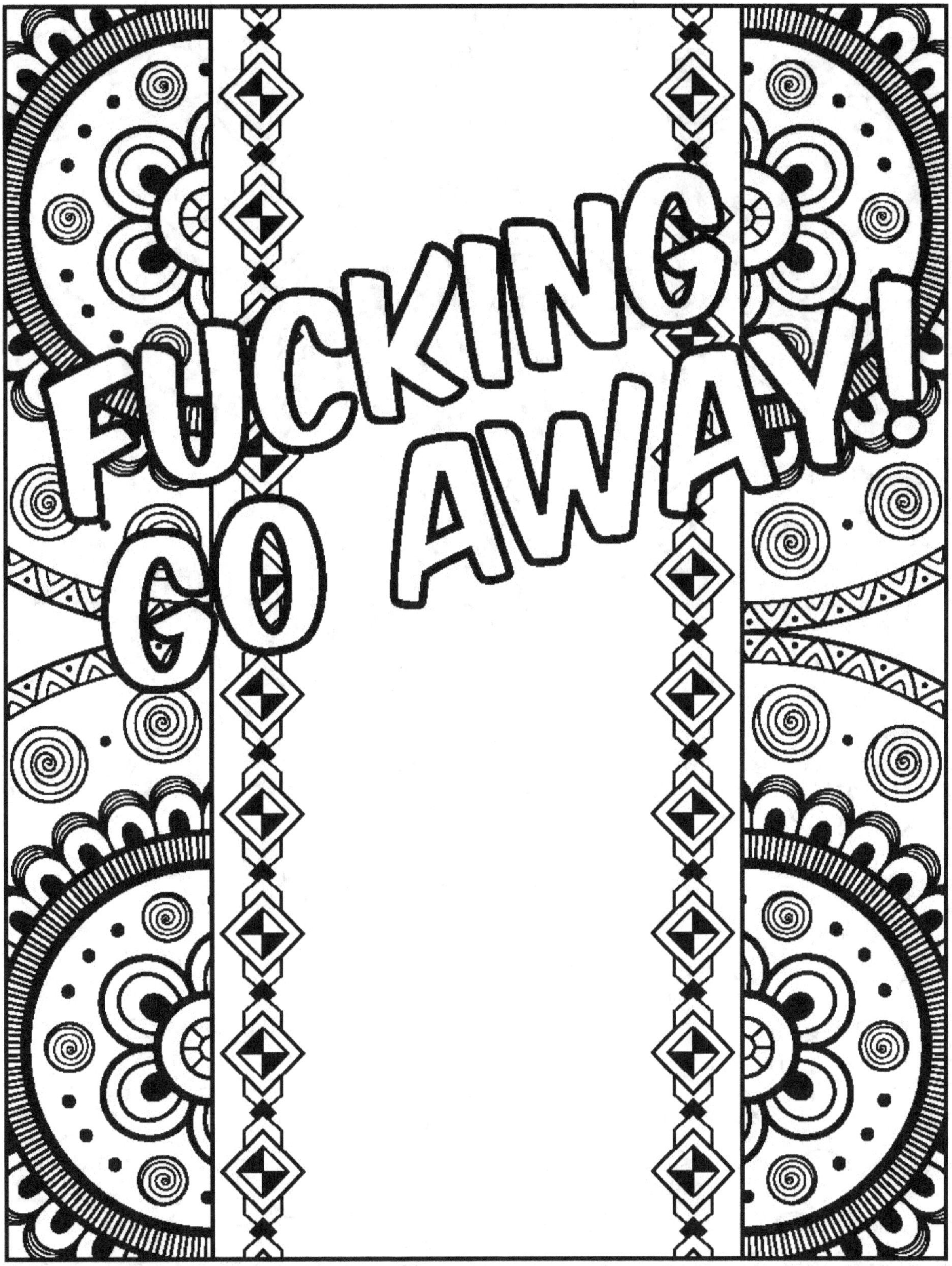
FUCKING GO AWAY!

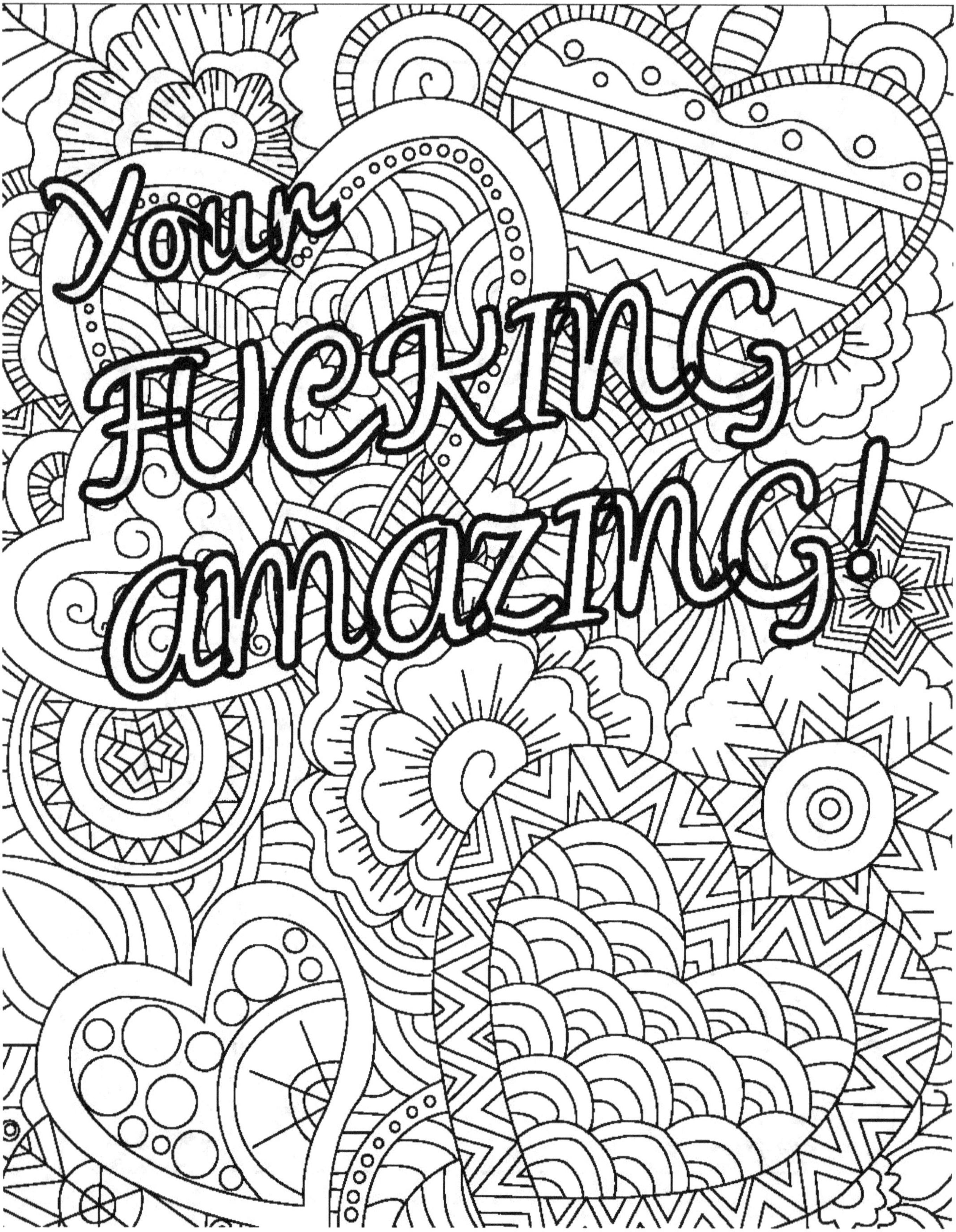
Your
FUCKING
amazing!

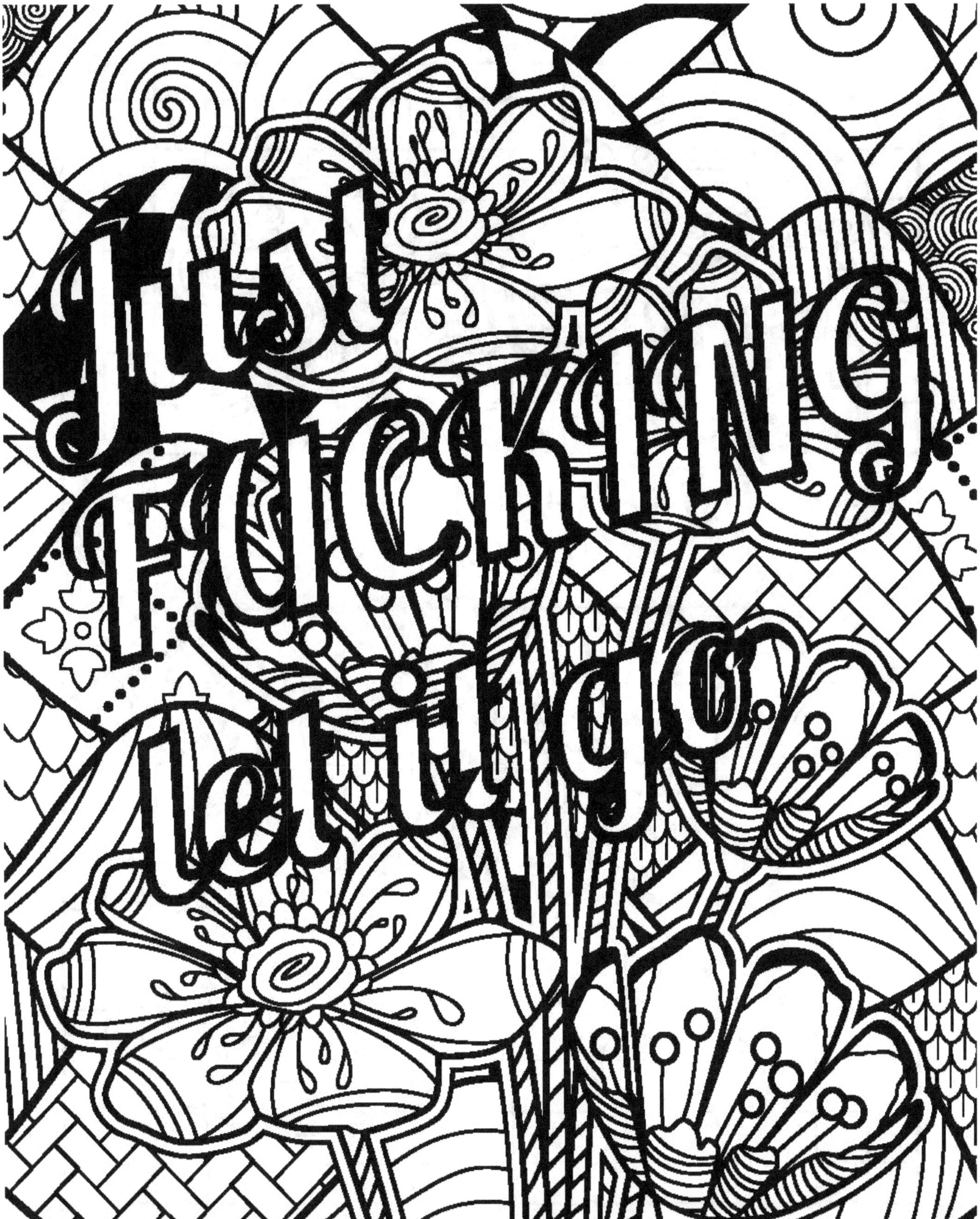
Just
FUCKING
let it go.

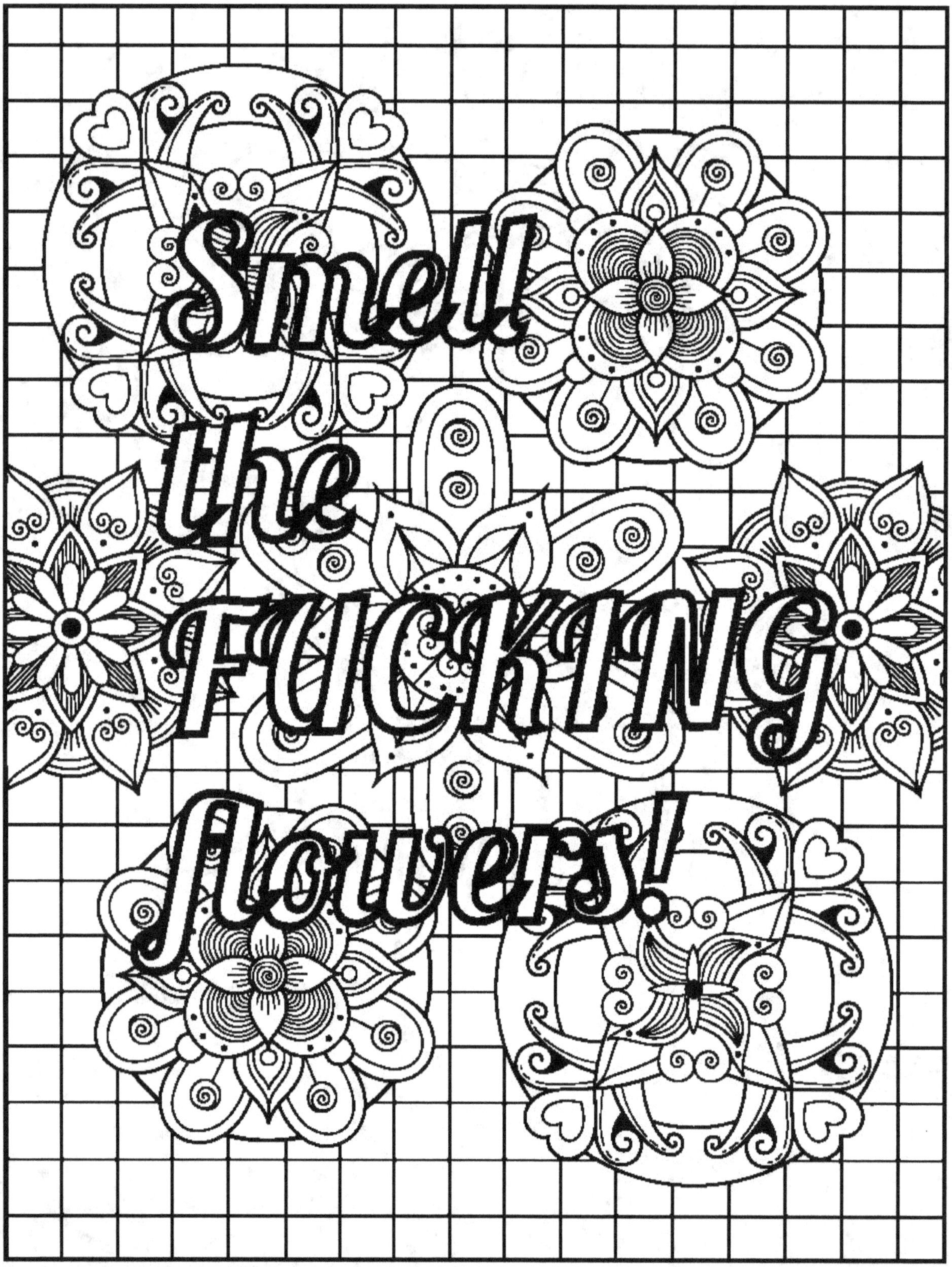
Smell
the
FUCKING
flowers!

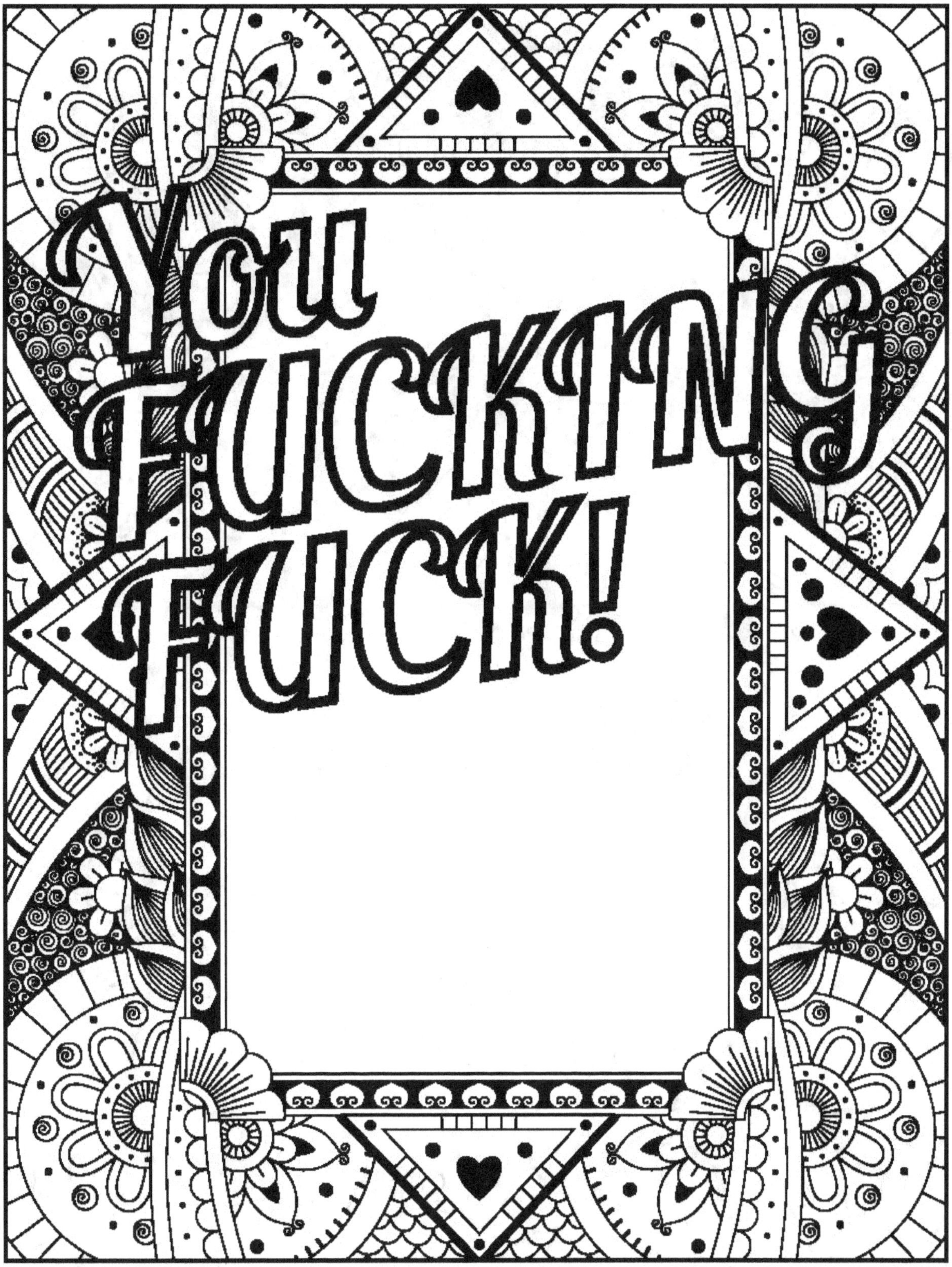
You
FUCKING
FUCK!

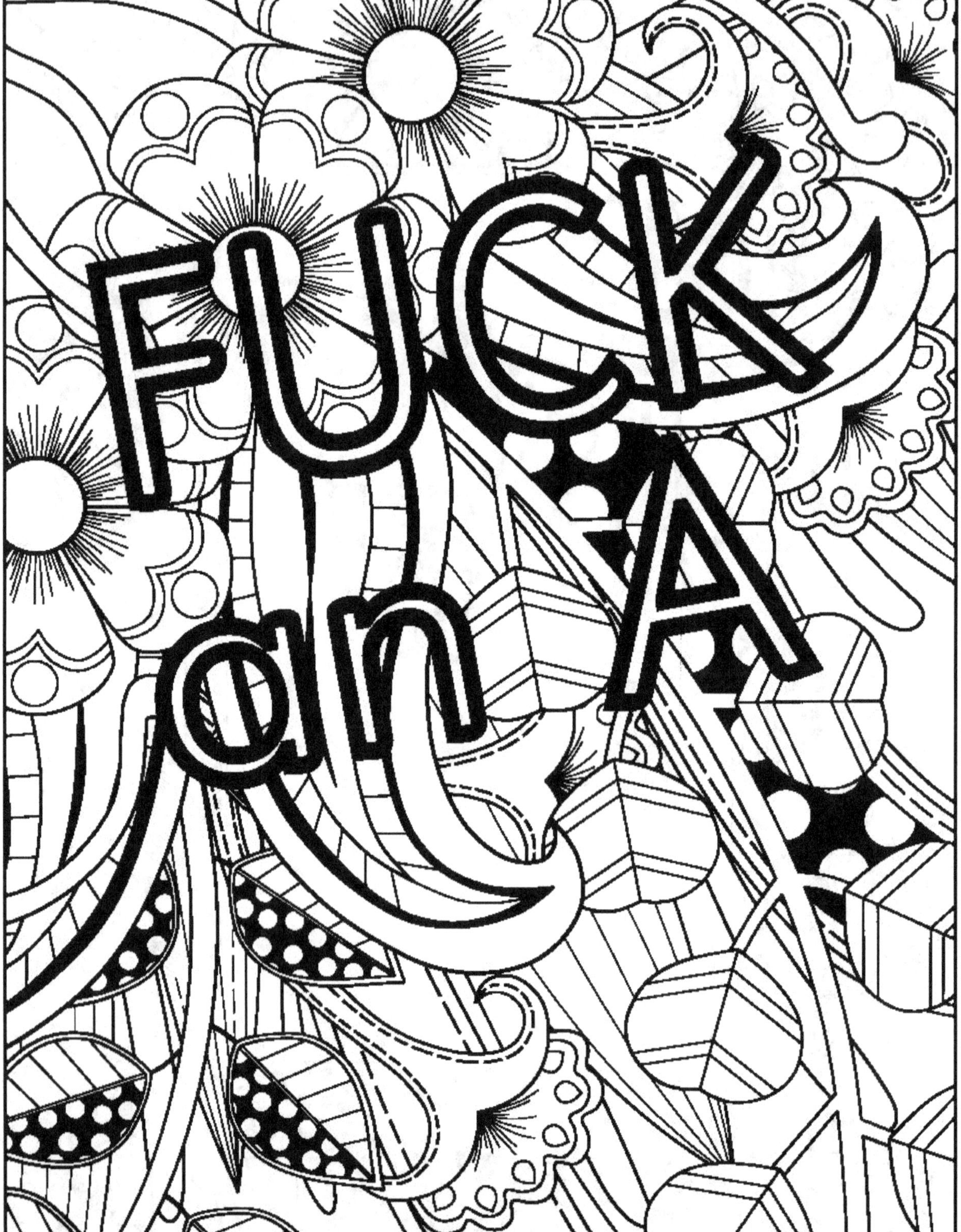
FUCK
an A

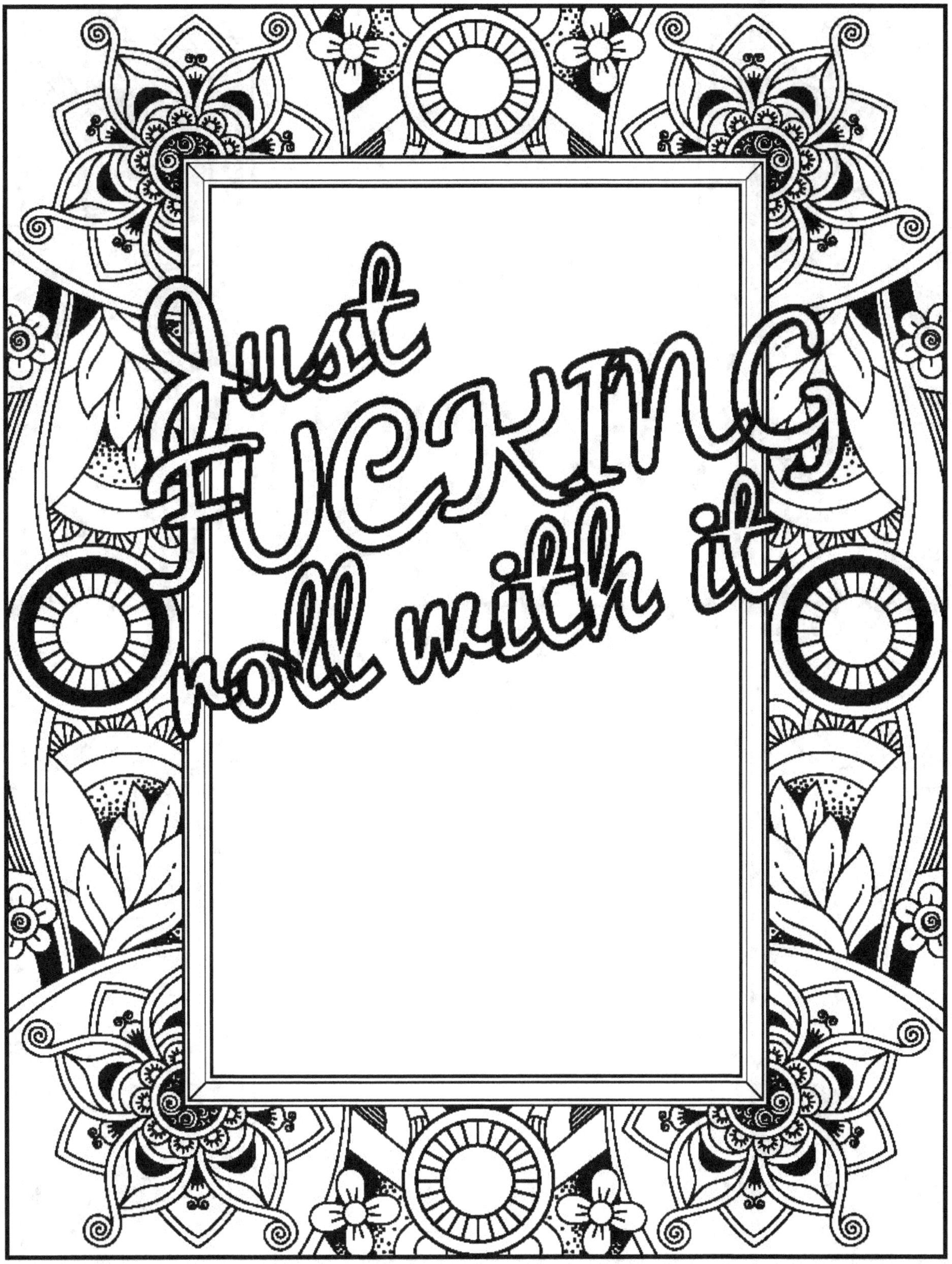
Just
FUCKING
roll with it

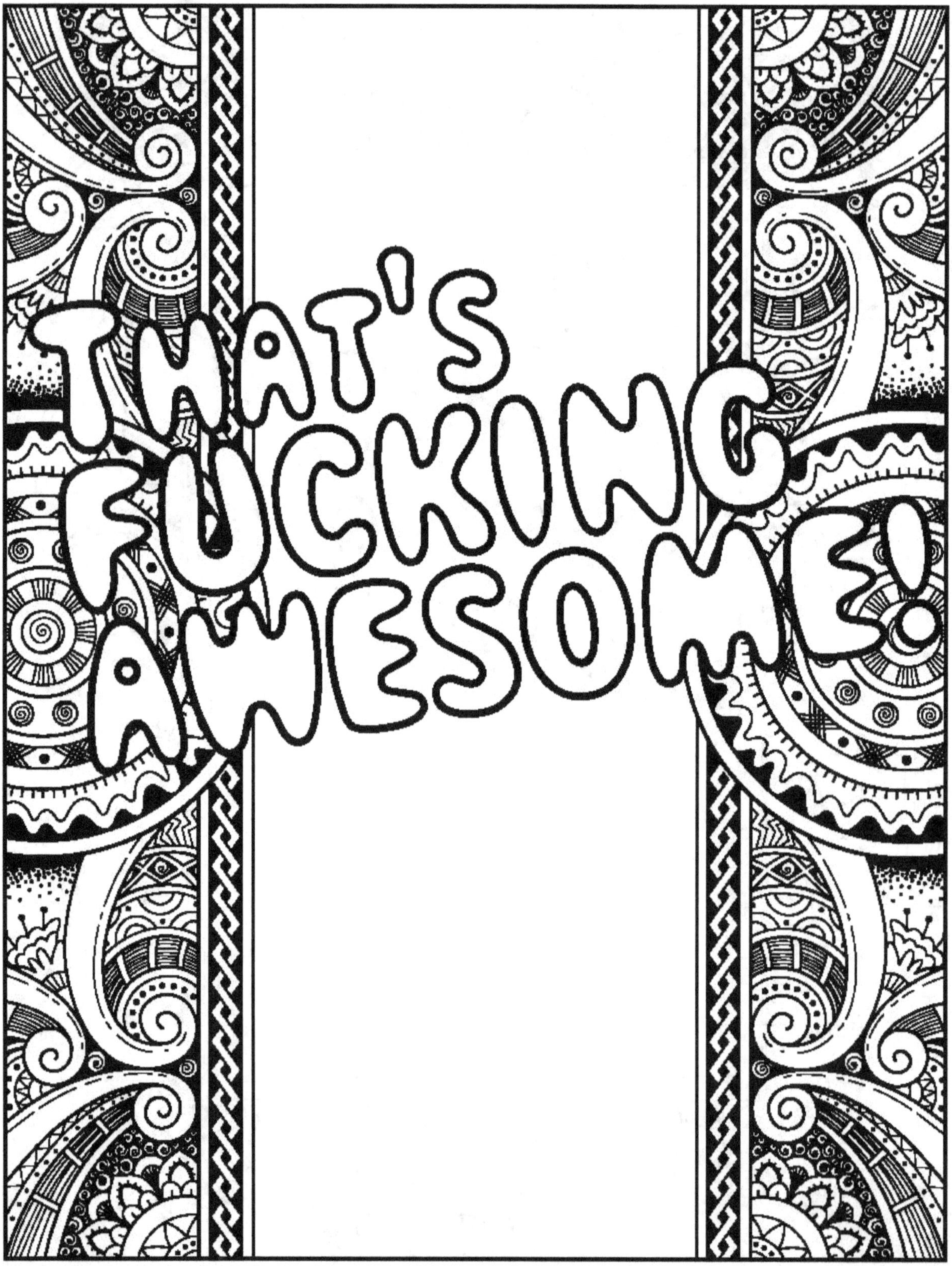
THAT'S
FUCKING
AWESOME!

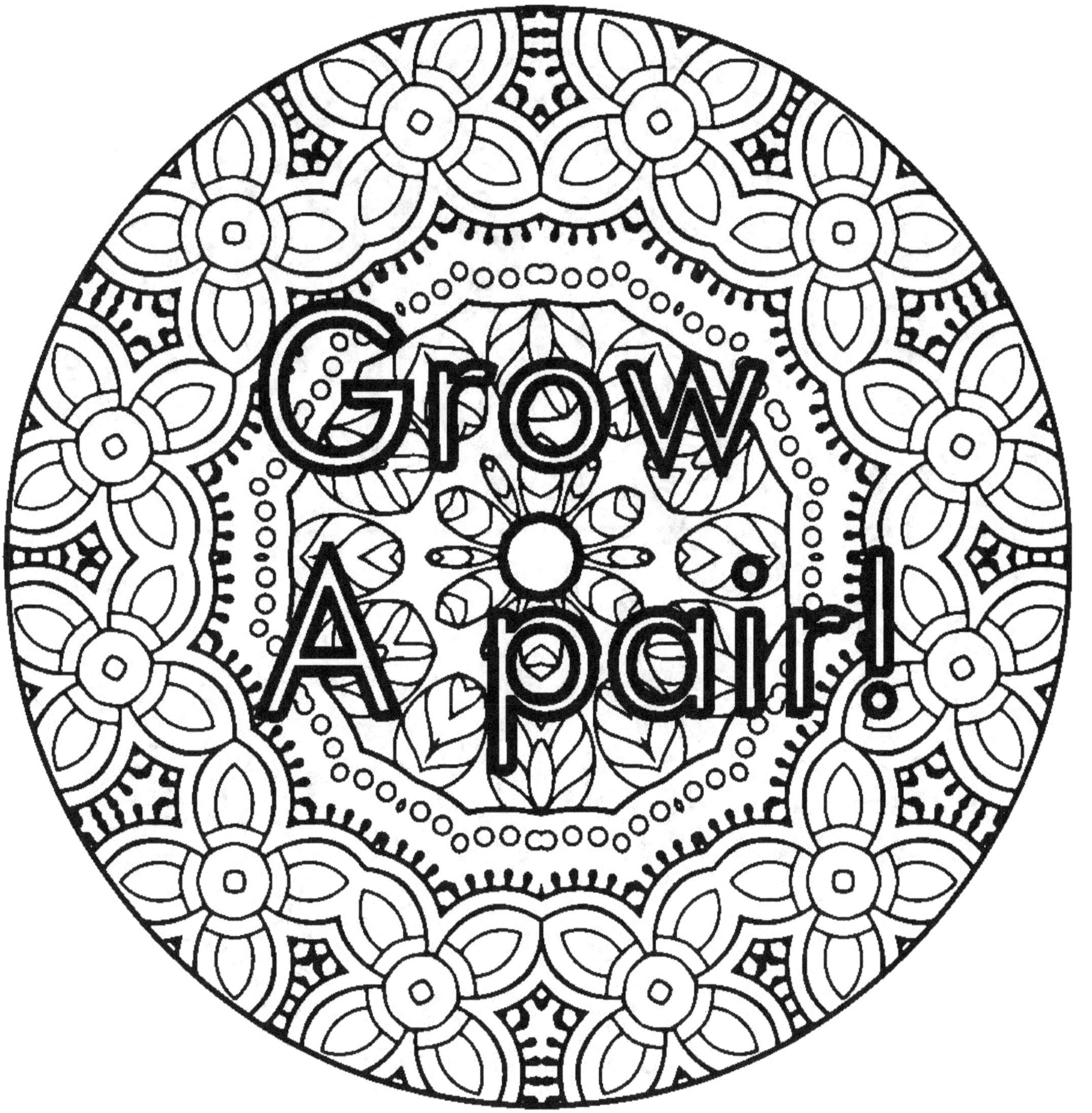
Grow
A pair!

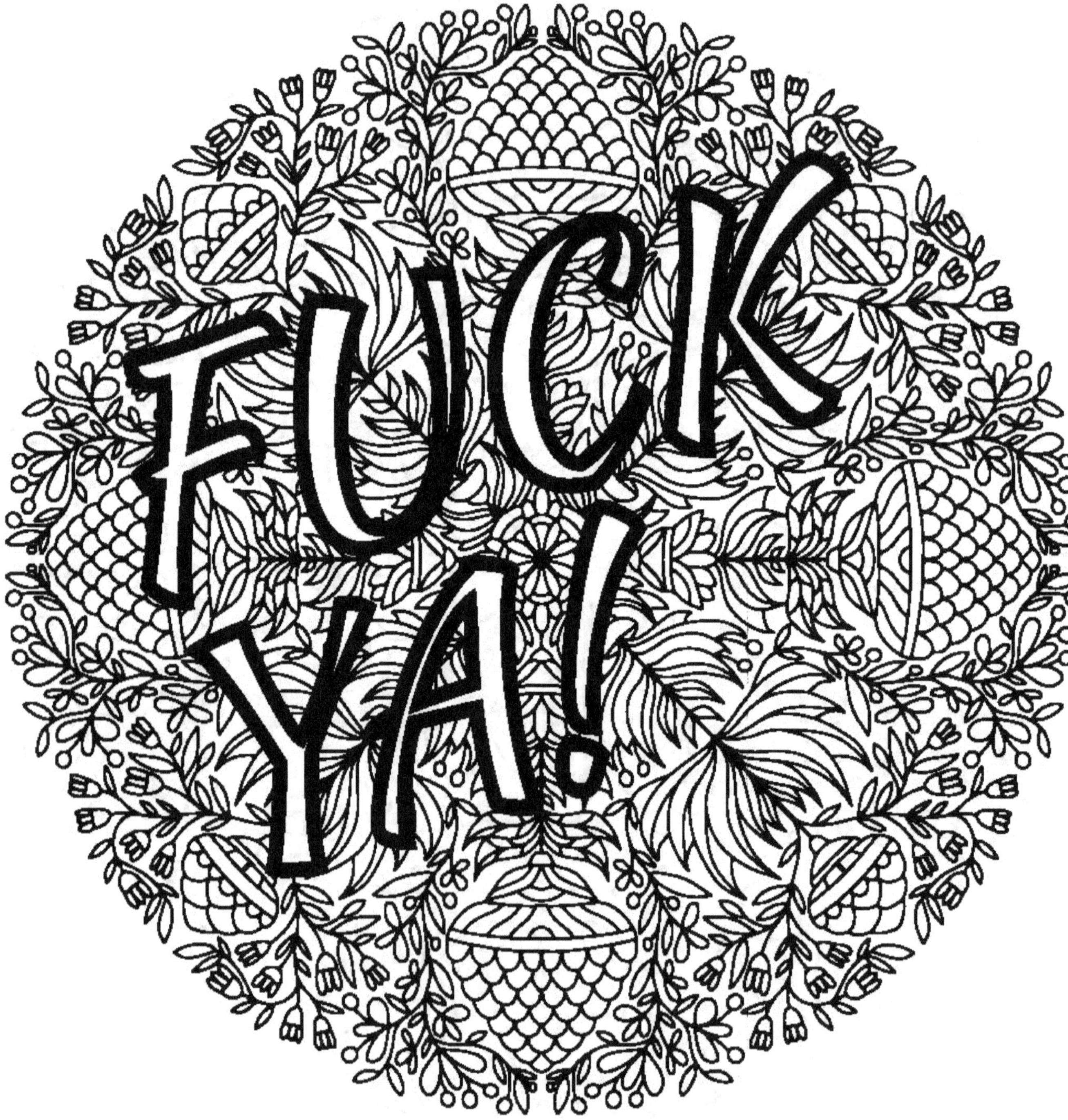
FUCK
YA!

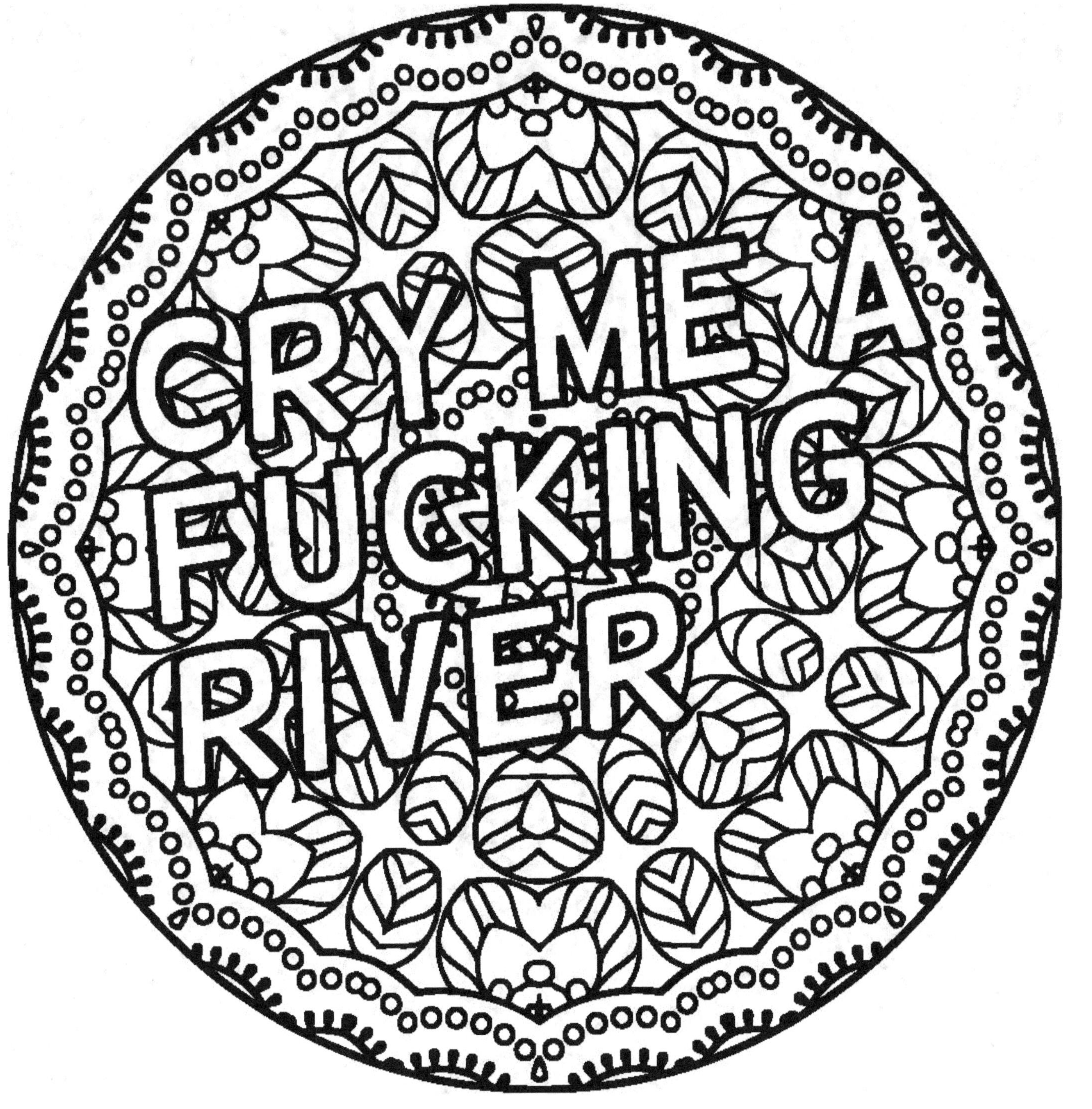
CRY ME A
FUCKING
RIVER

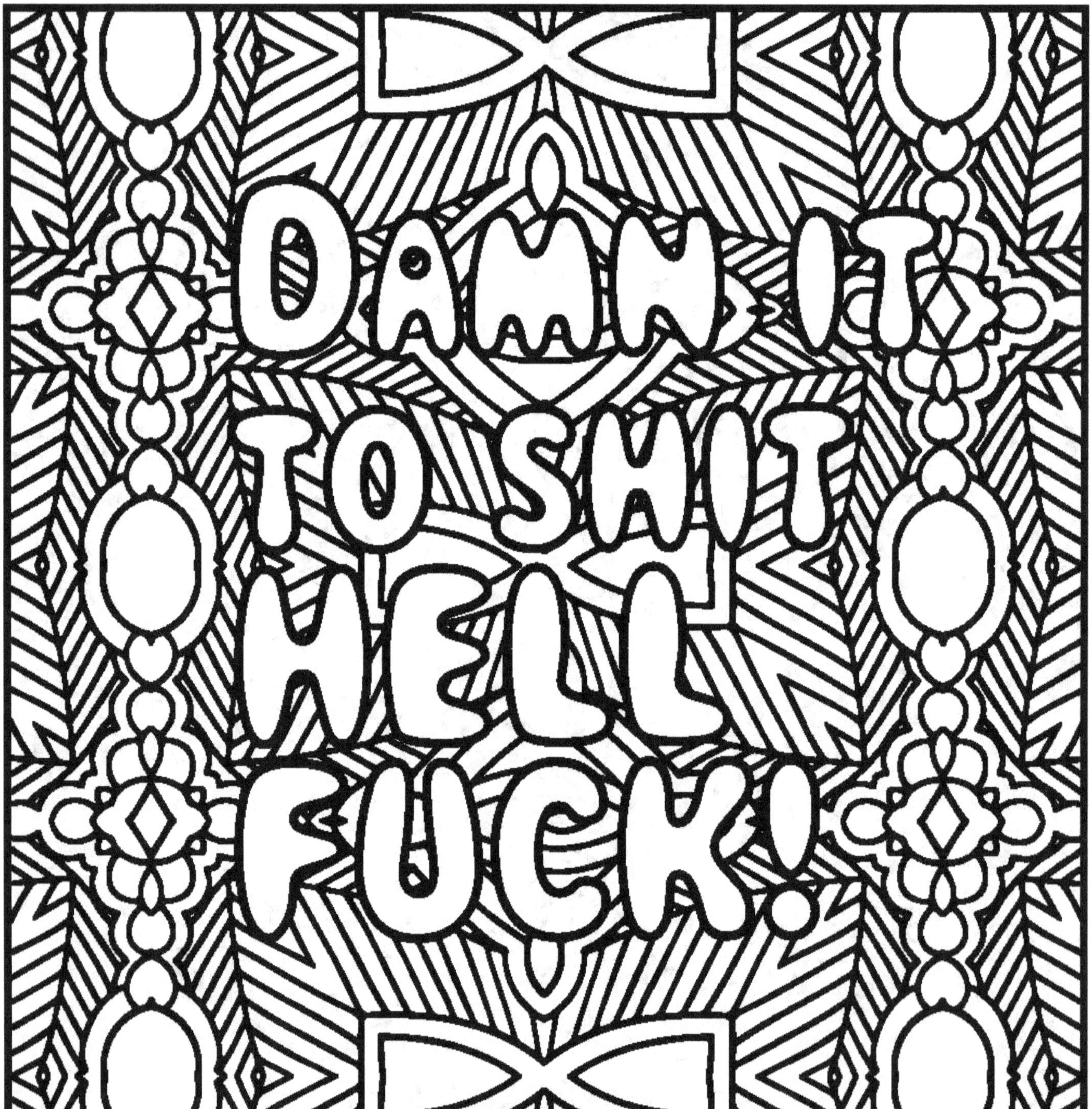
DAMN IT
TO SHIT
HELL
FUCK!

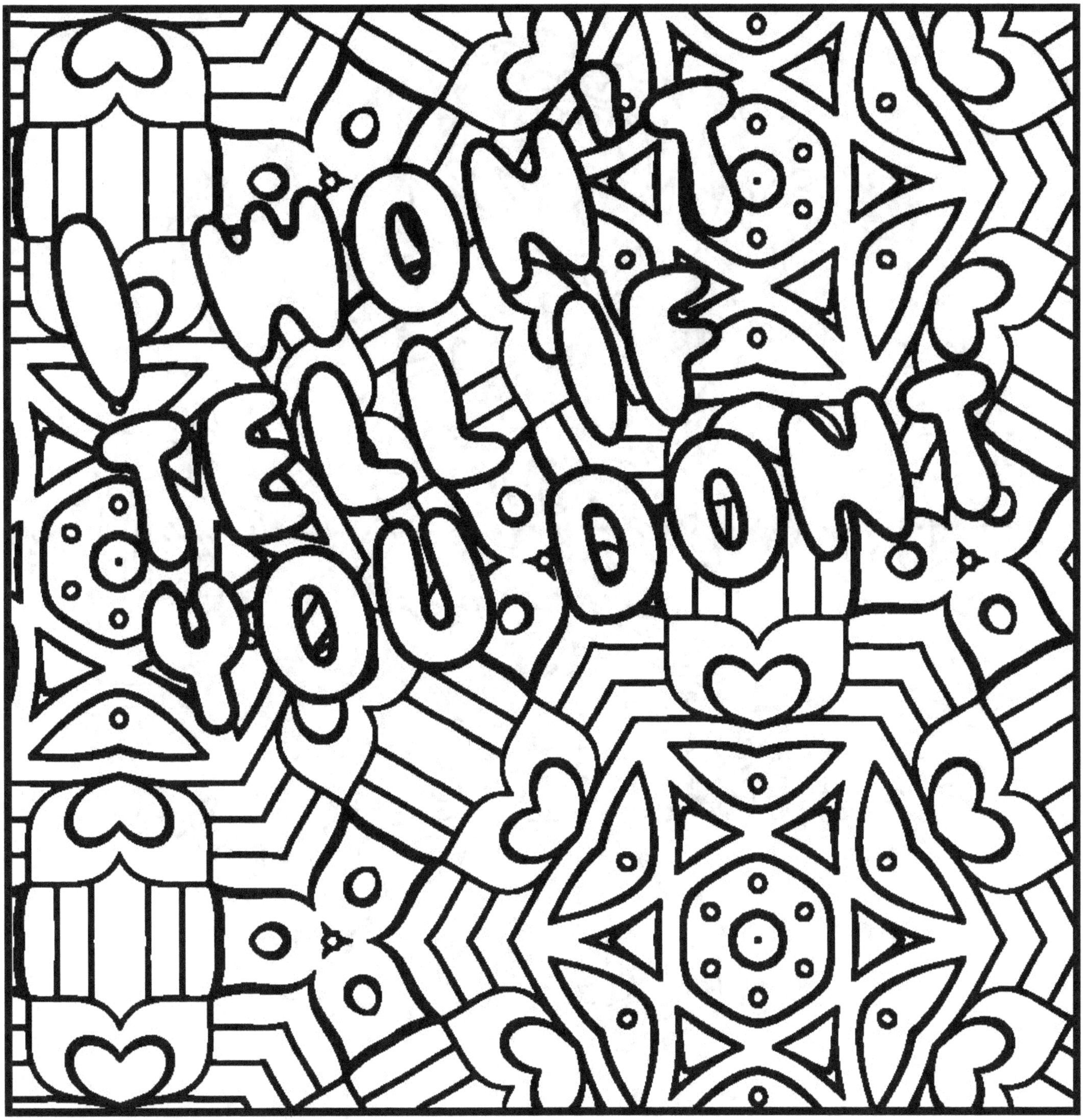
I WON'T
TELL IF
YOU DON'T

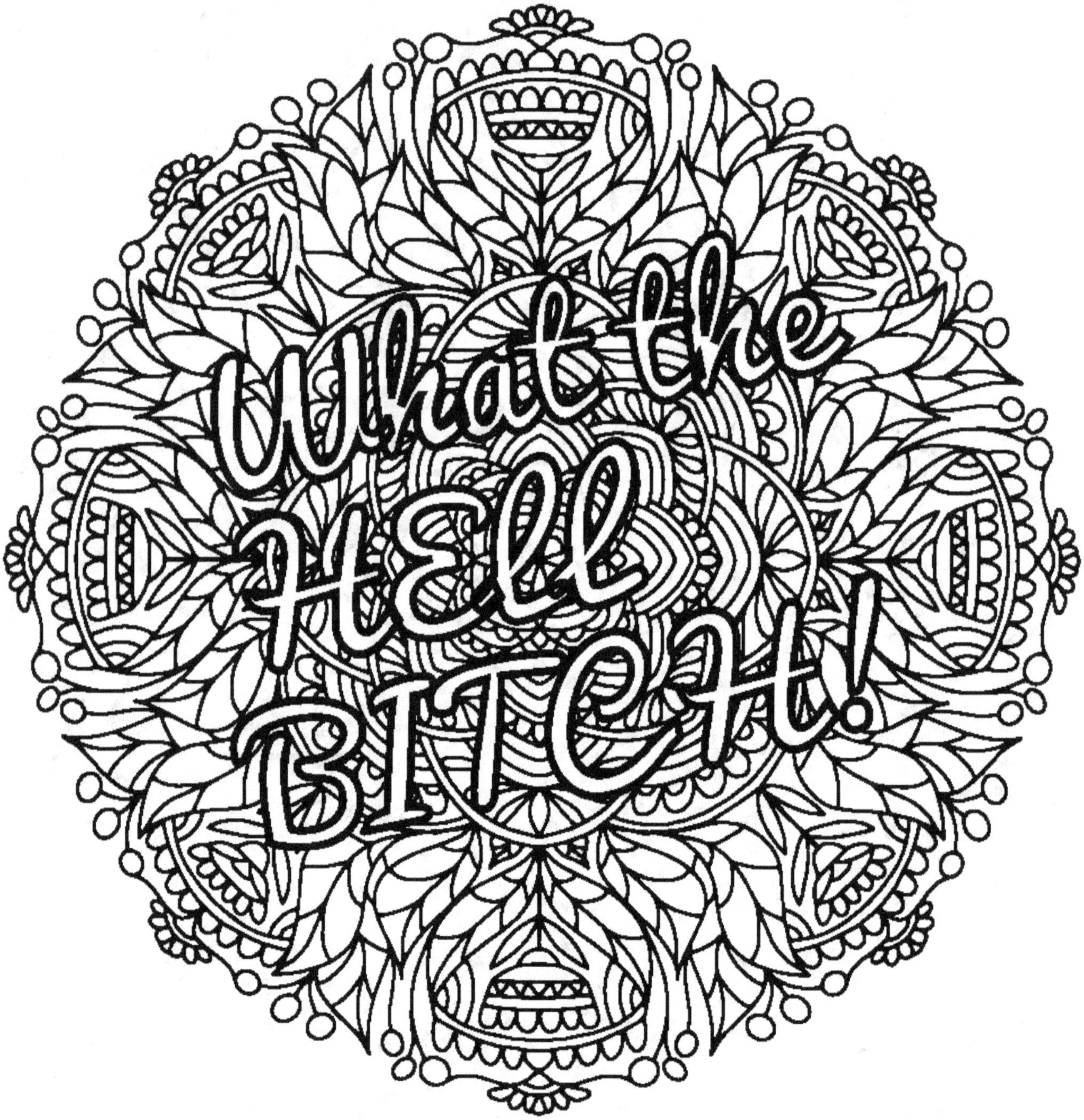
What the
HELL
BITCH!

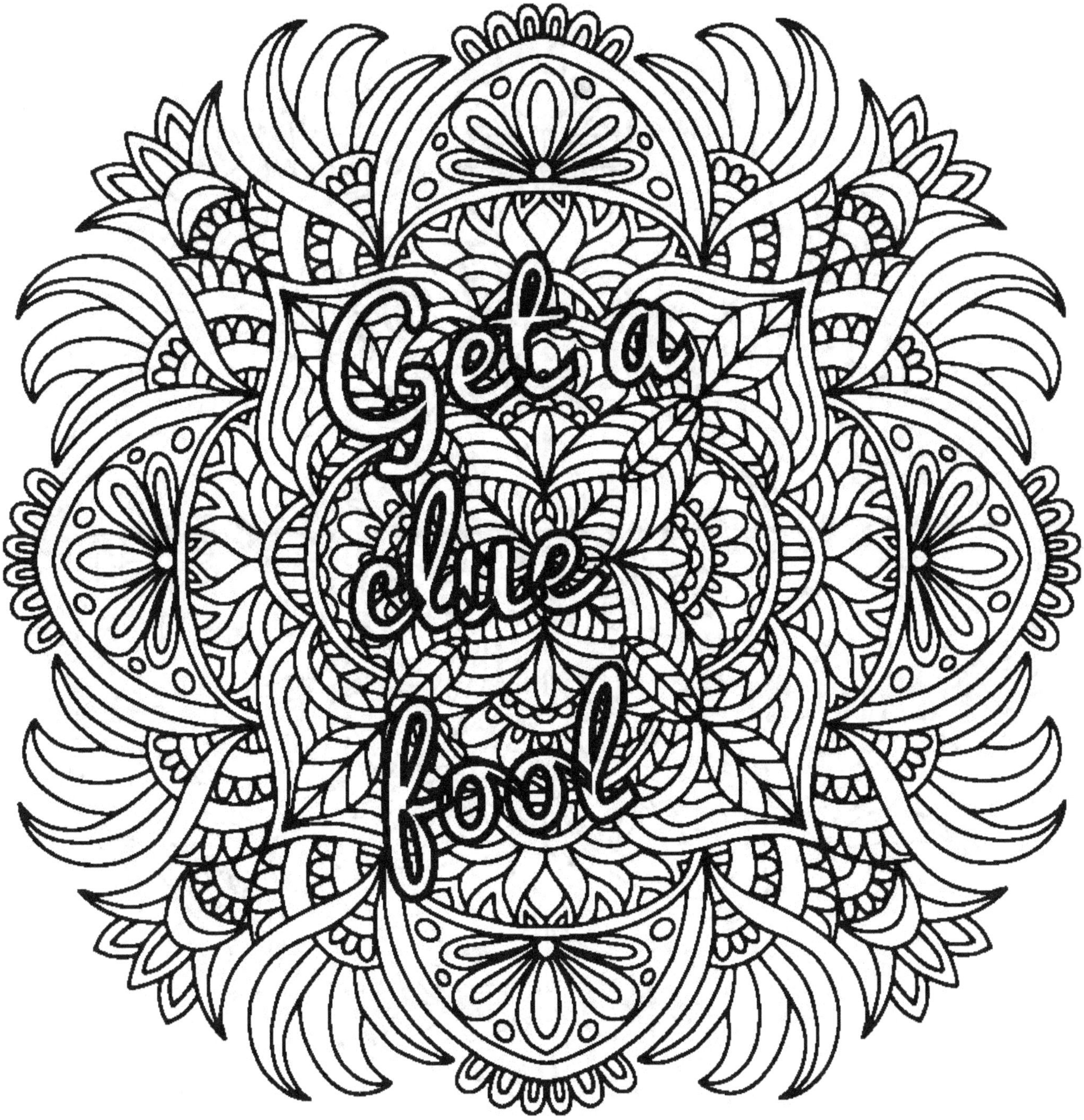
Get a
clue
fool

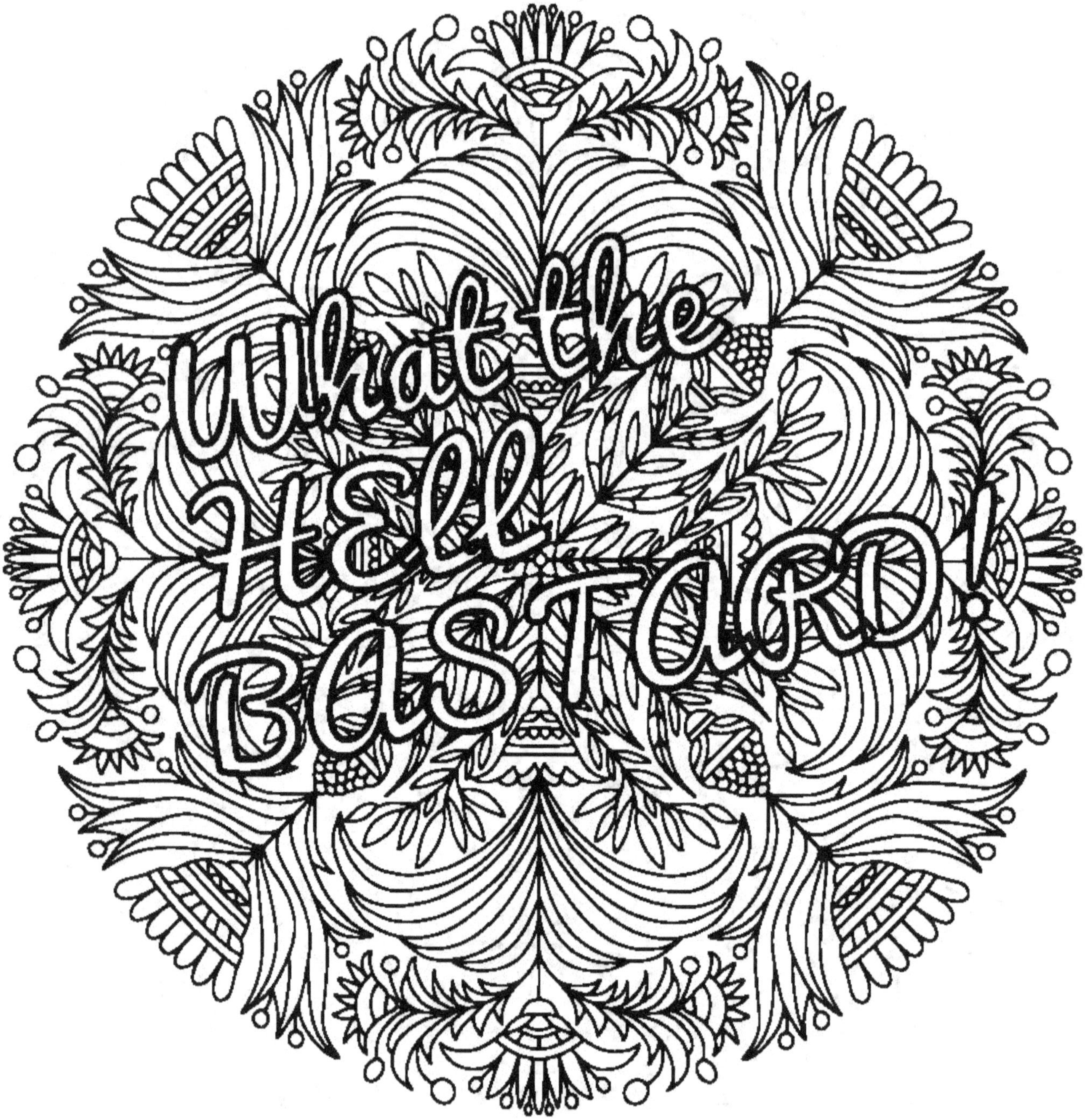
What the
HELL
BASTARD!

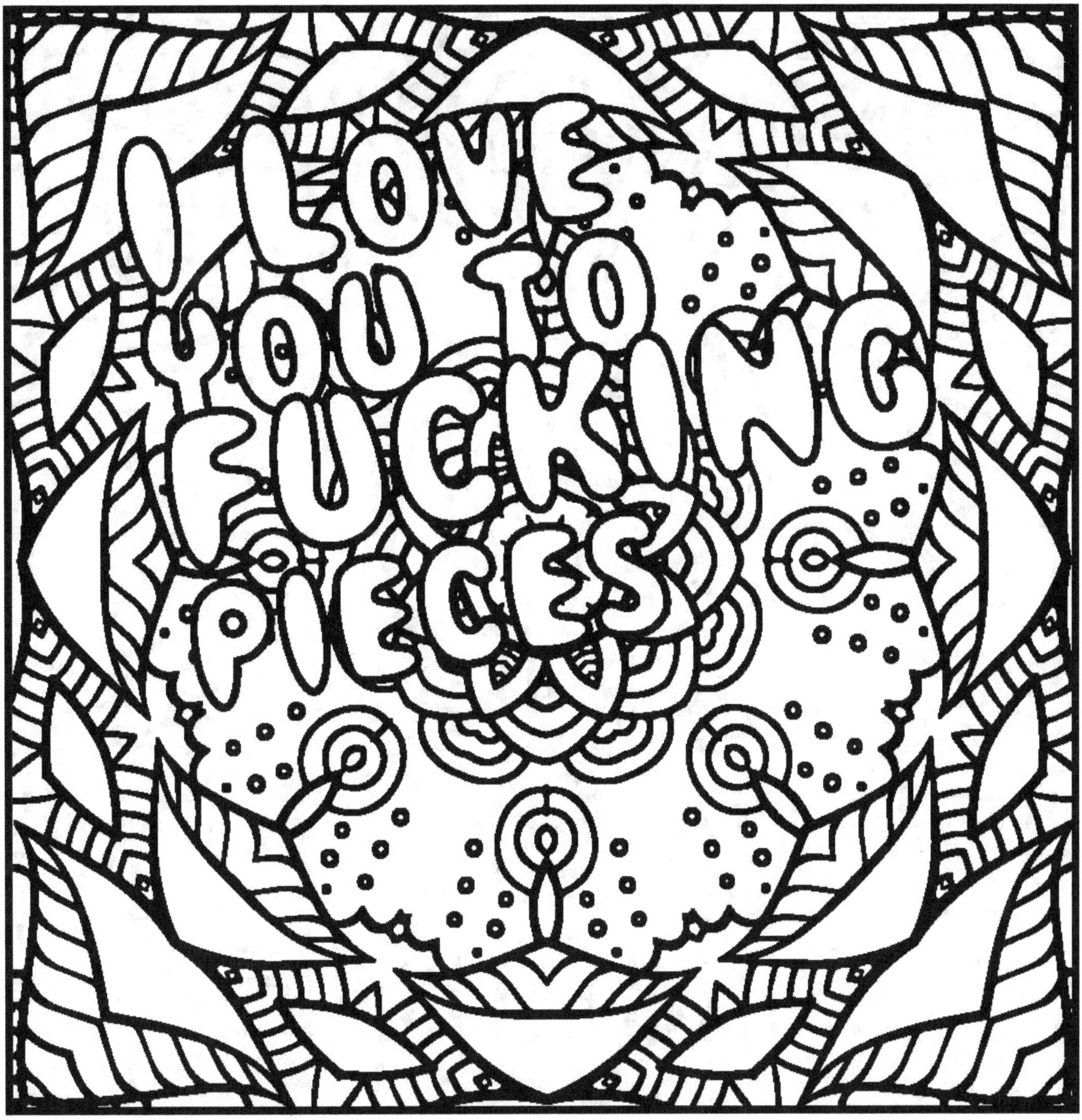
I LOVE YOU TO FUCKING PIECES

CLEAN YOUR FUCKING HOUSE!

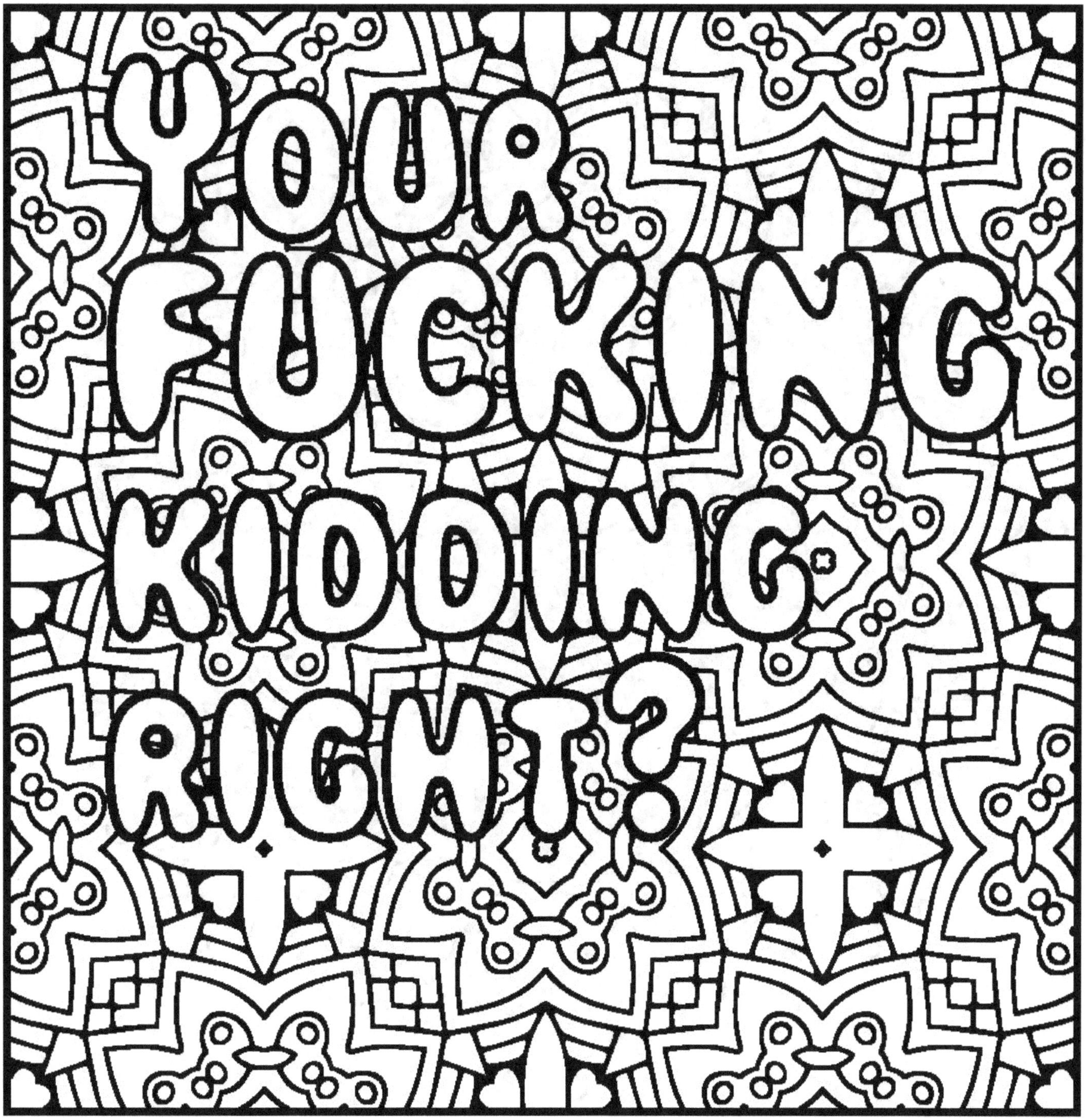
YOUR
FUCKING
KIDDING
RIGHT?

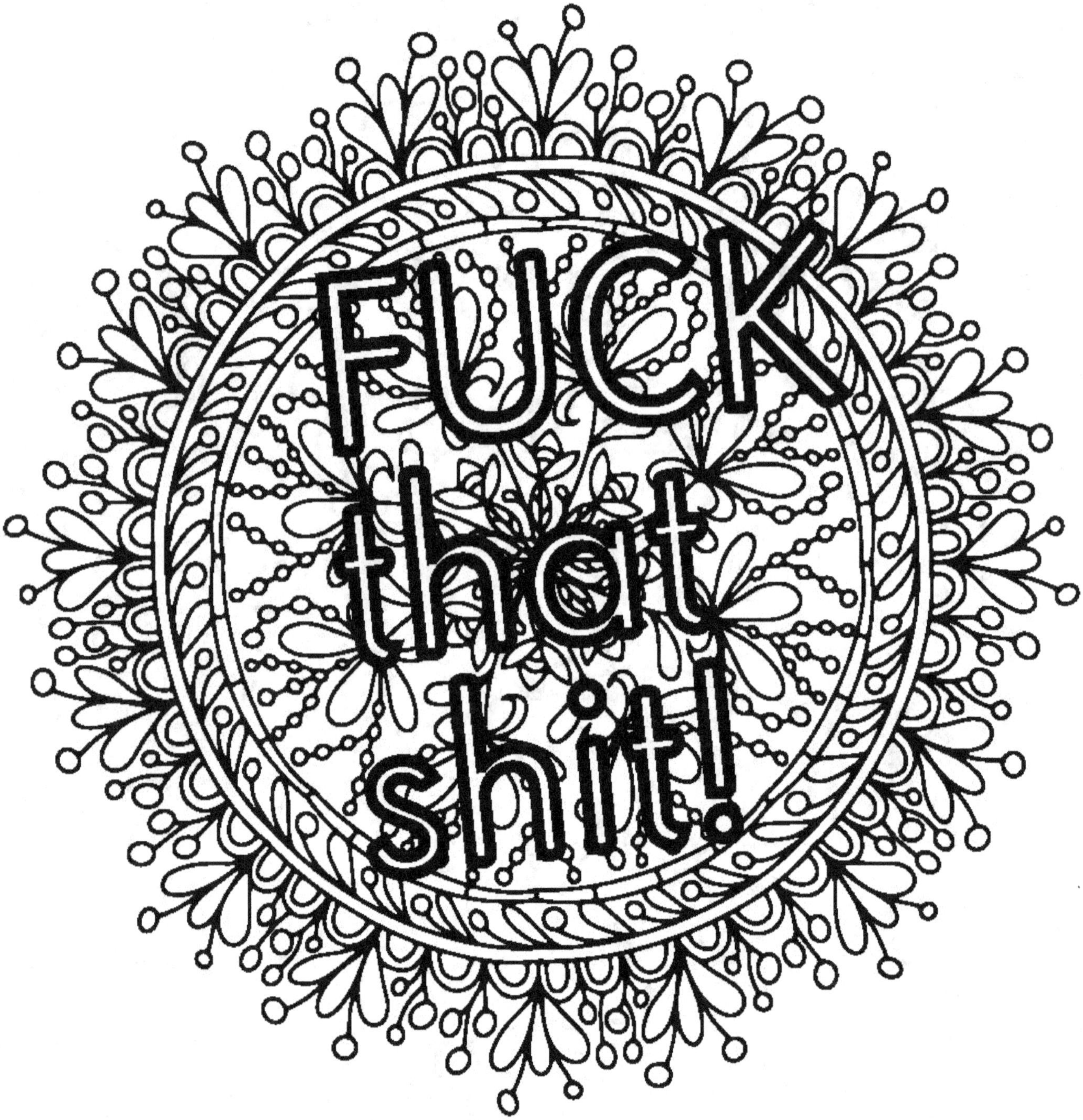
FUCK
that
shit!

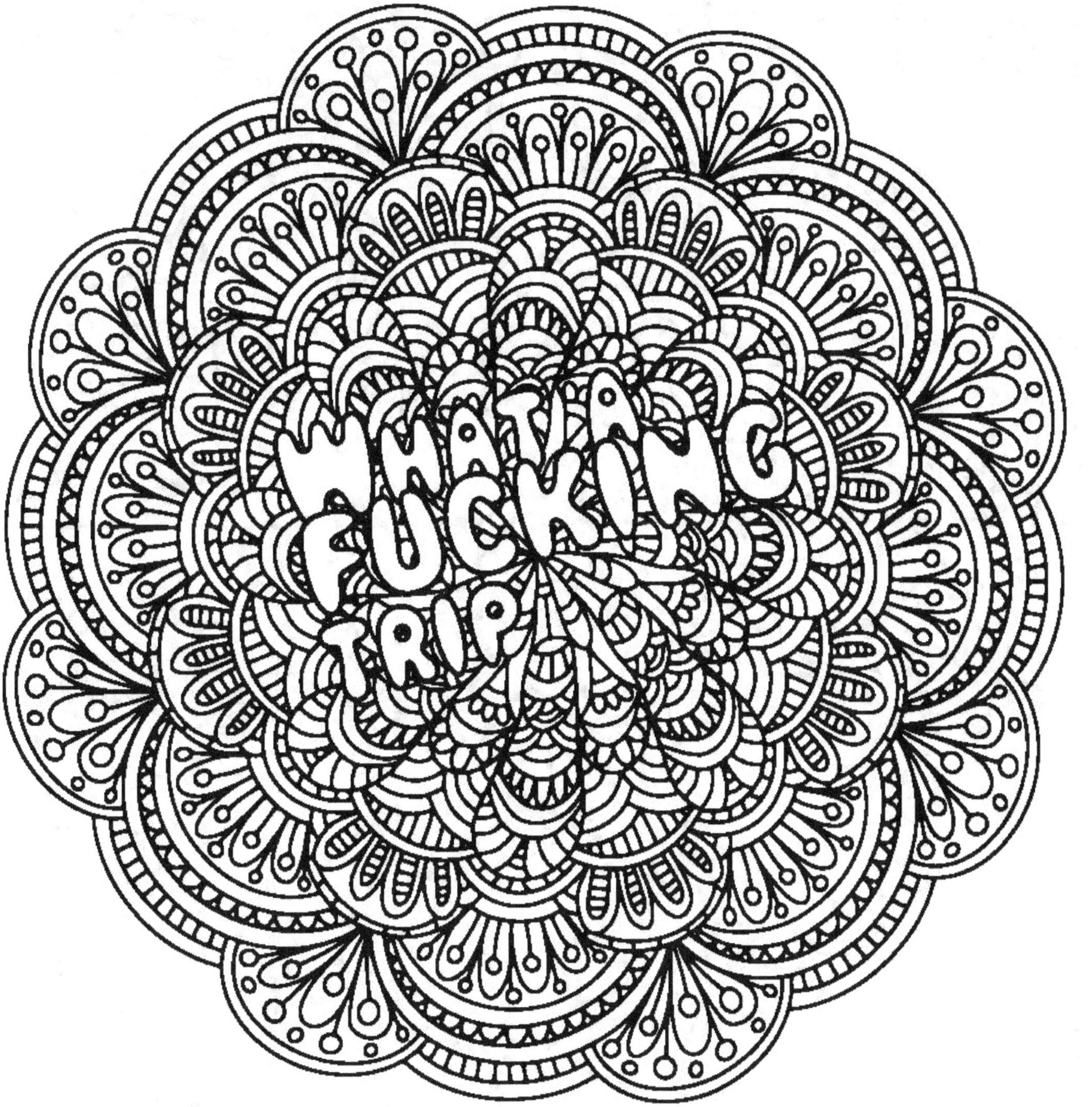
WHAT A
FUCKING
TRIP

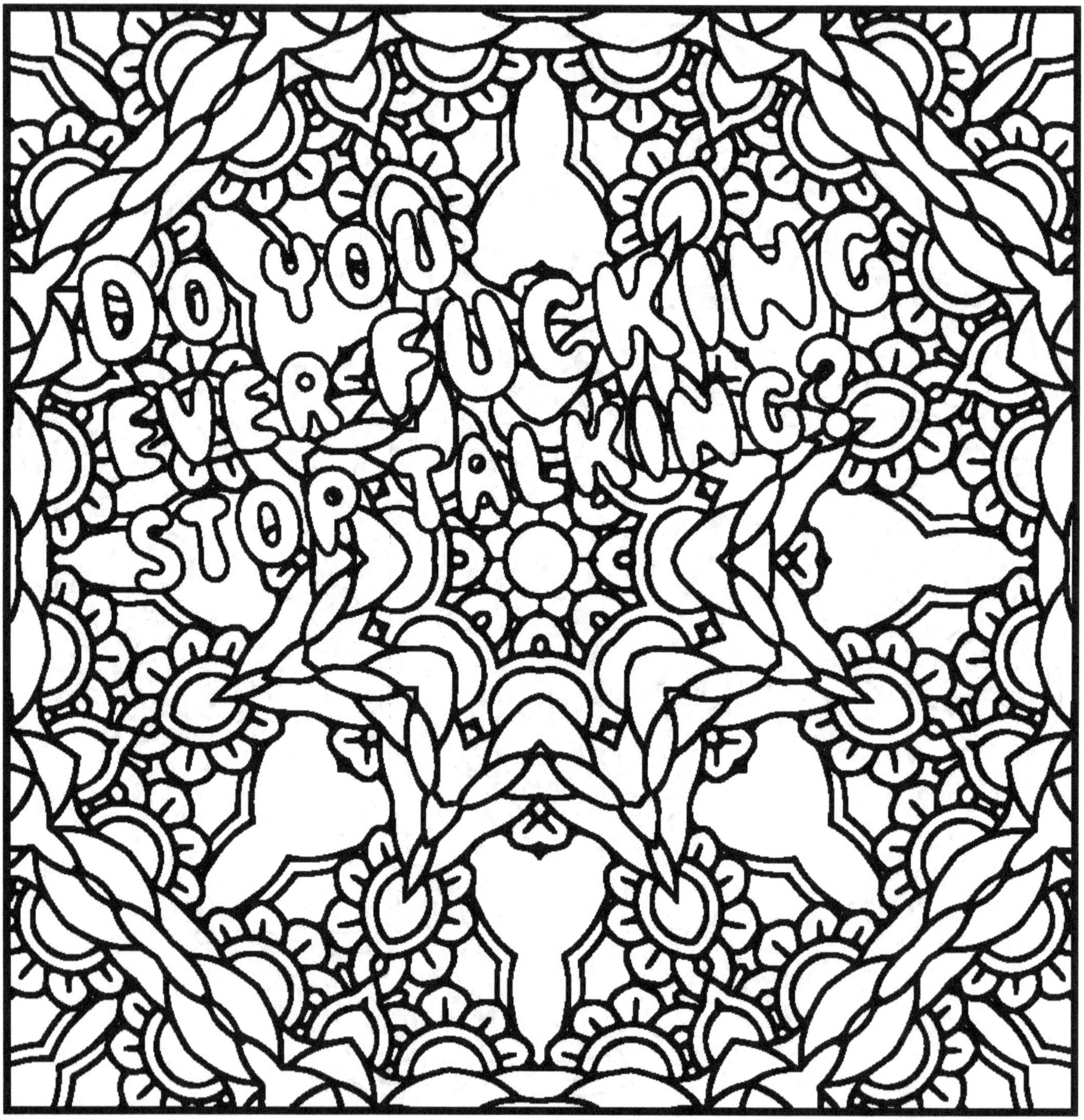
DO YOU
EVER FUCKING
STOP TALKING?

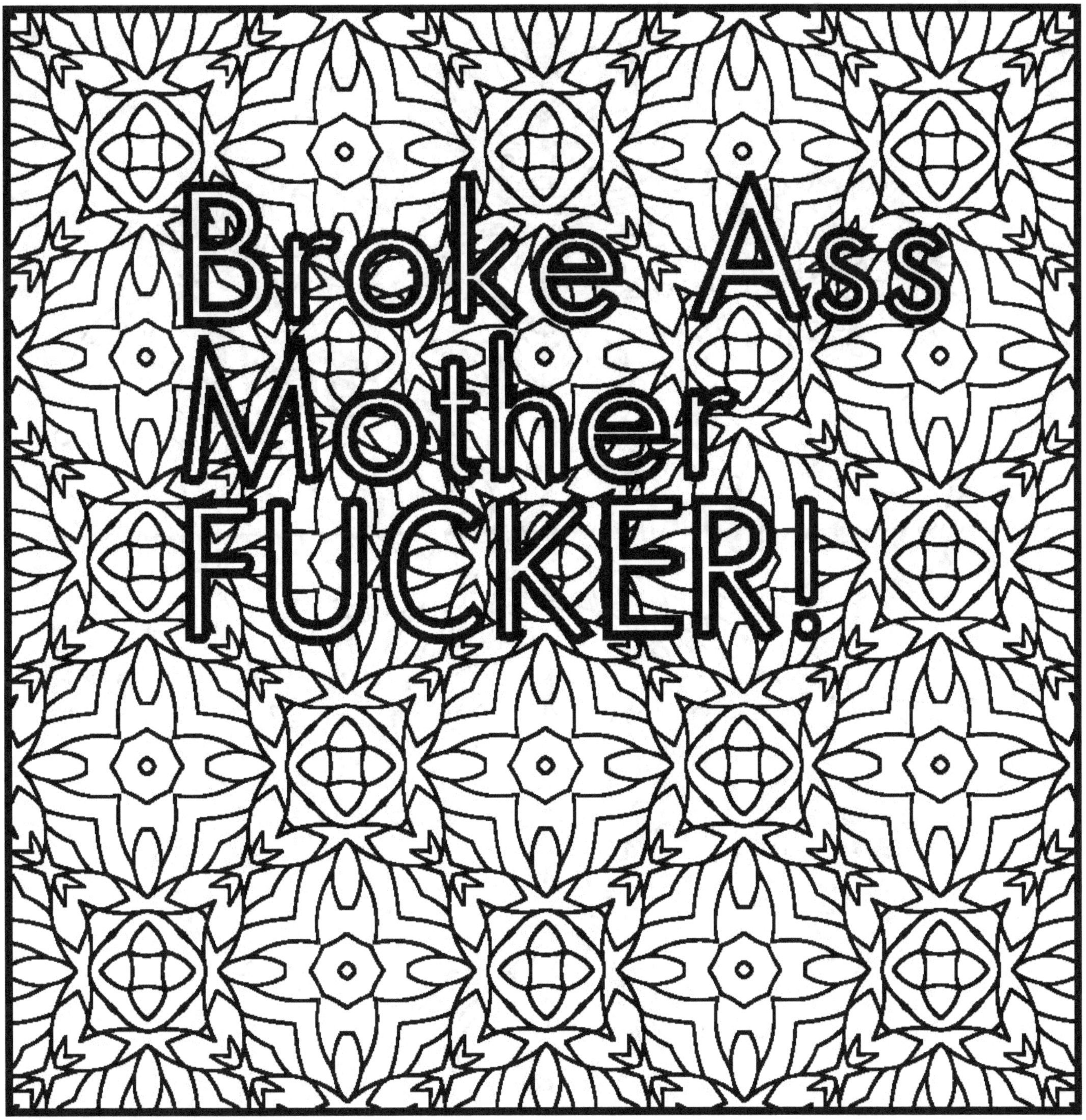
Broke Ass
Mother
FUCKER!

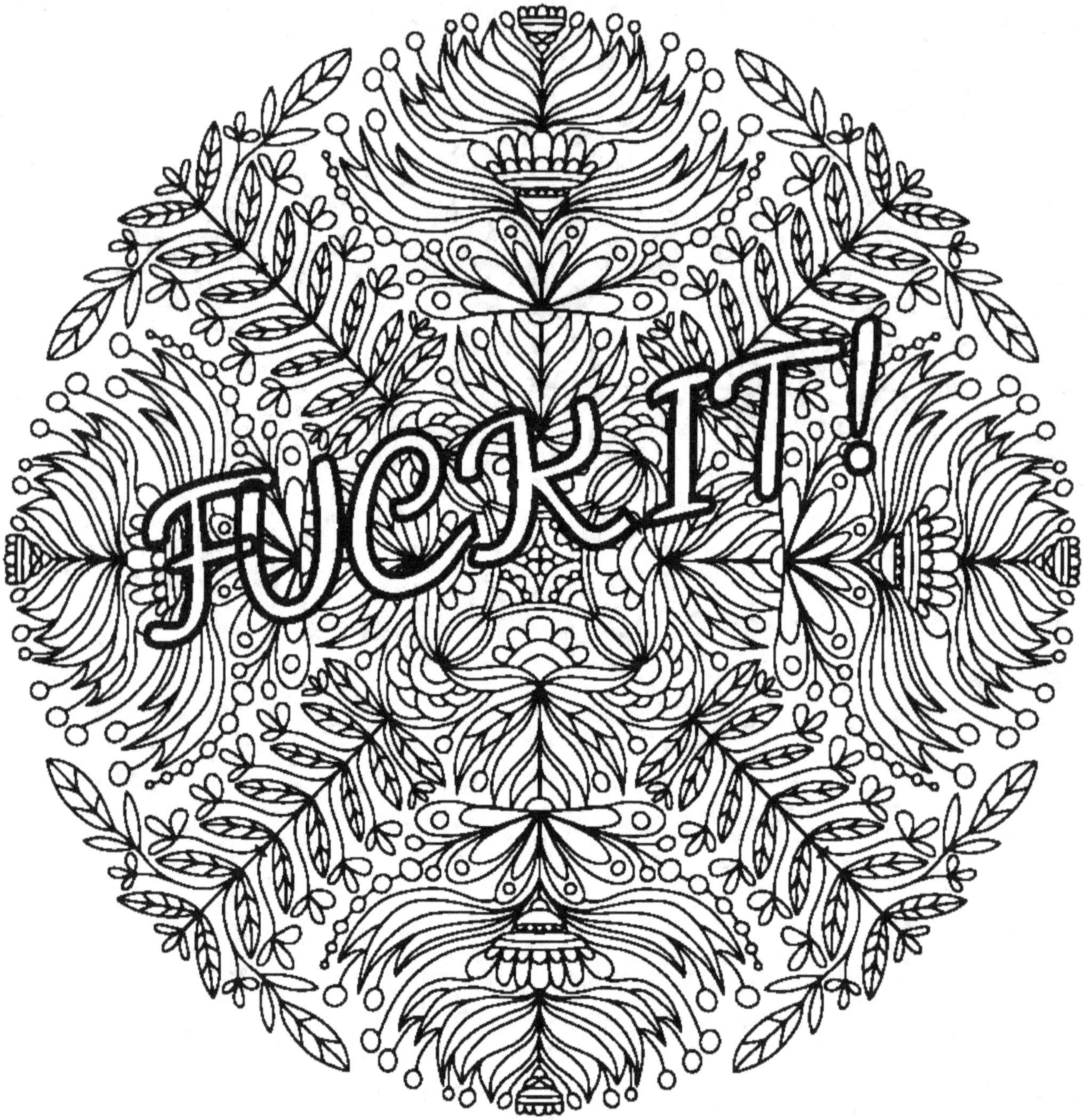
FUCK IT!

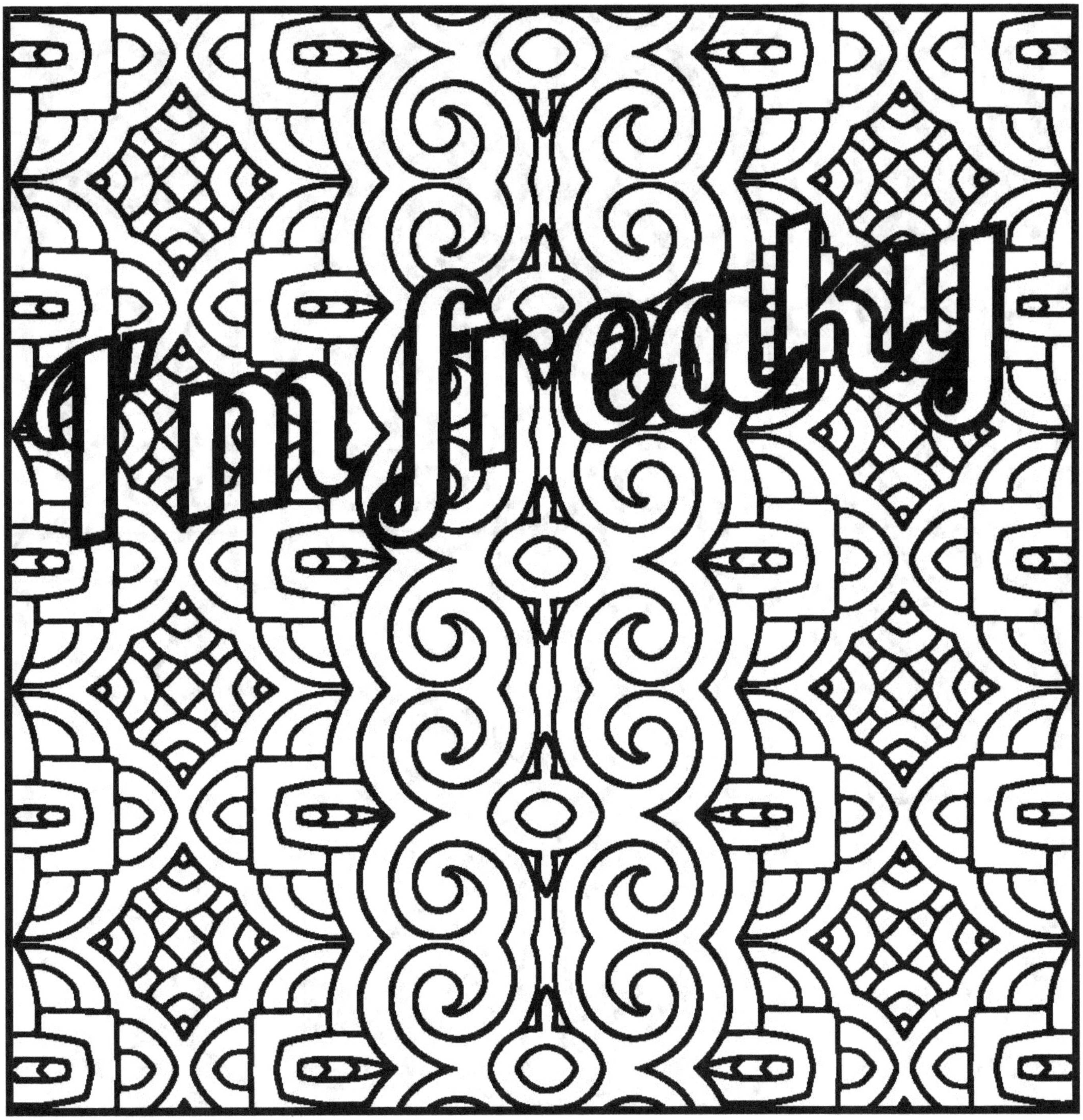
I'm freaky

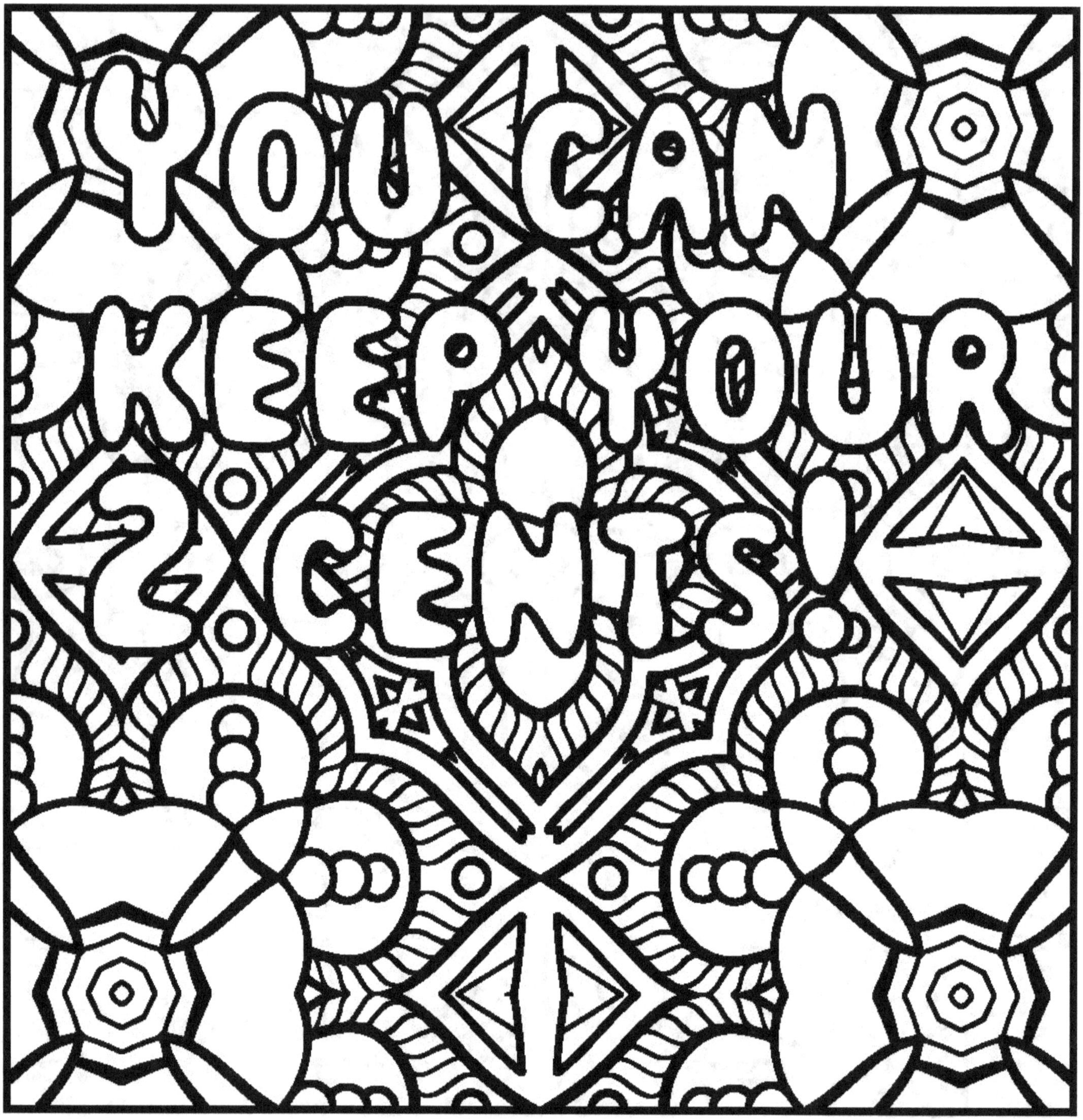
YOU CAN
KEEP YOUR
2 CENTS!

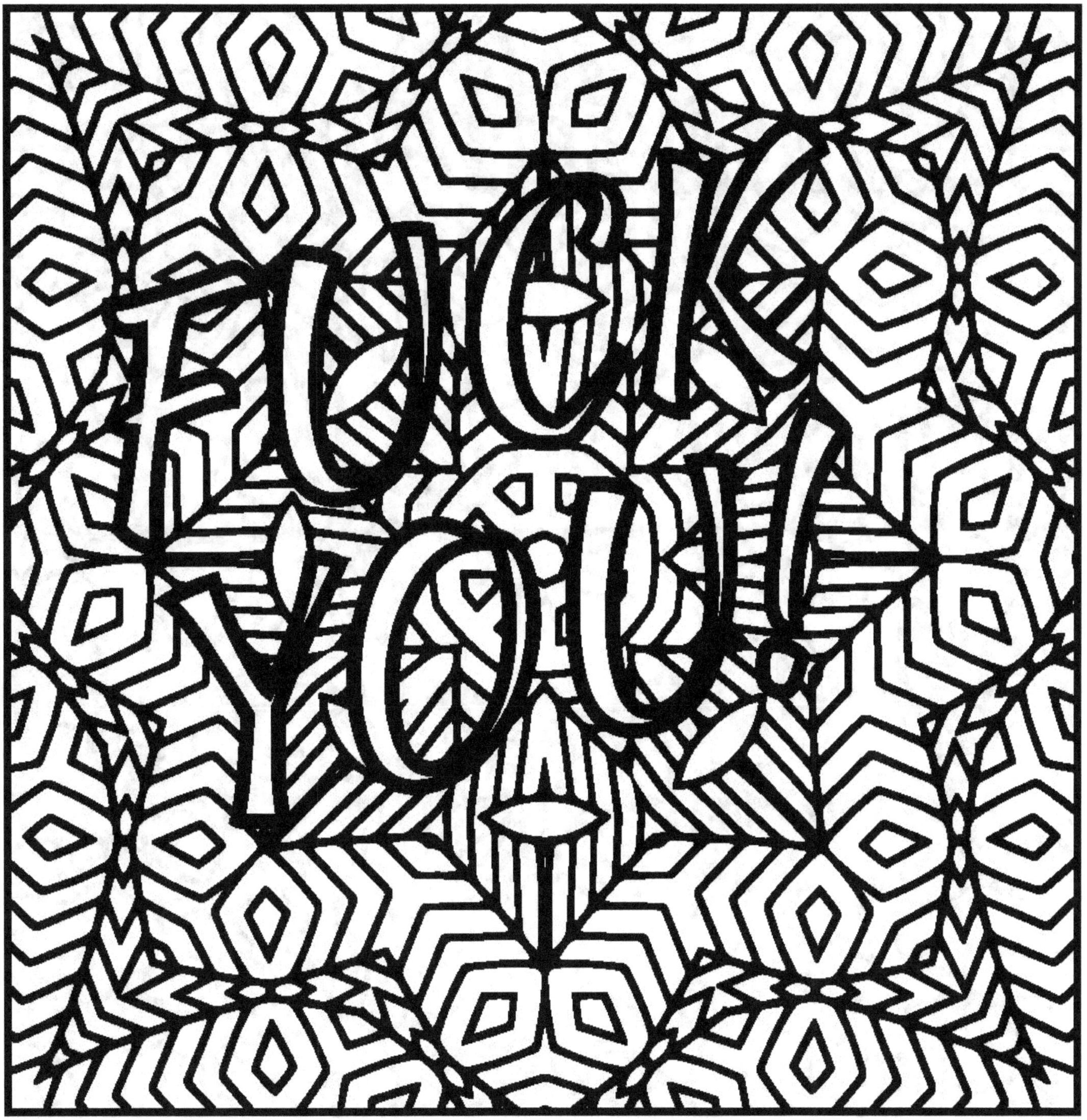
FUCK
YOU!

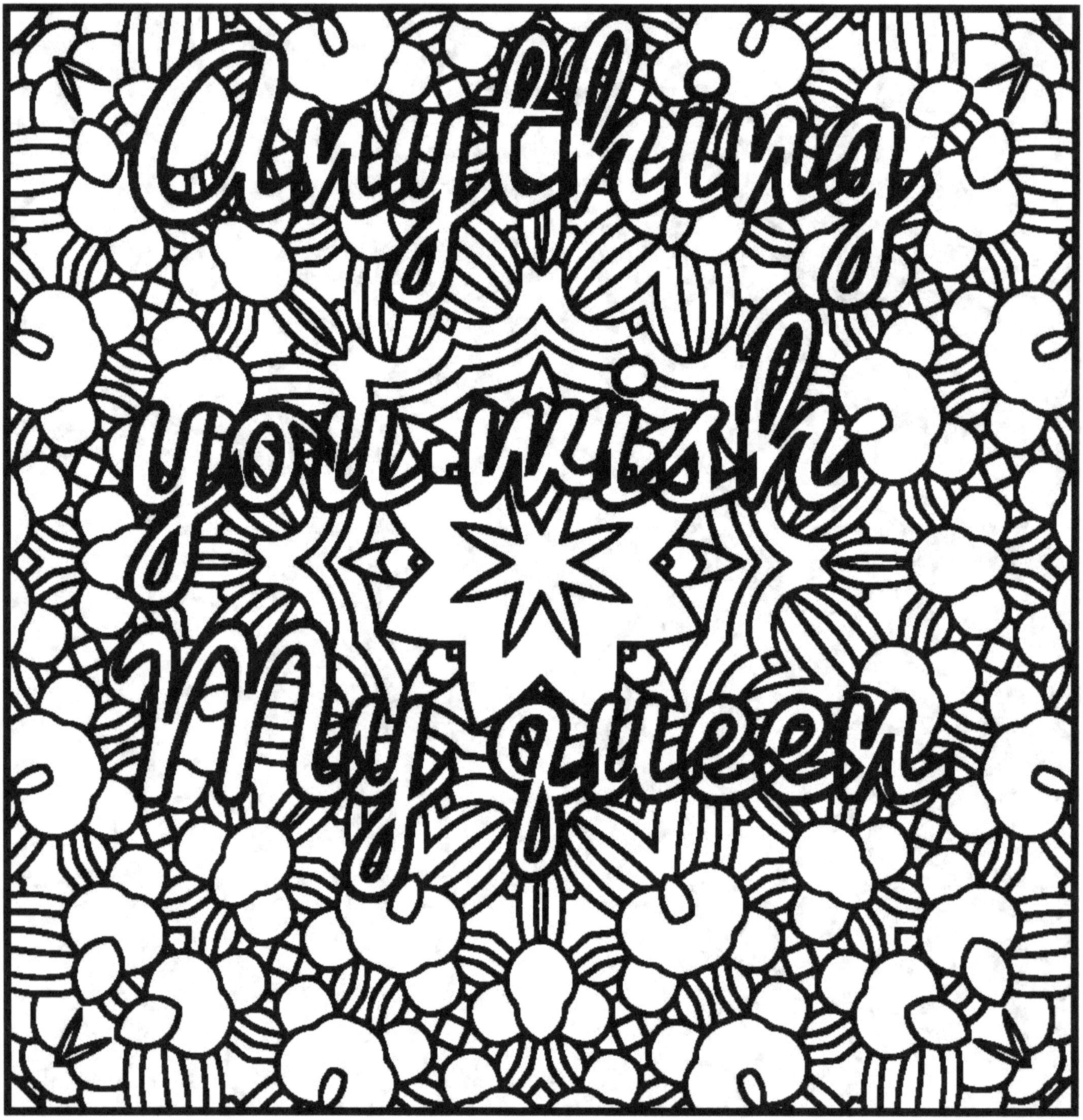
Anything
you wish
My queen

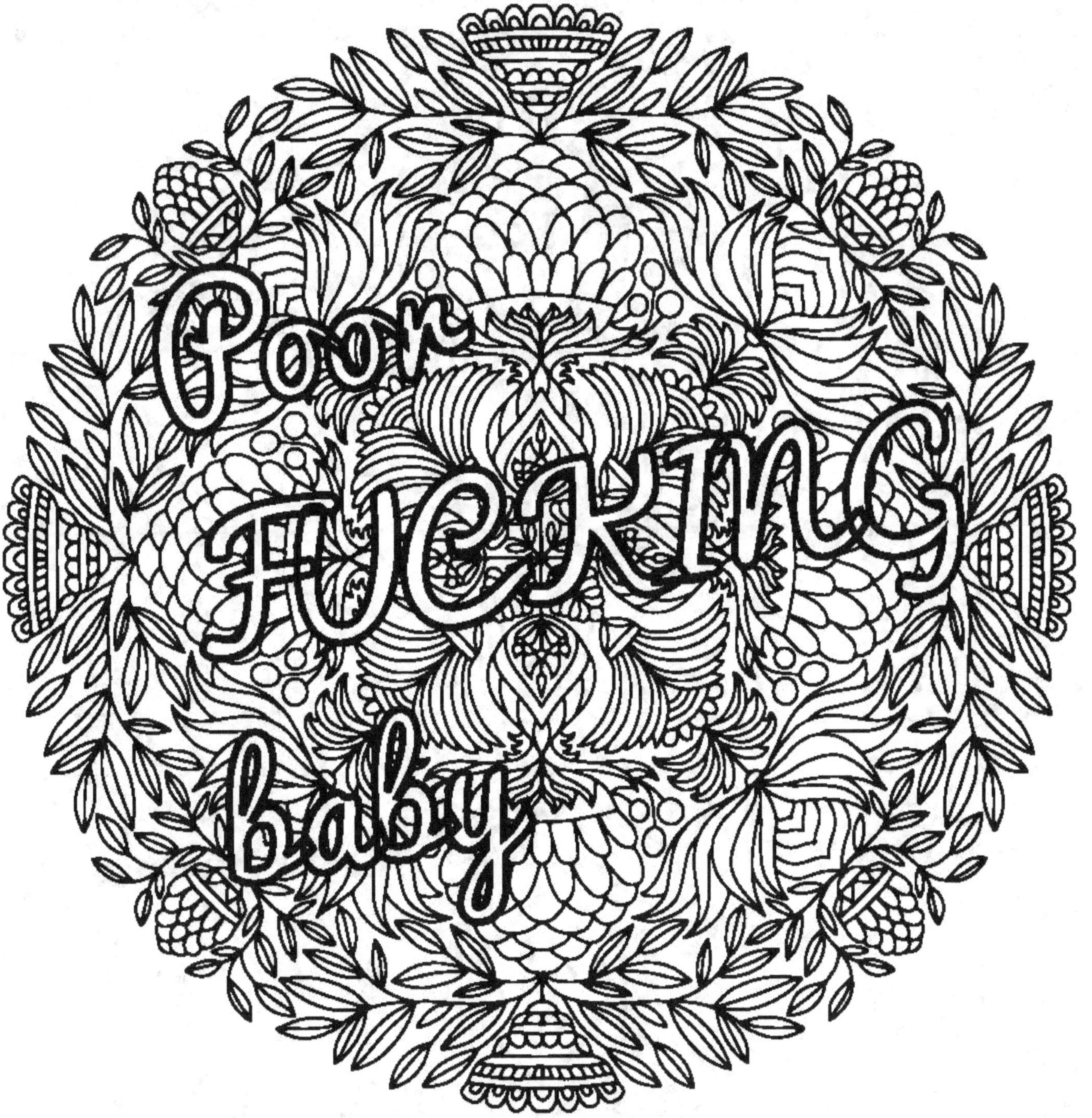
Poor
FUCKING
baby

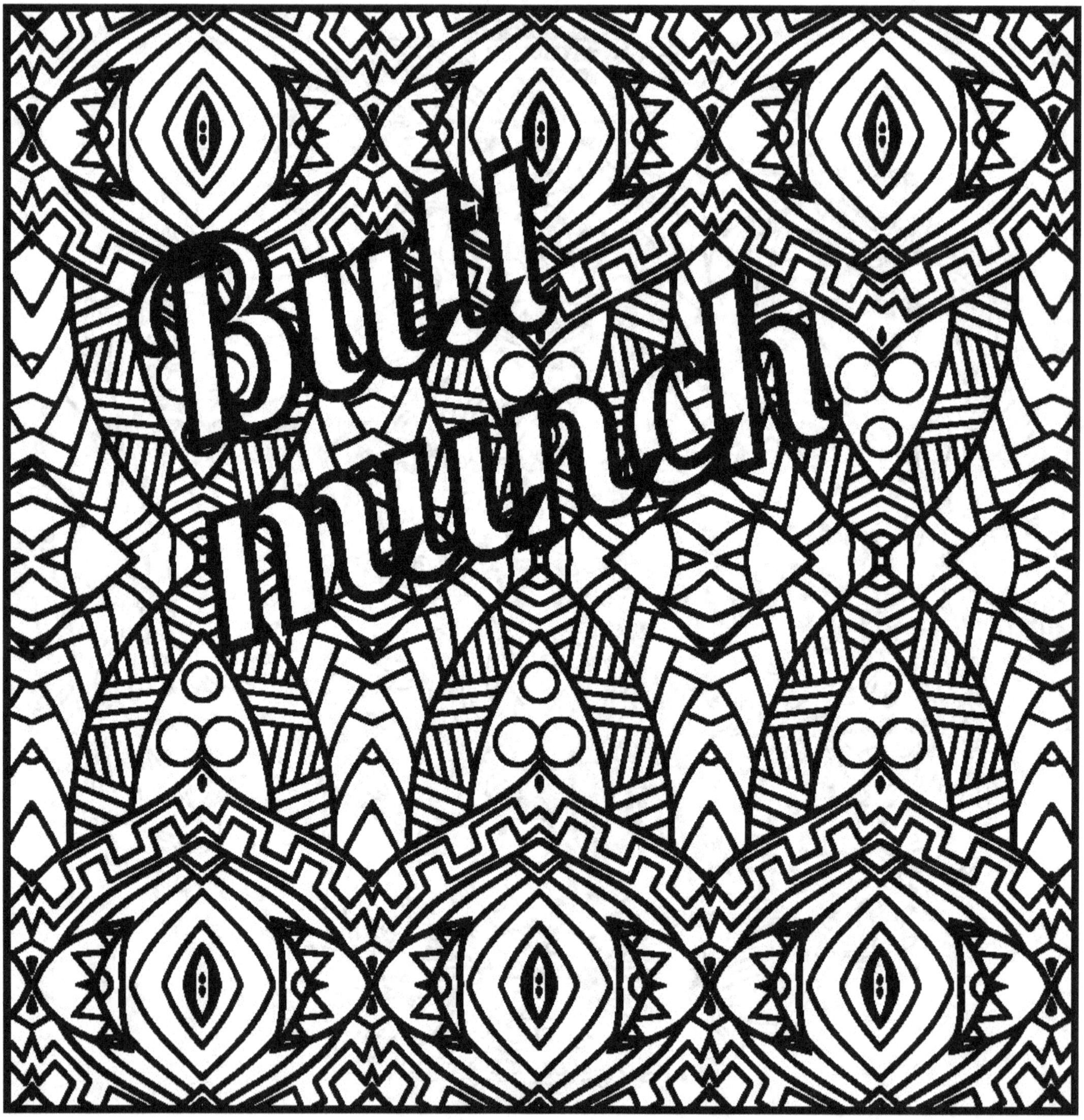
Butt
munch

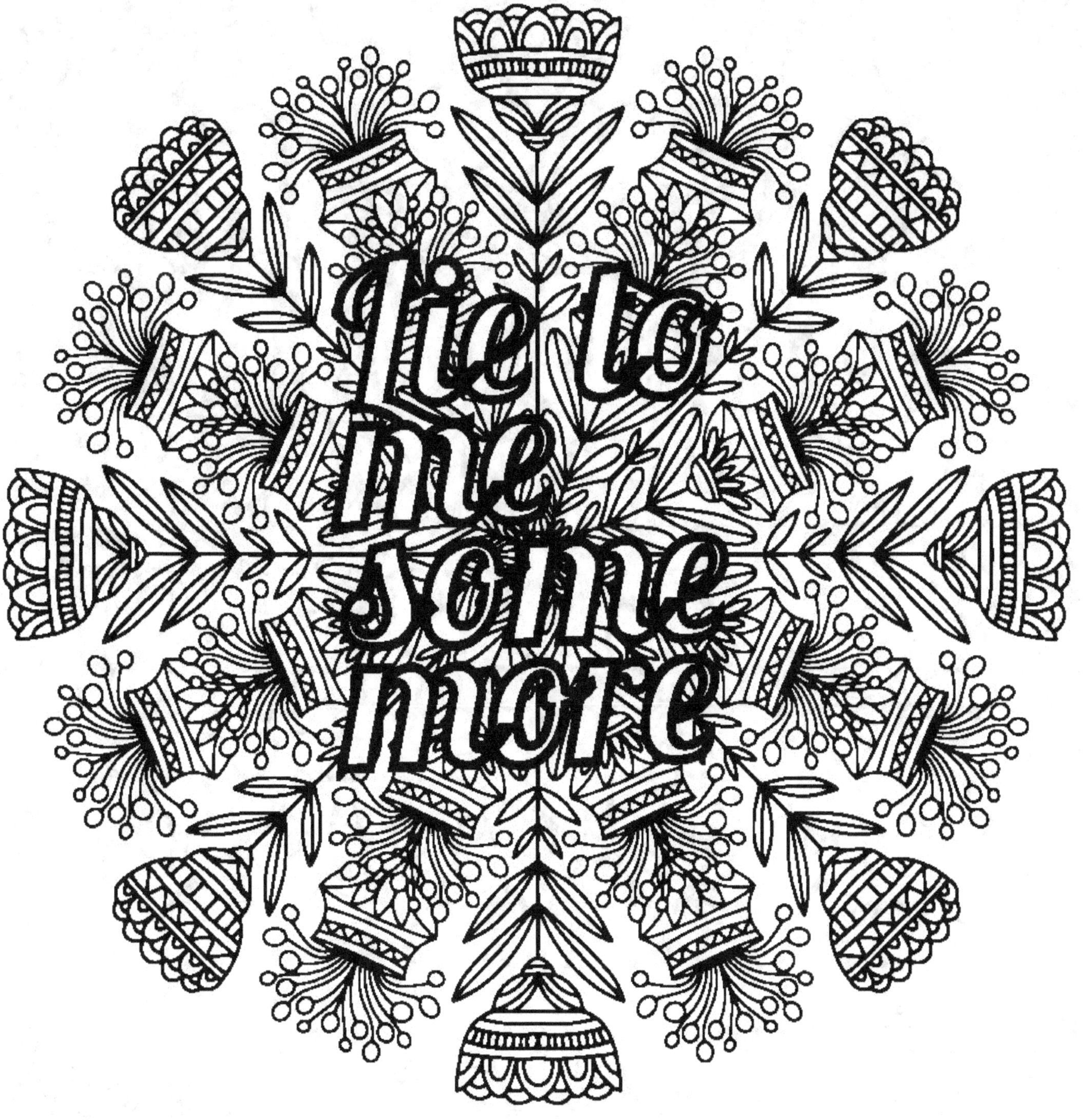
lie to
me
some
more

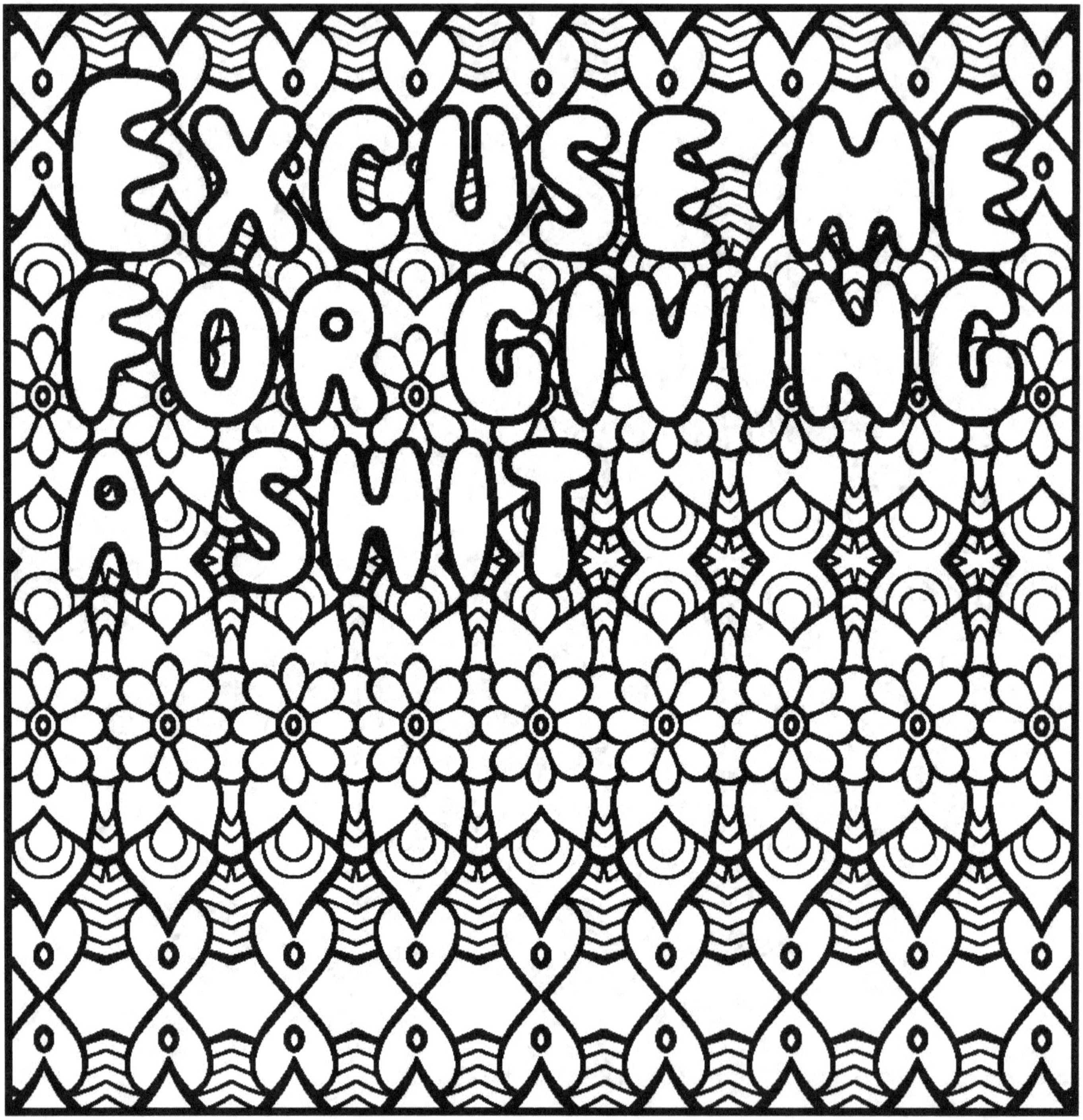
EXCUSE ME
FOR GIVING
A SHIT

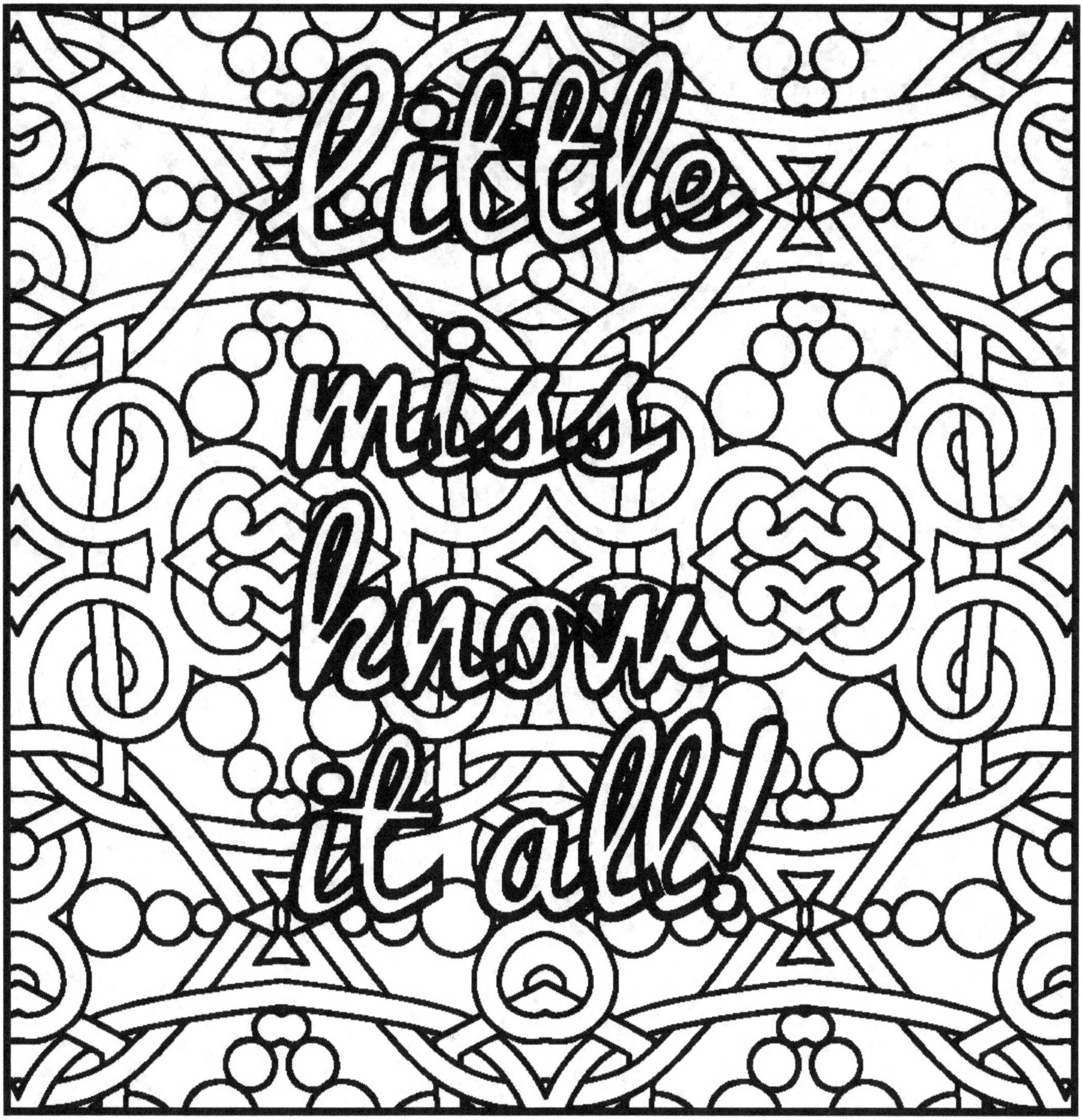
little
miss
know
it all!

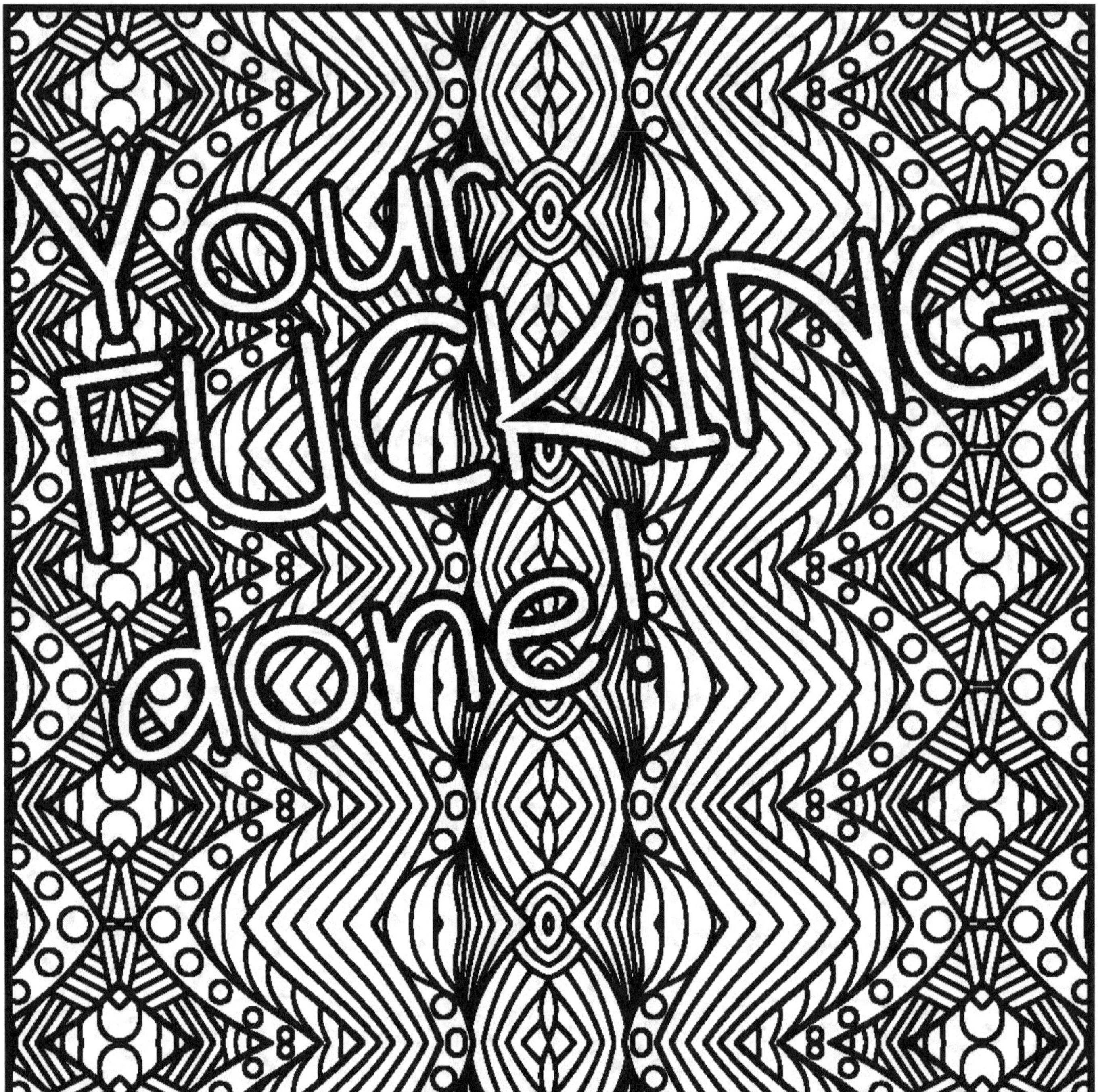
Your
FUCKING
done!

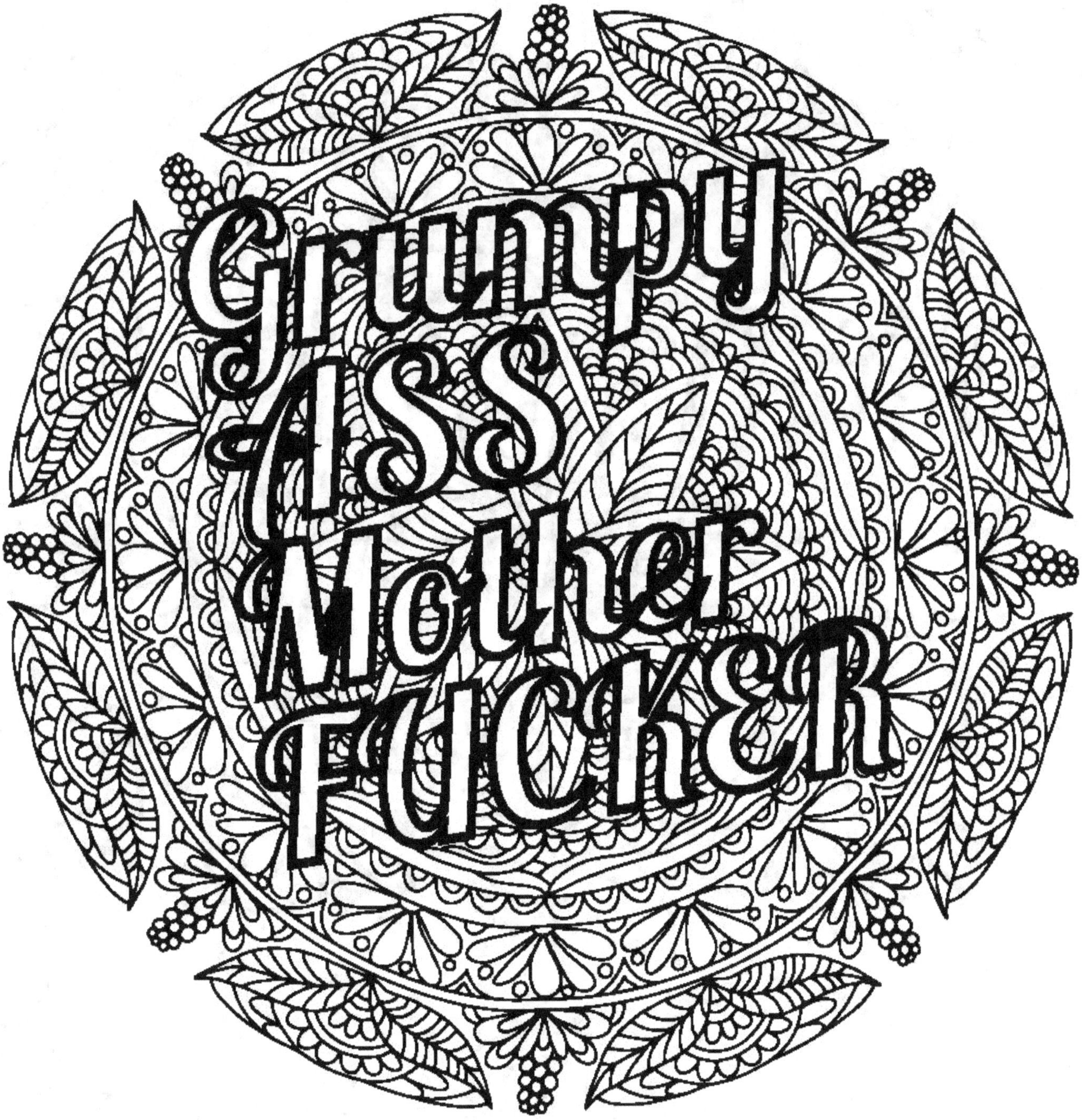
Grumpy
ASS
Mother
FUCKER

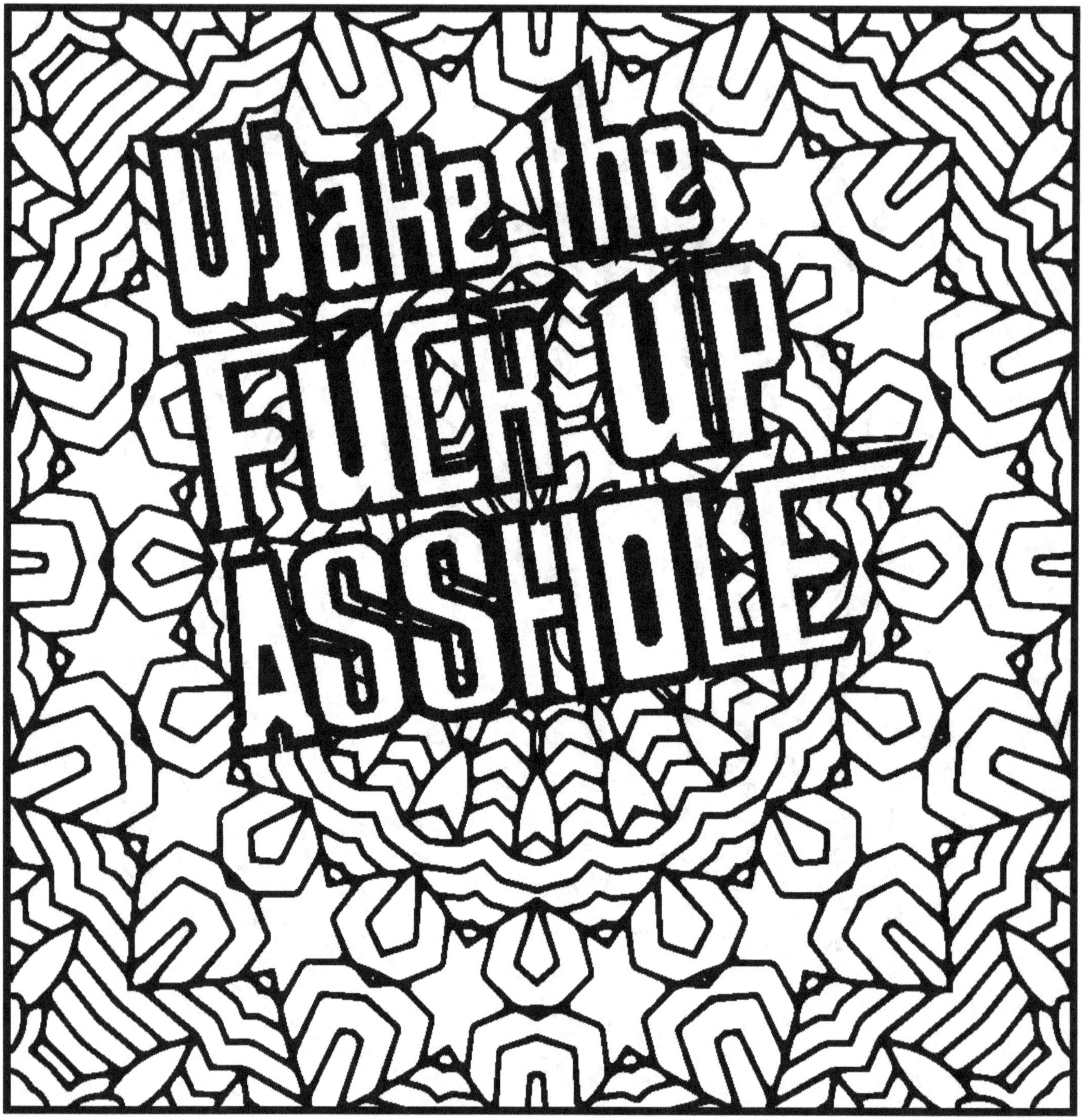
Wake the
FUCK UP
ASSHOLE

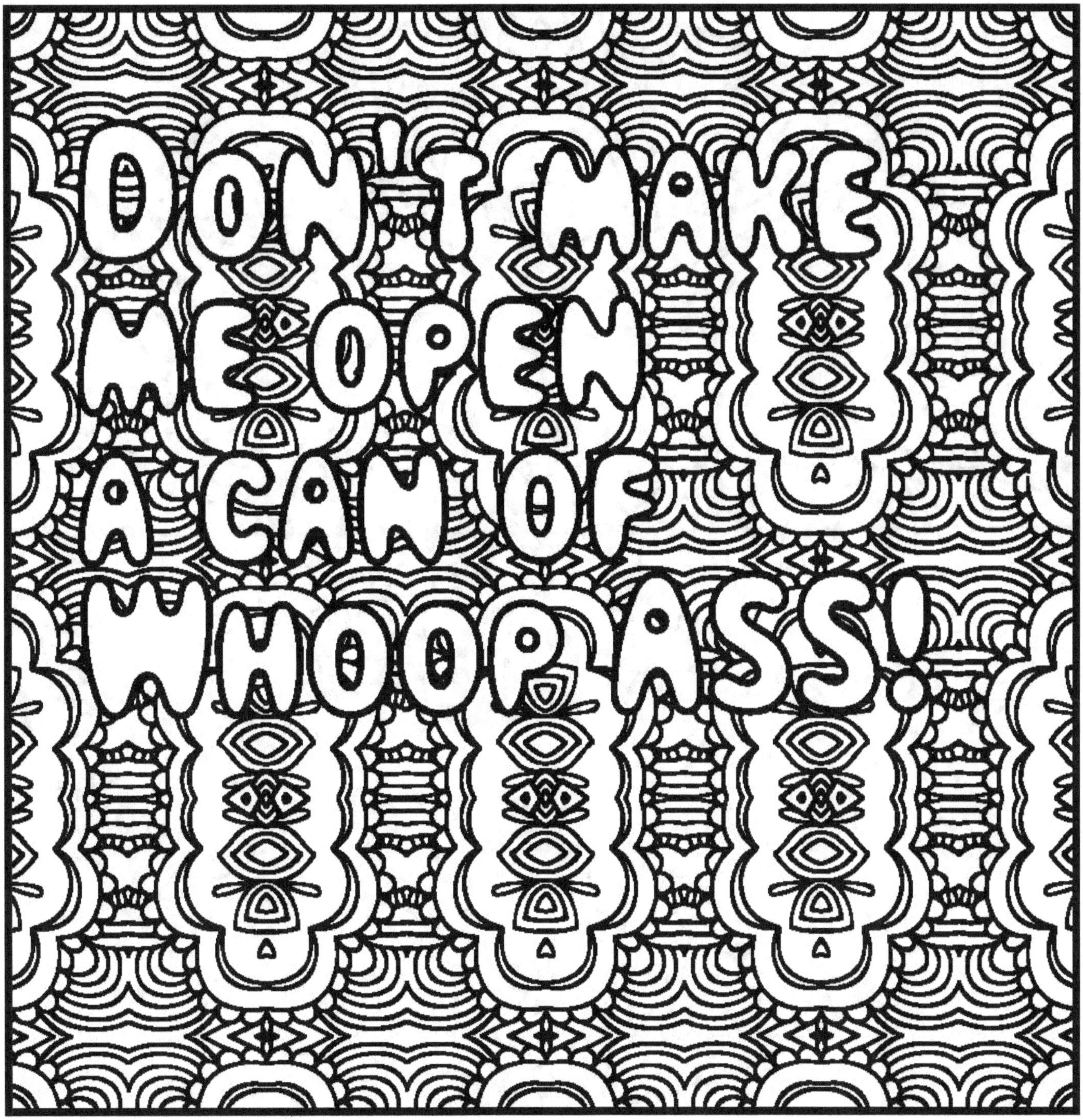
DON'T MAKE
ME OPEN
A CAN OF
WHOOP ASS!

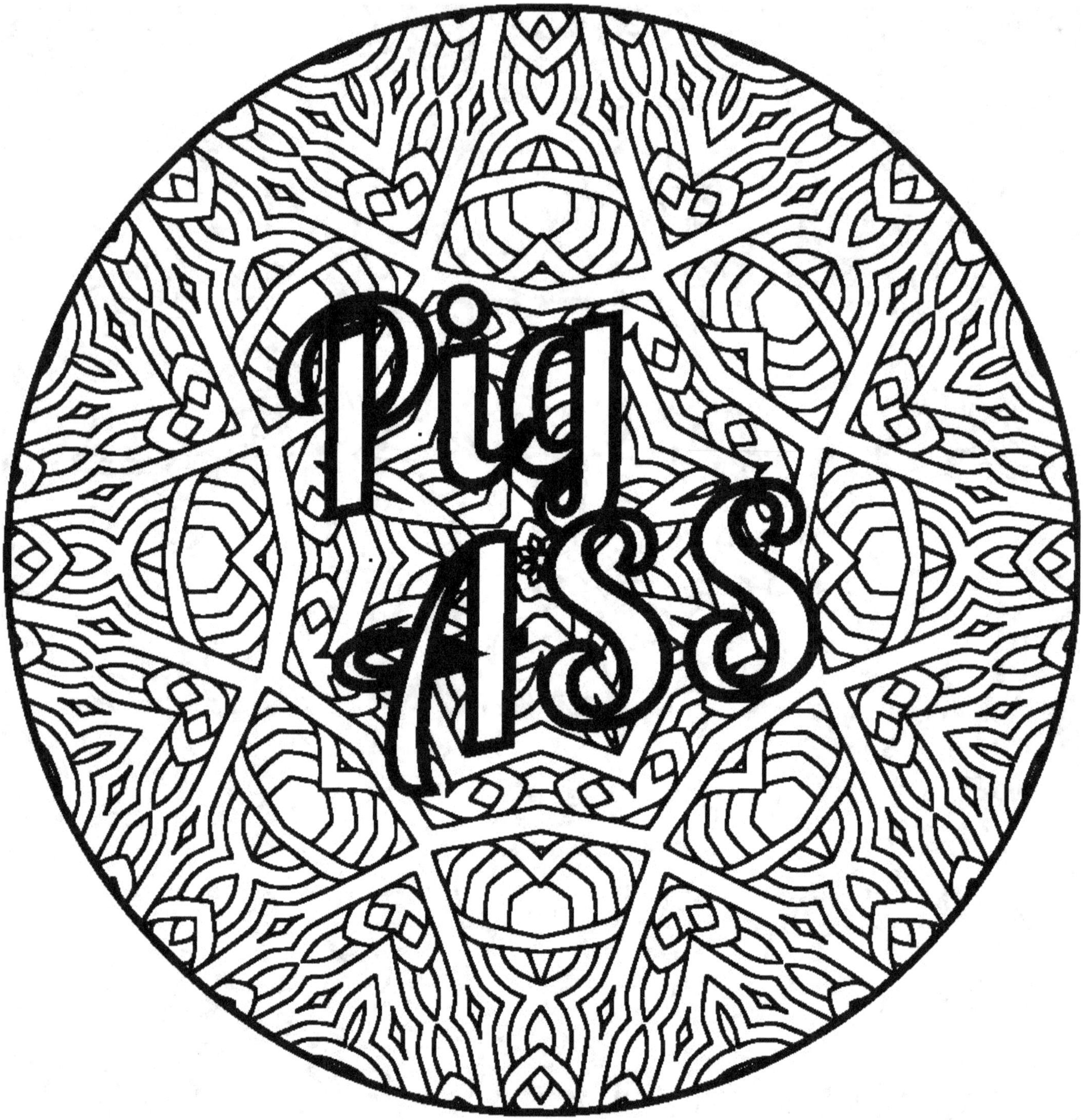
Pig
ASS

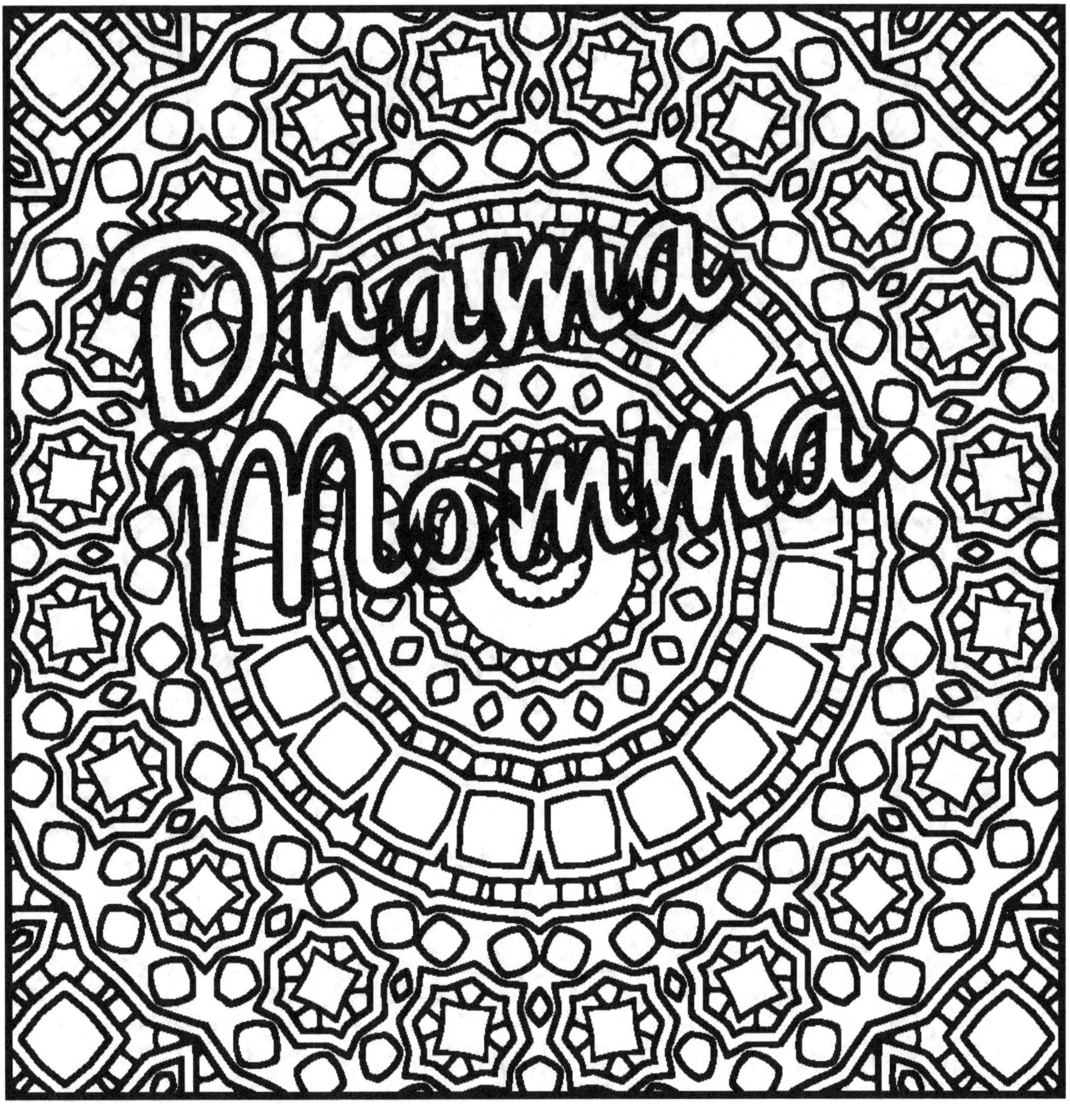
Drama Momma

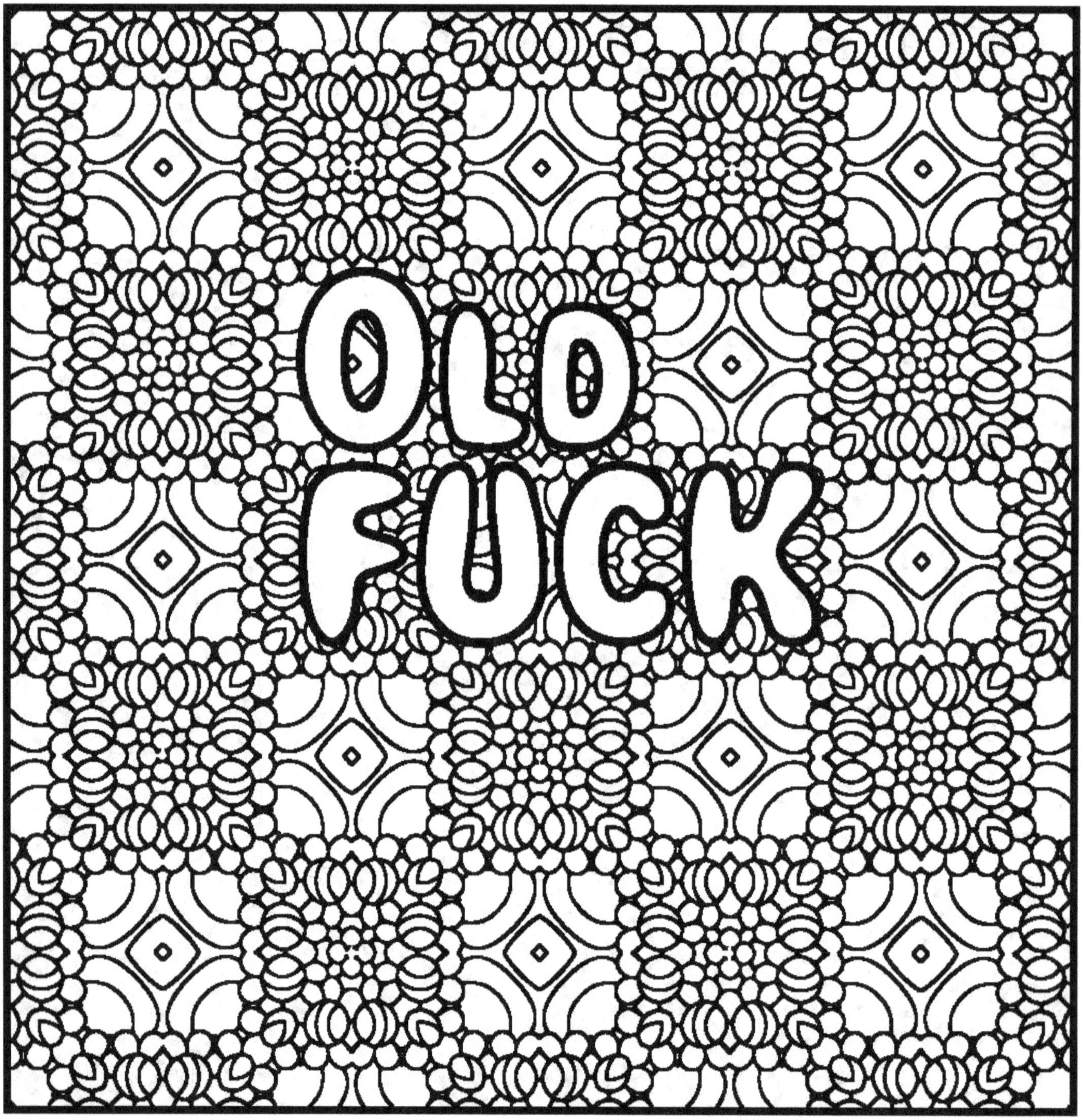
OLD
FUCK

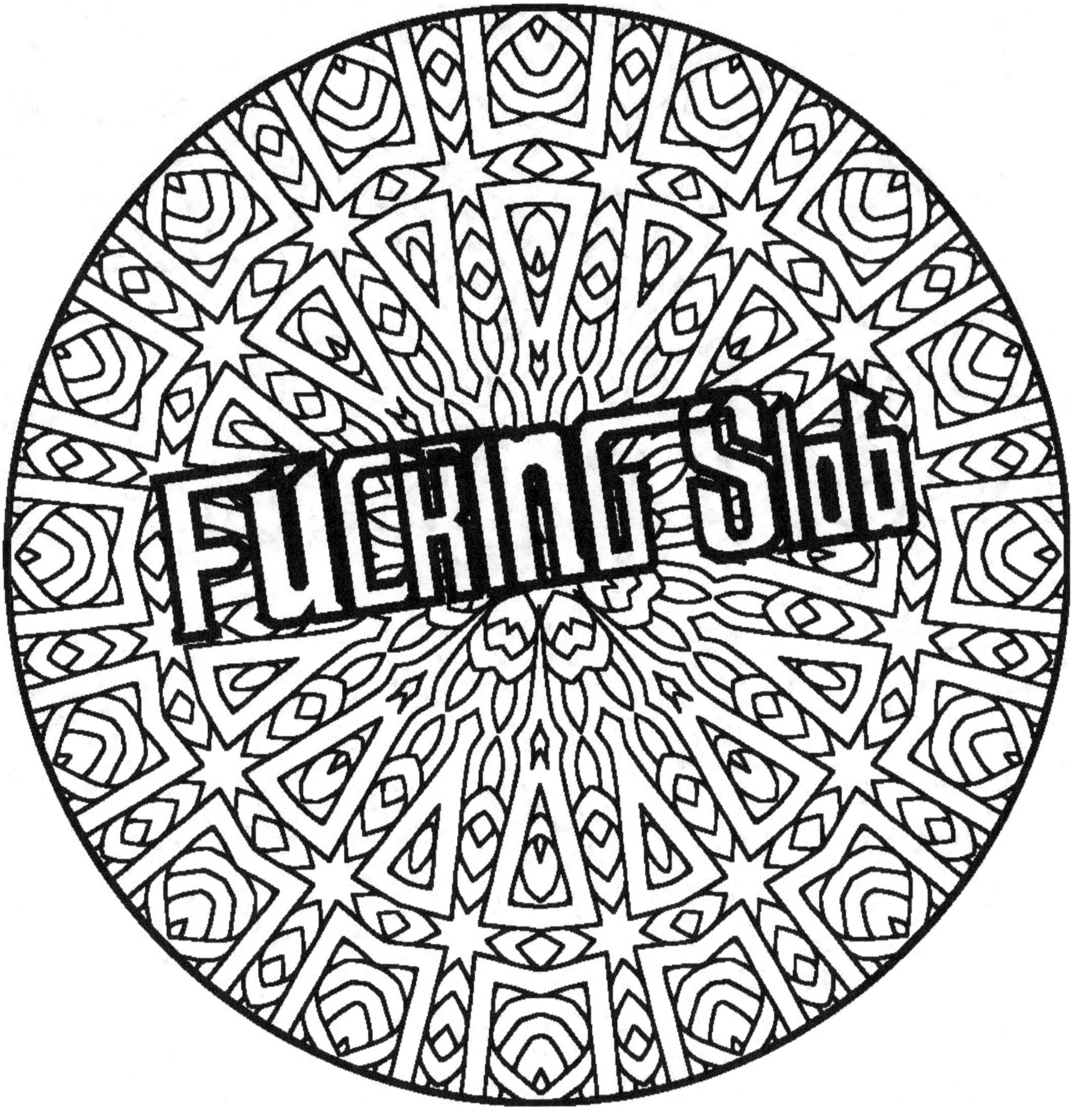
Fucking Slob

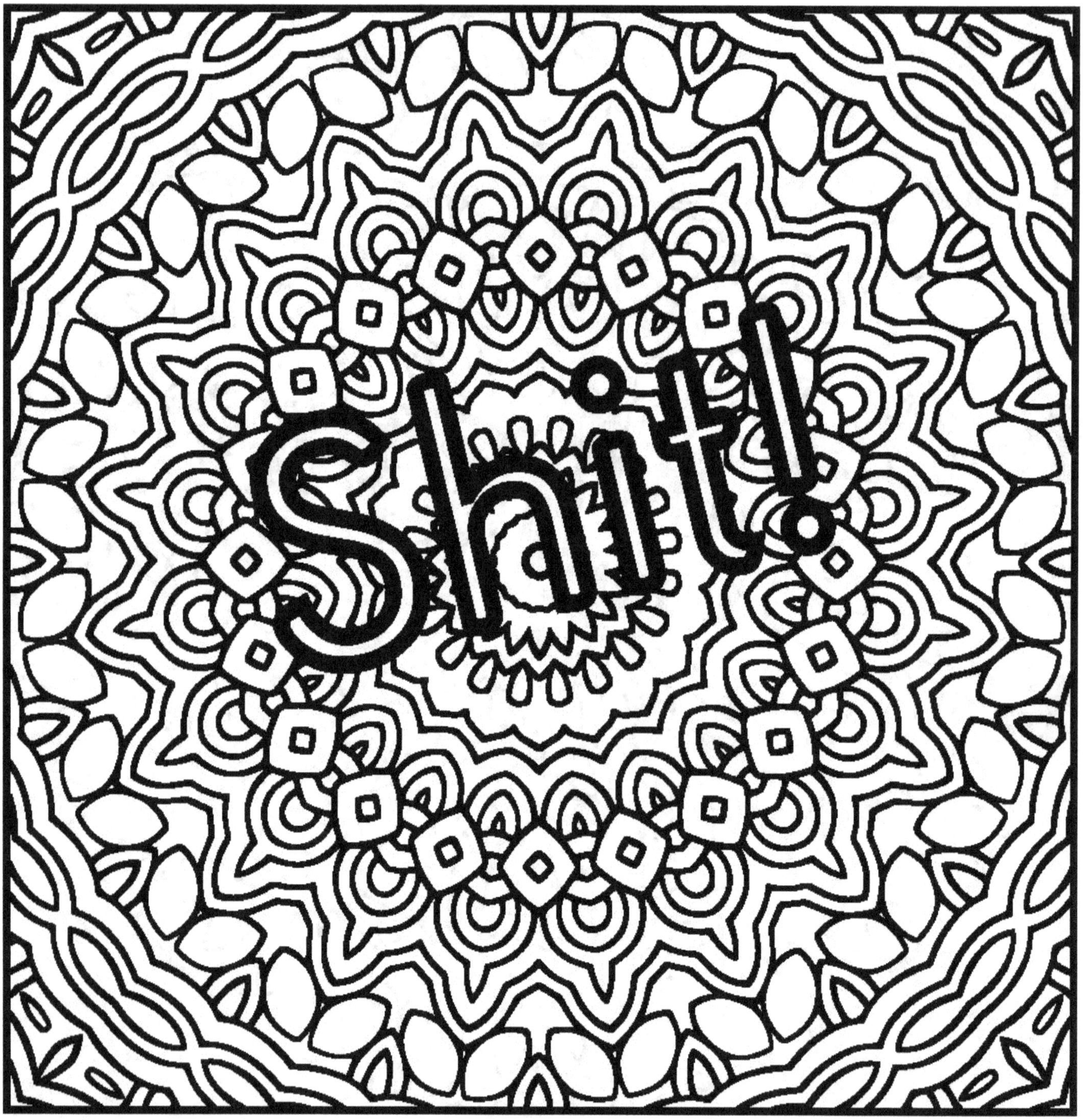
Shit!

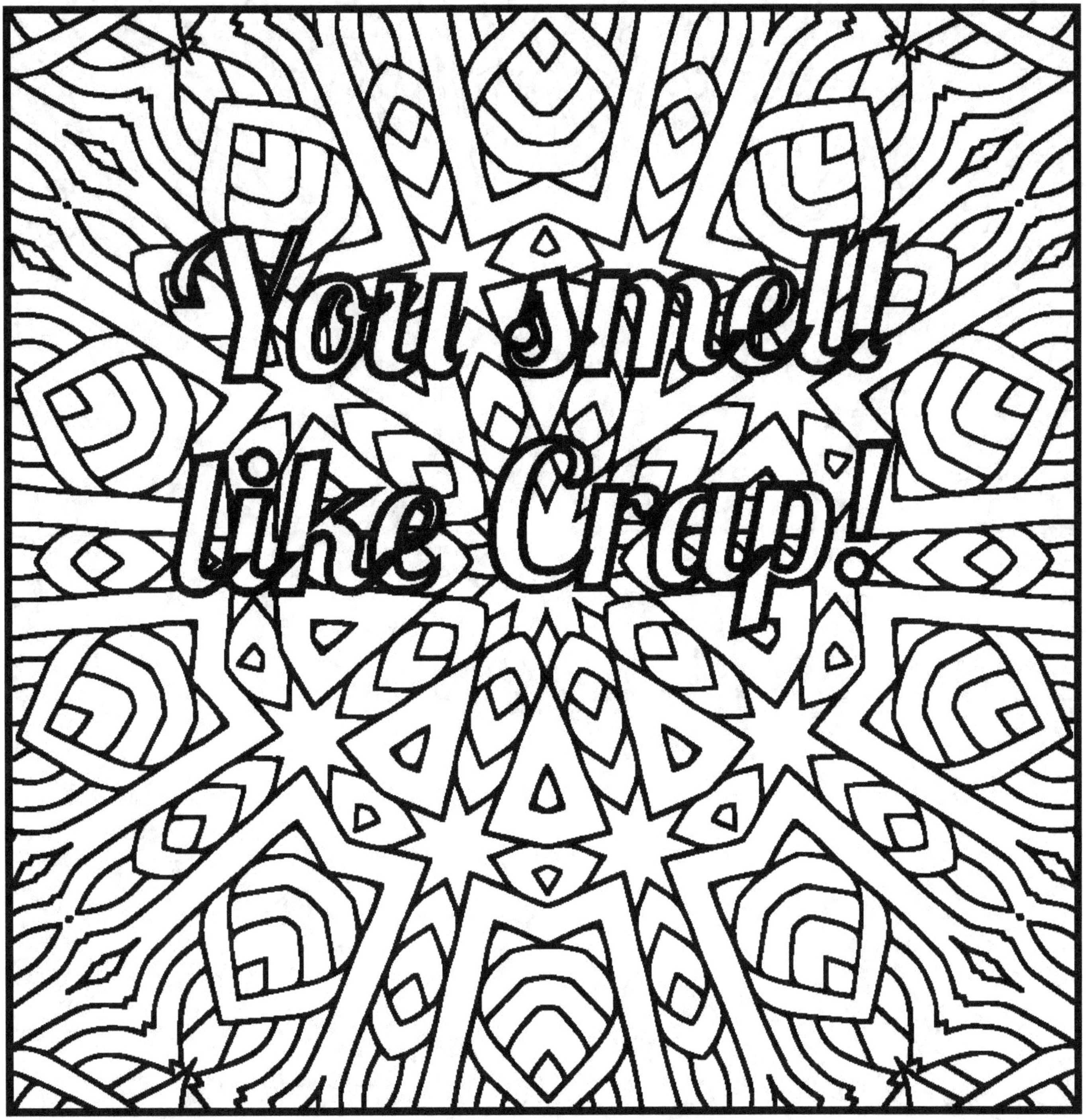
You smell
like Crap!

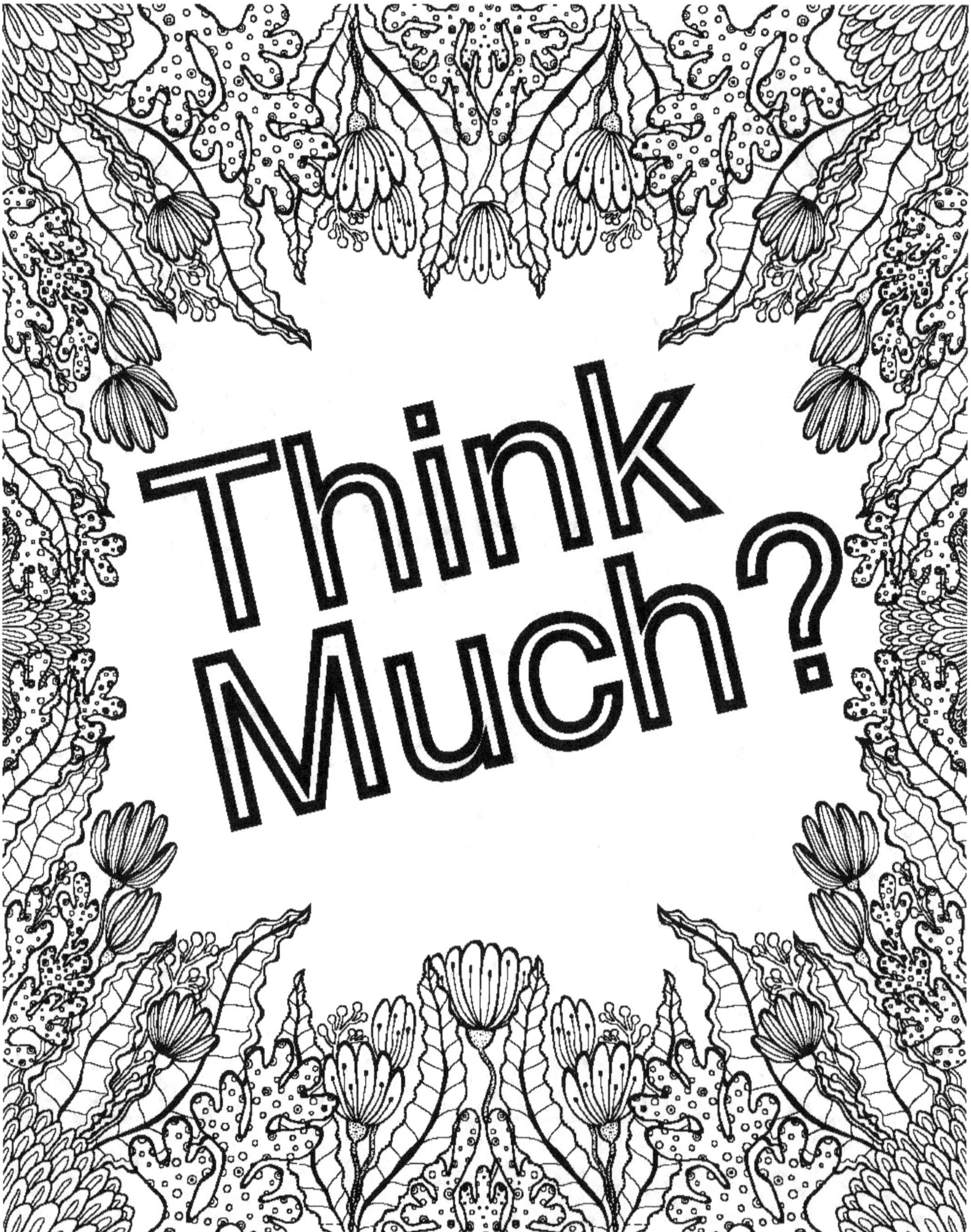
Think
Much?

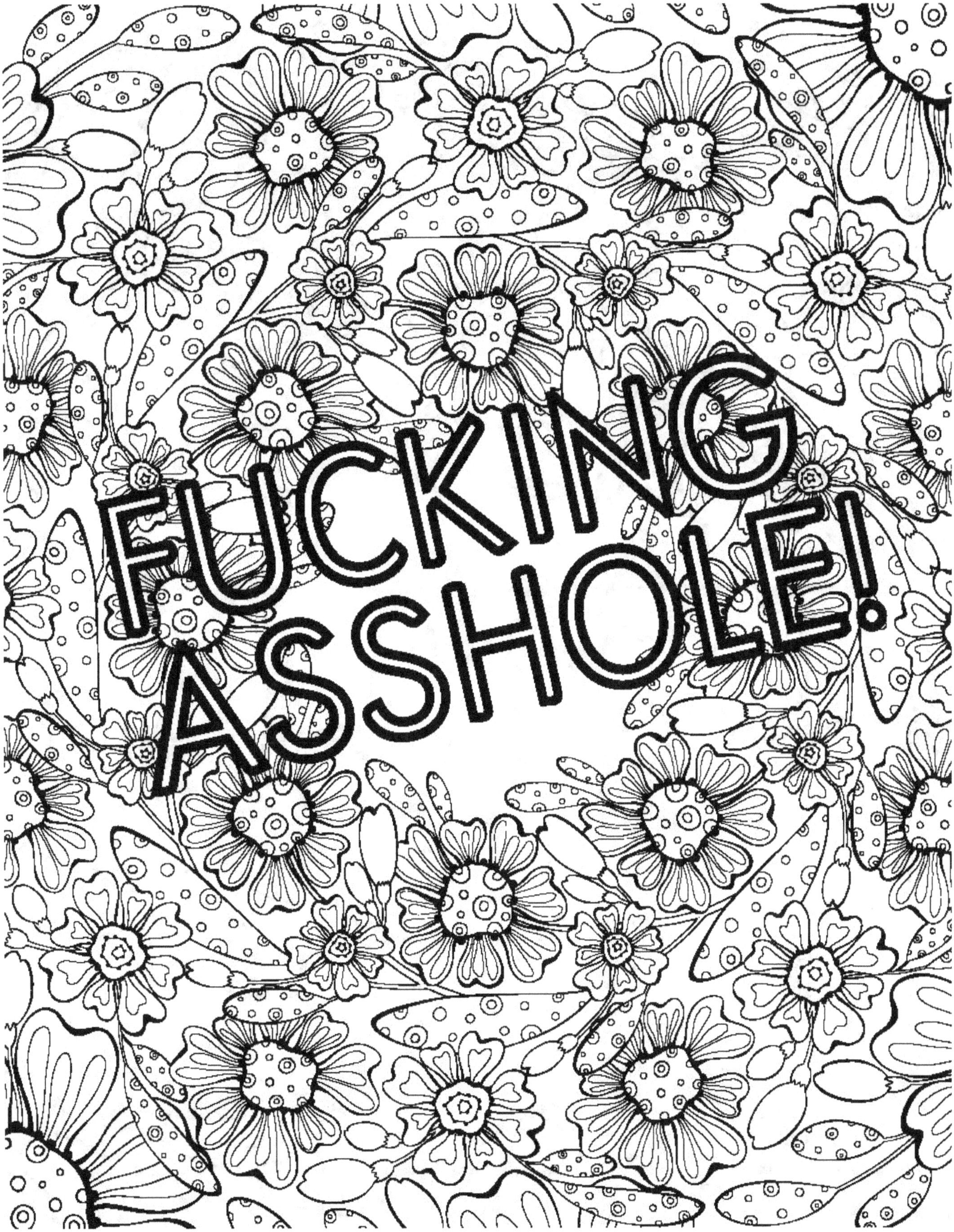
FUCKING ASSHOLE!

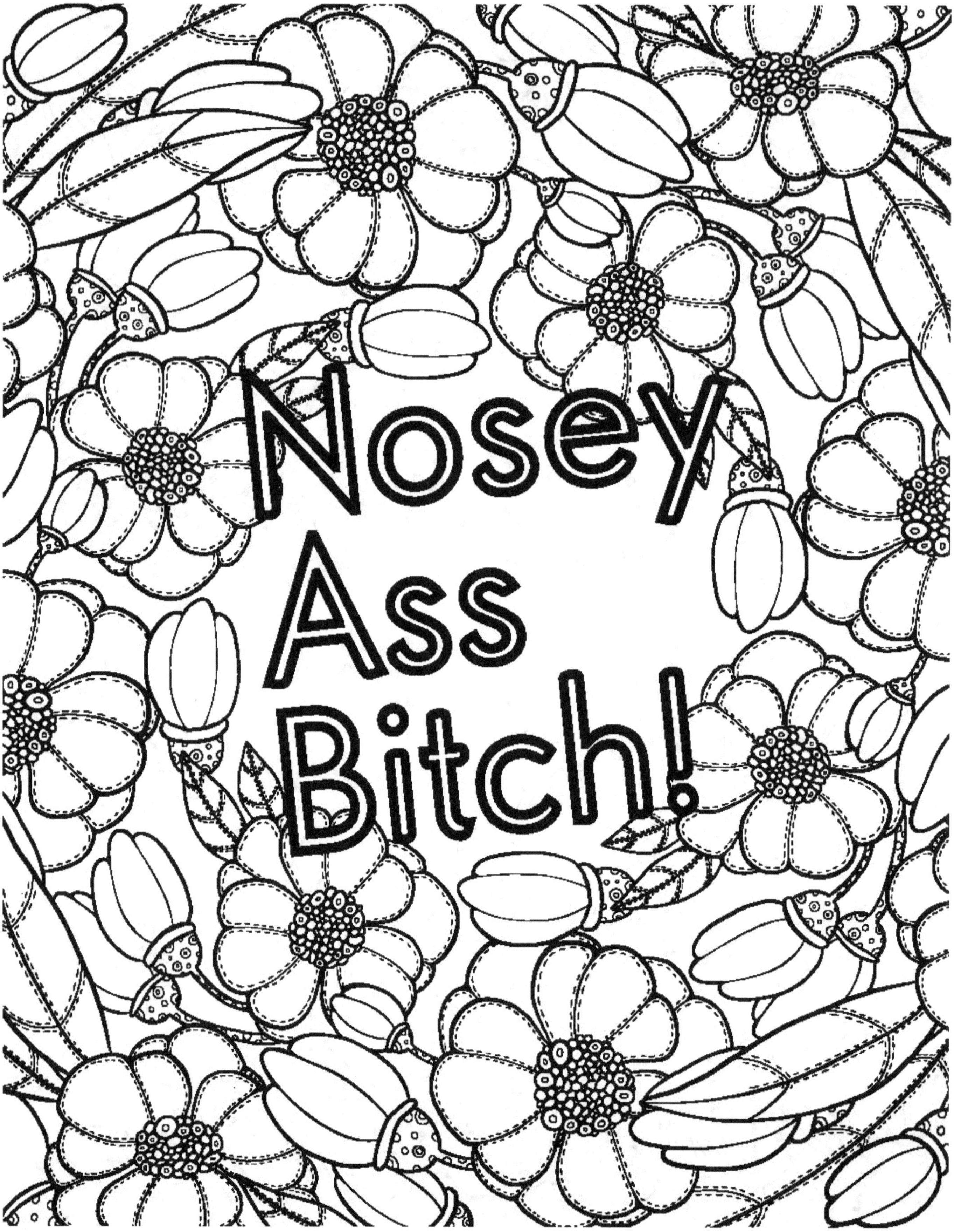
Nosey
Ass
Bitch!

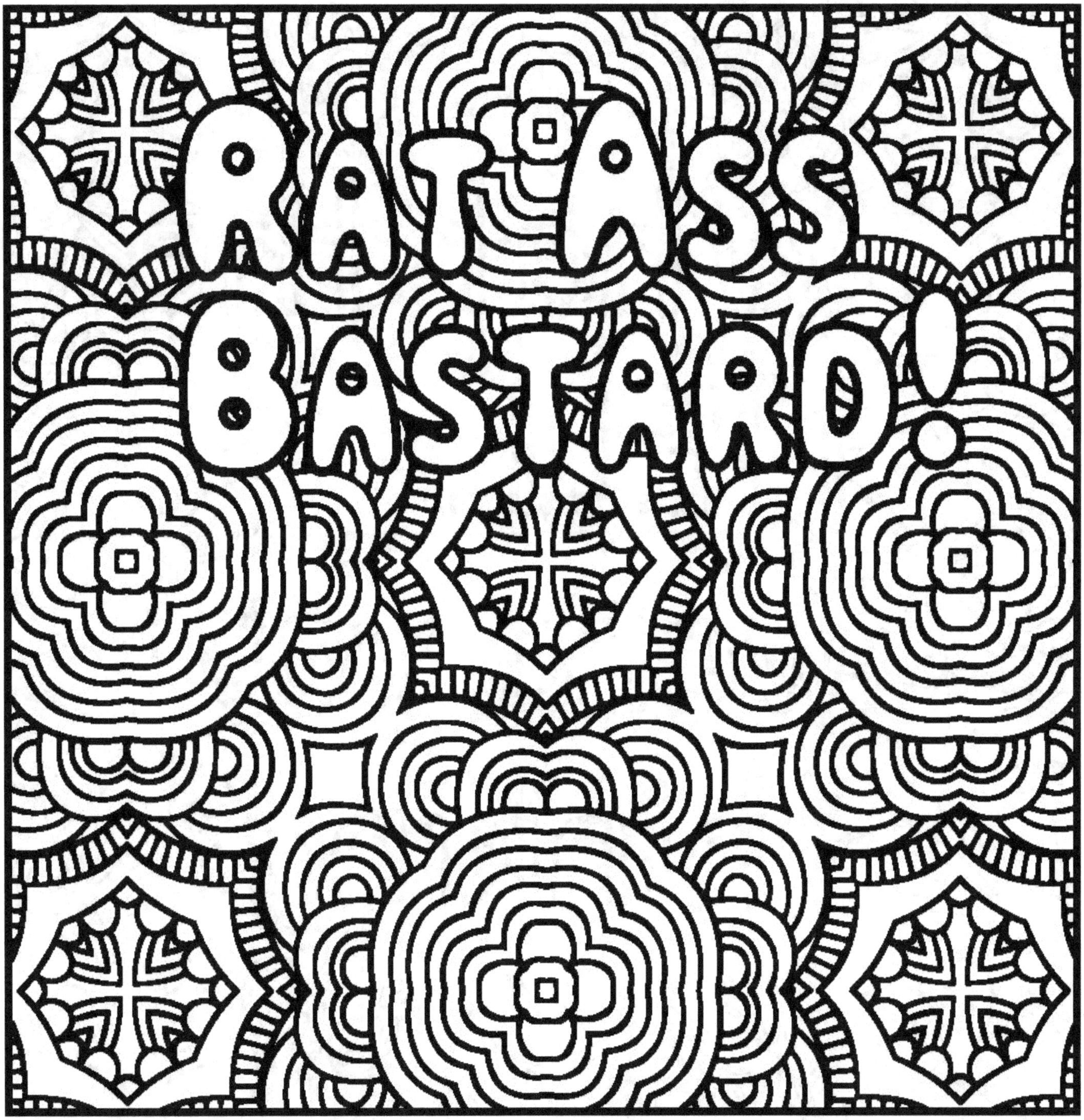
RAT ASS
BASTARD!

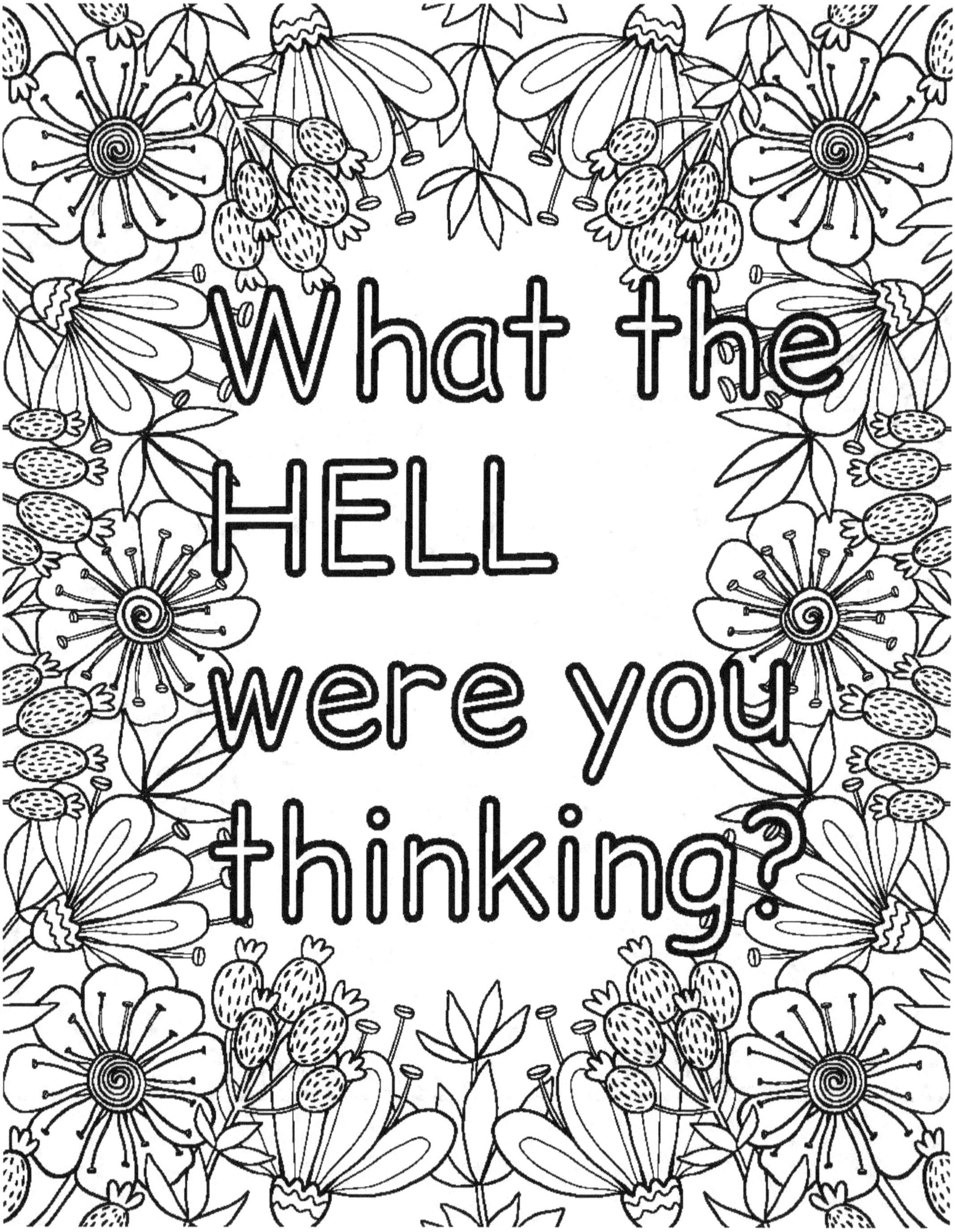
What the
HELL
were you
thinking?

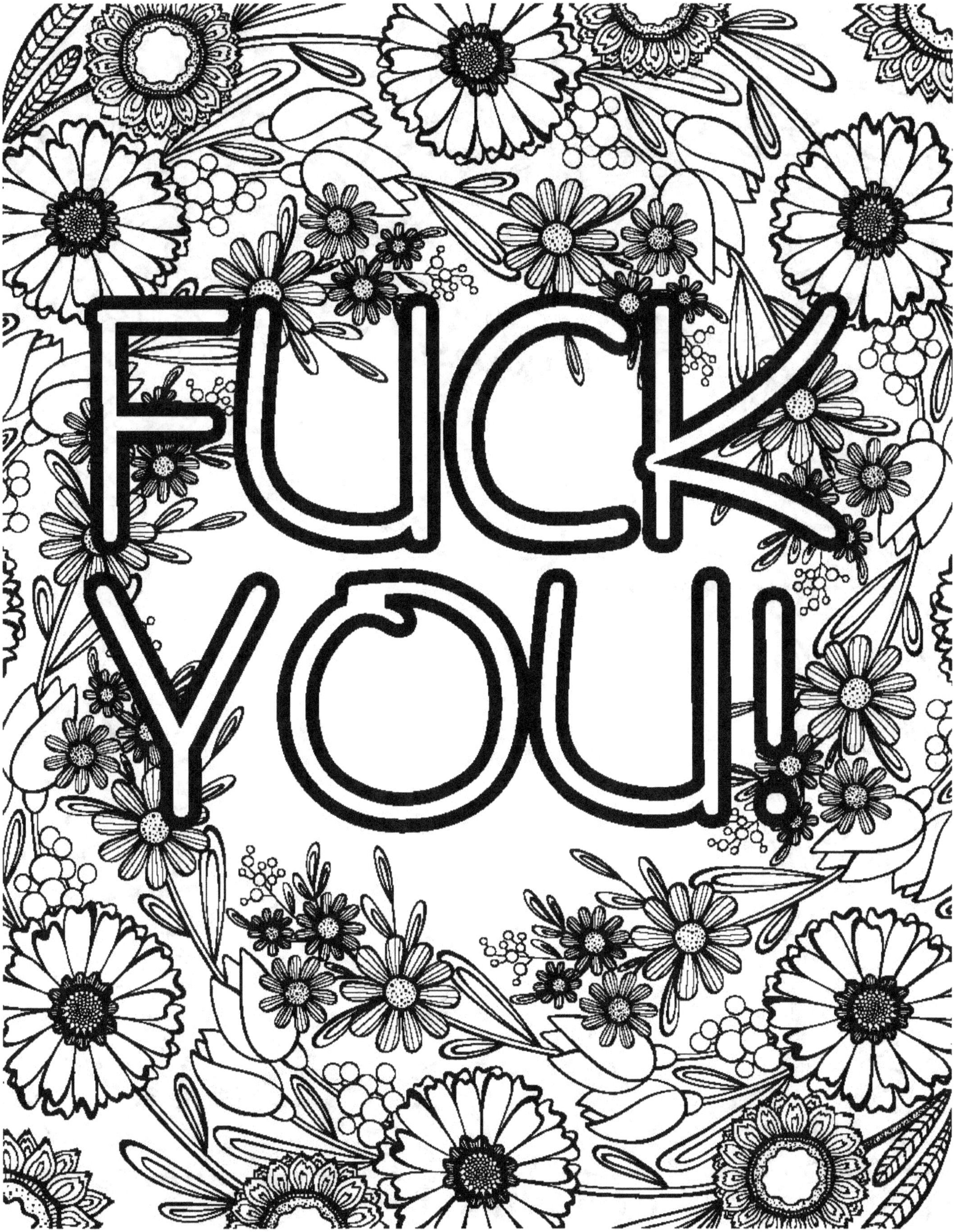
FUCK
YOU!

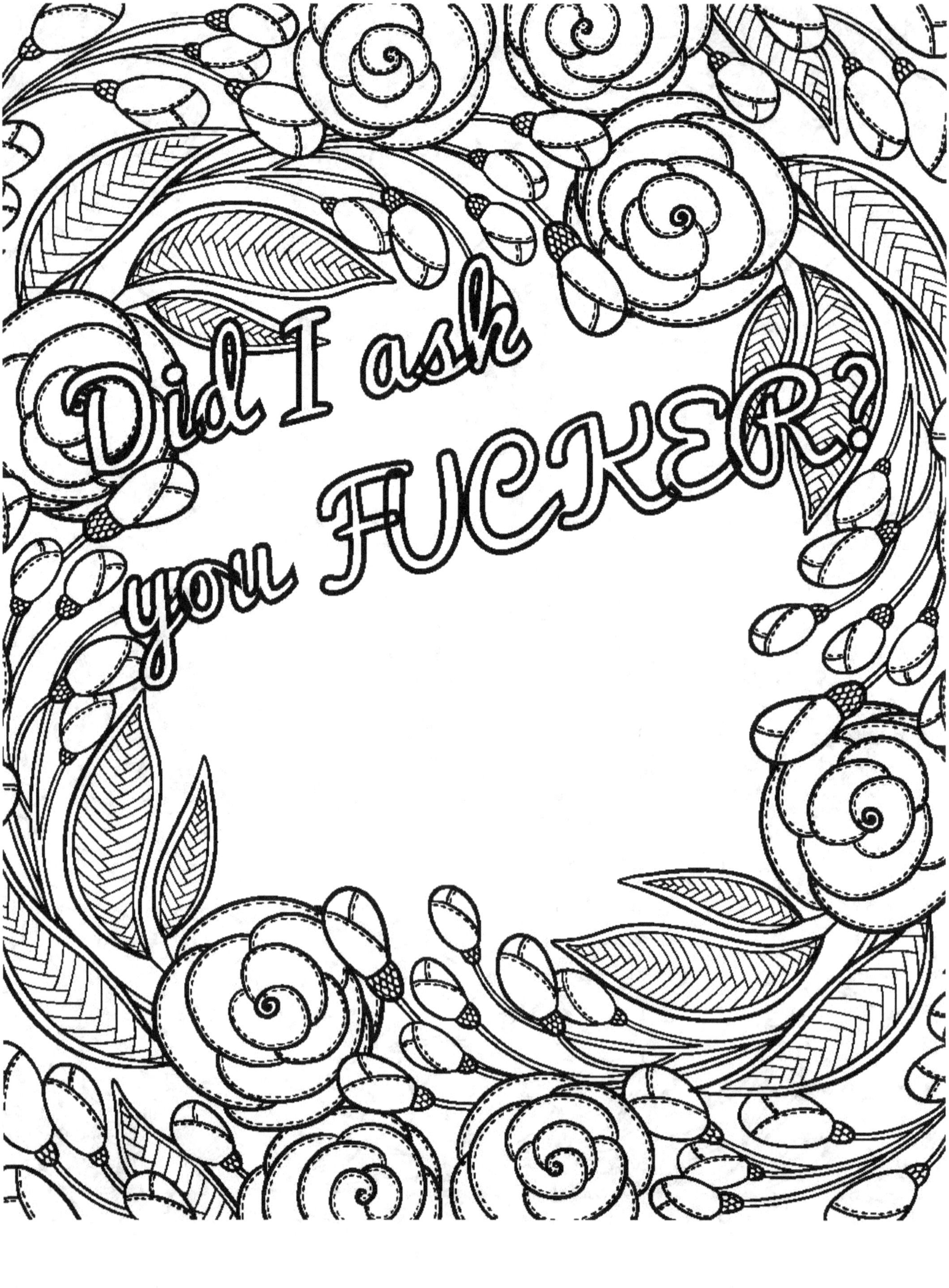
Did I ask
you FUCKER?

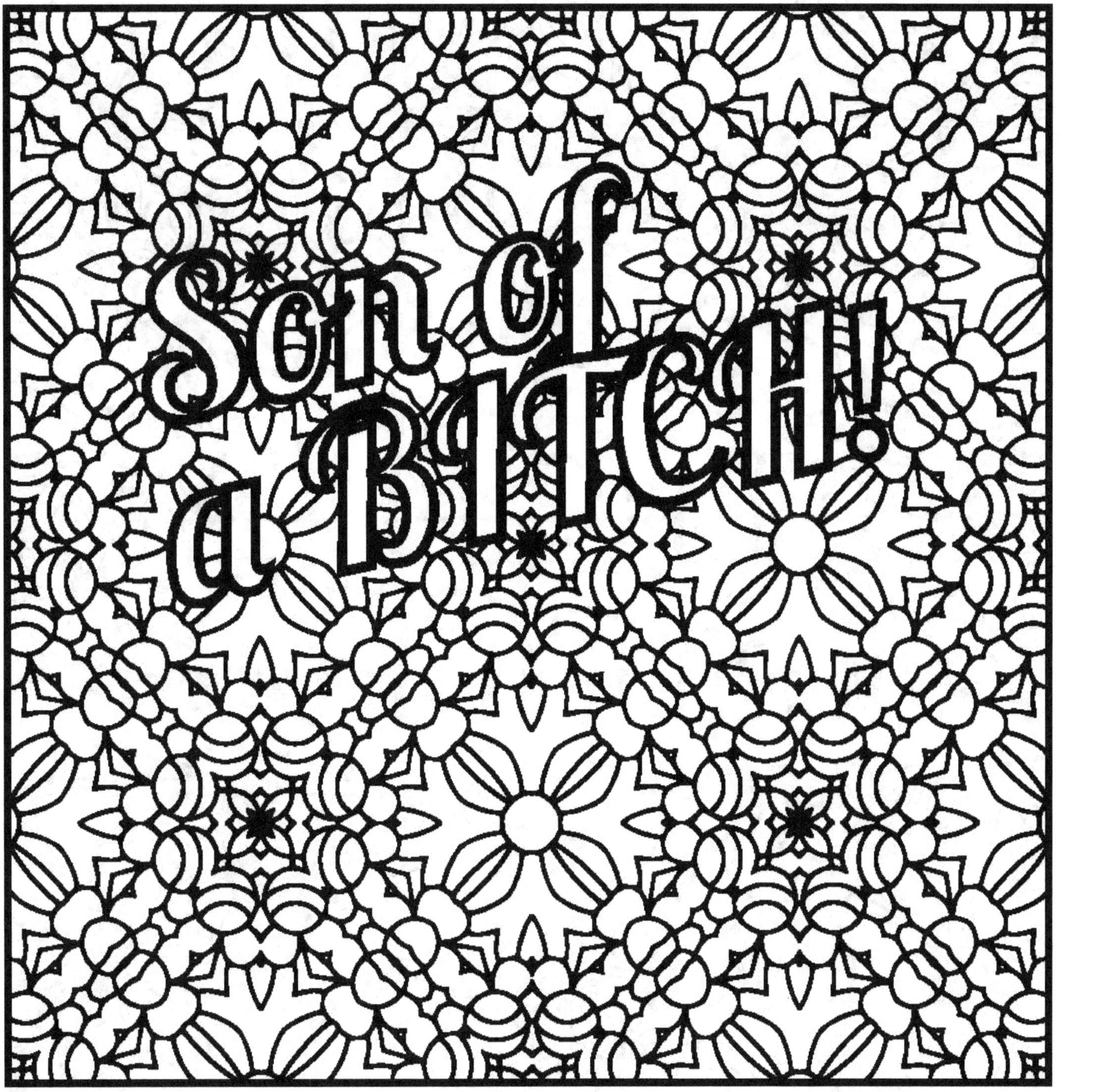
Son of
a BITCH!

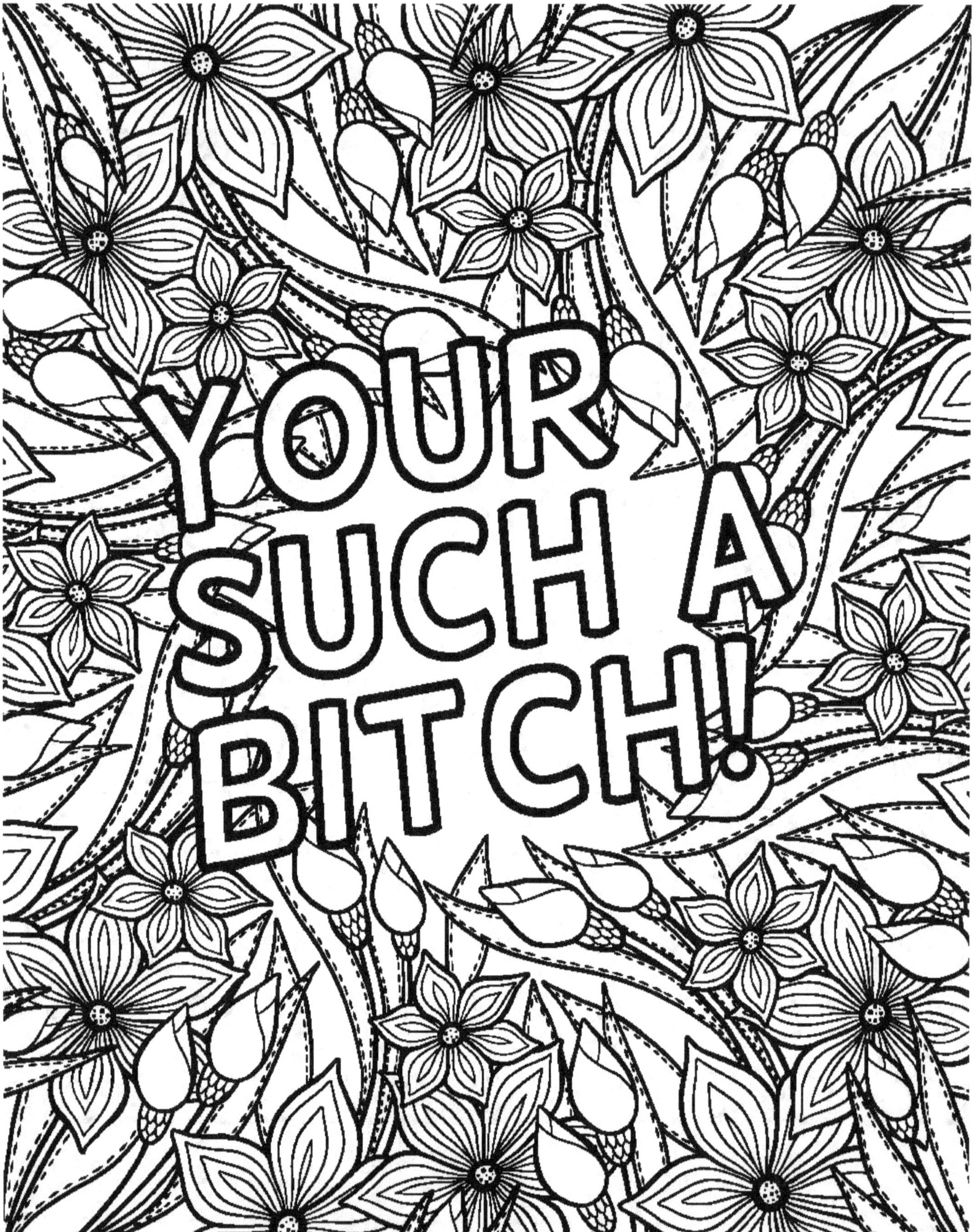
YOUR
SUCH A
BITCH!

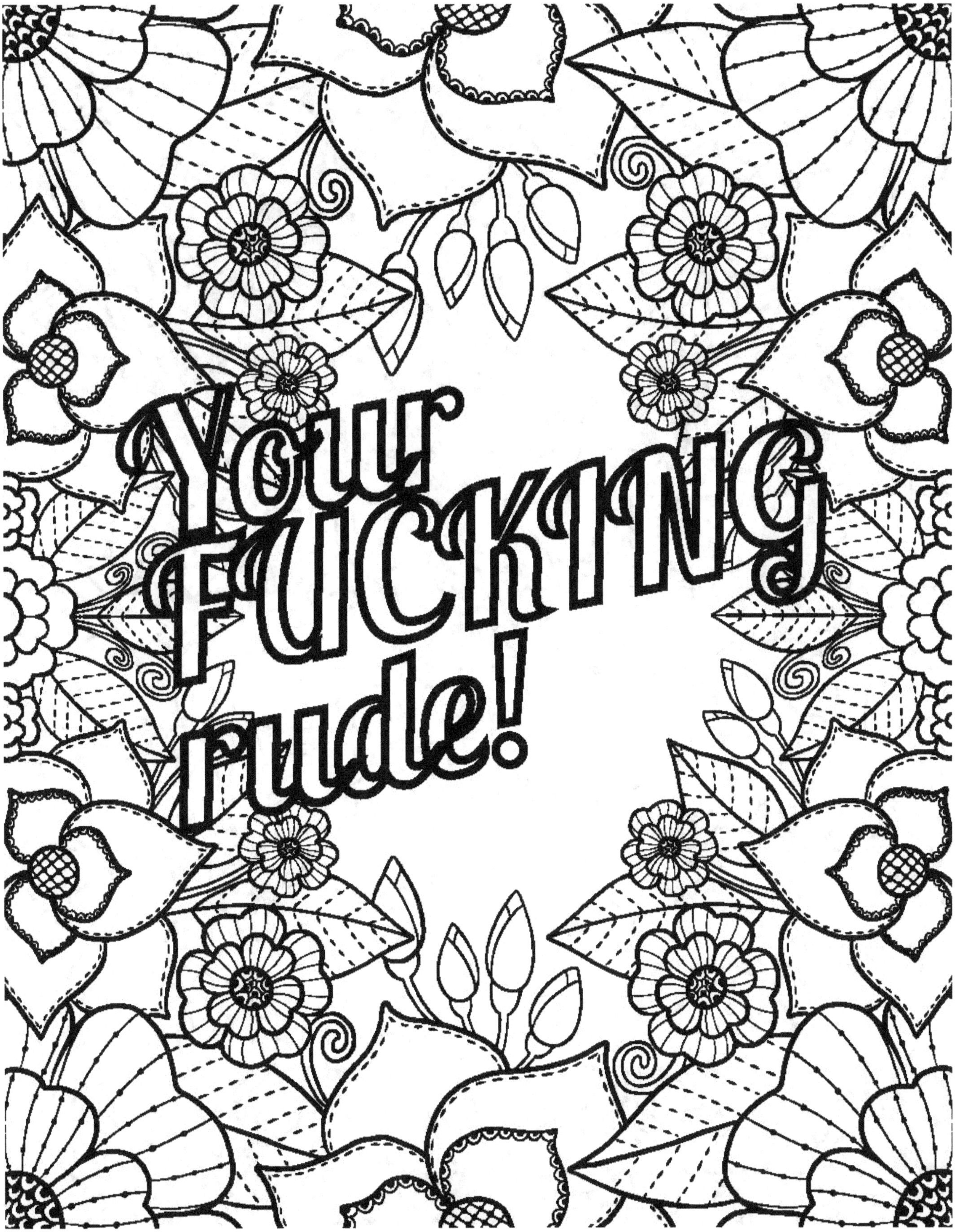
Your
FUCKING
rude!

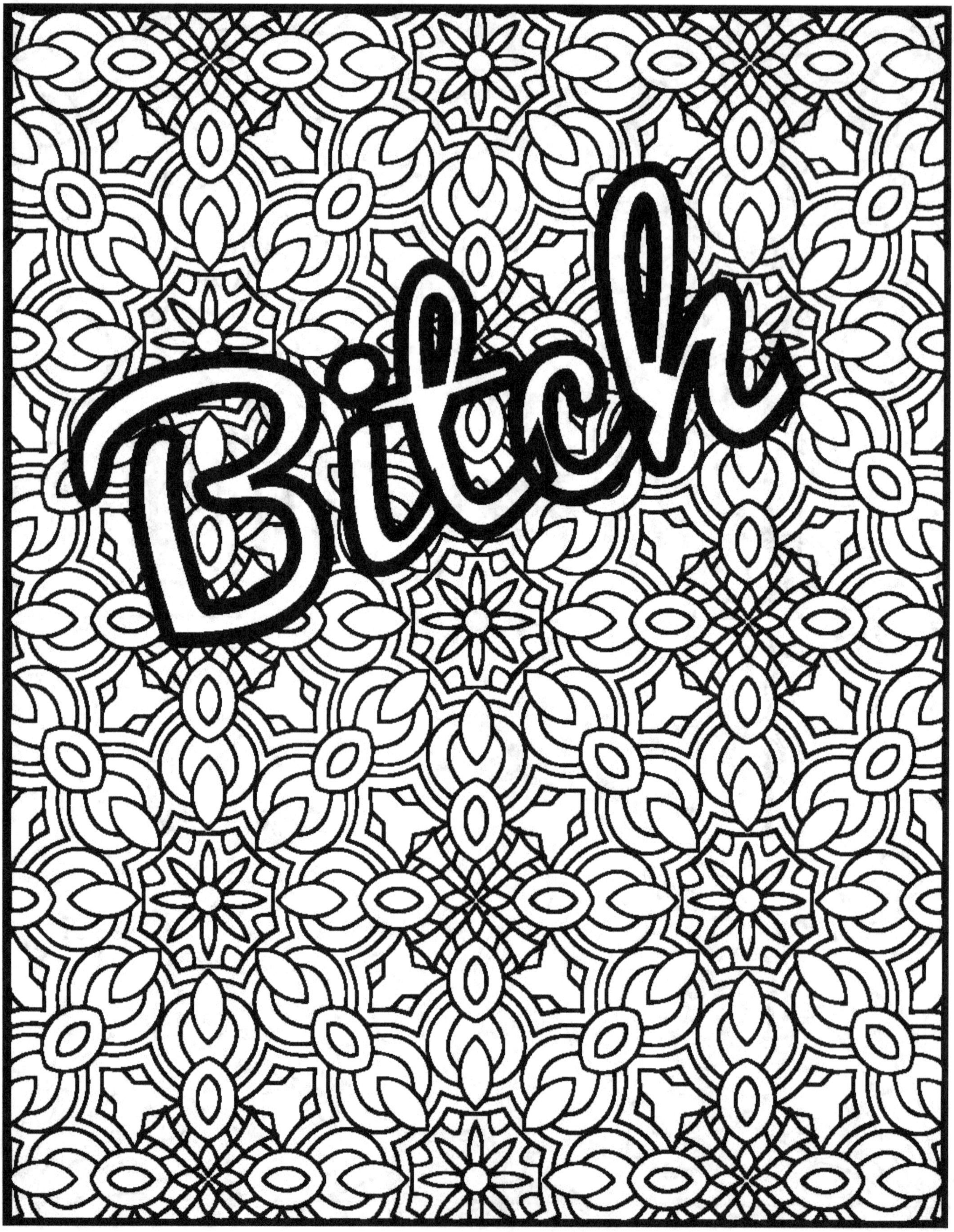
Bitch

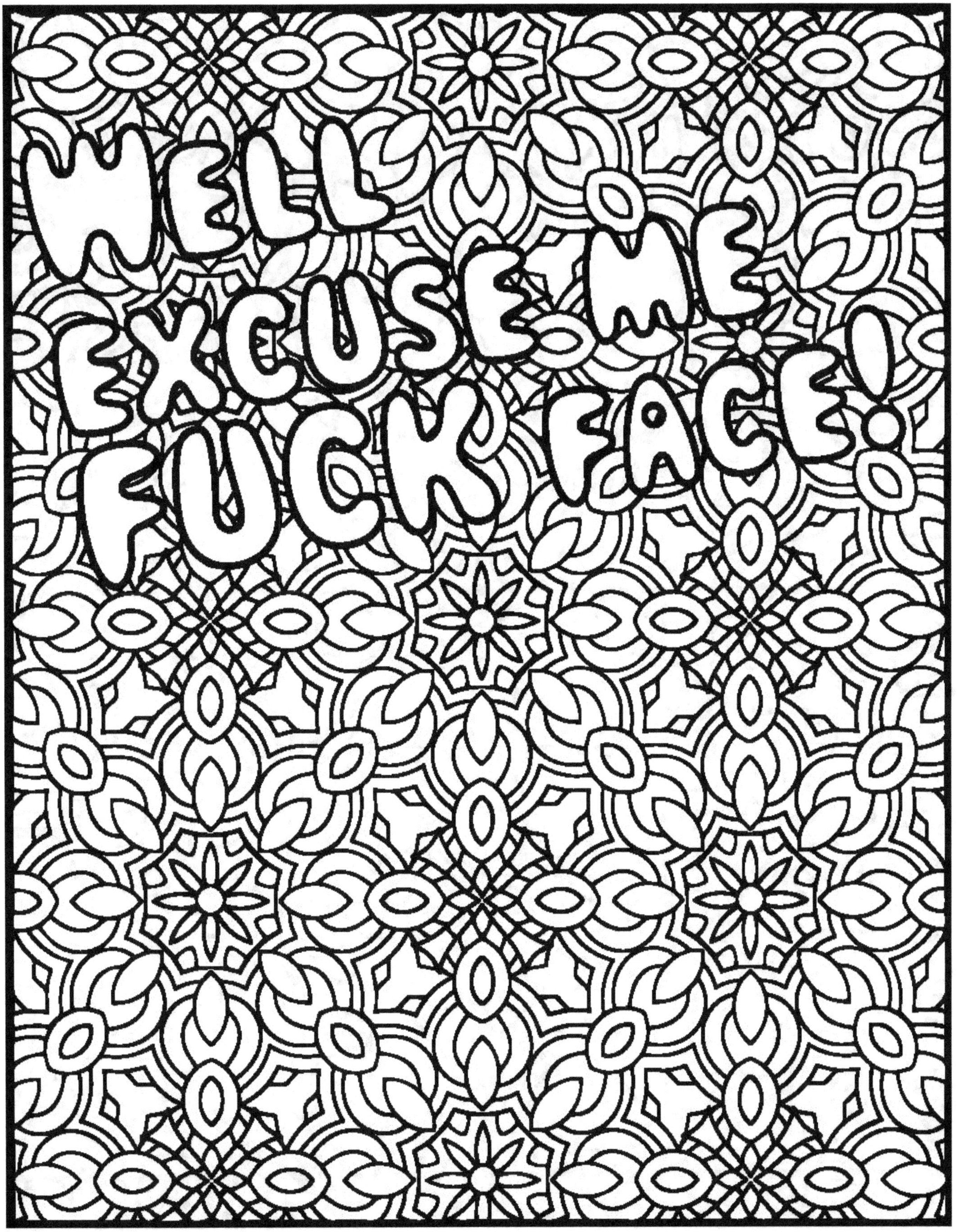
WELL EXCUSE ME FUCK FACE!

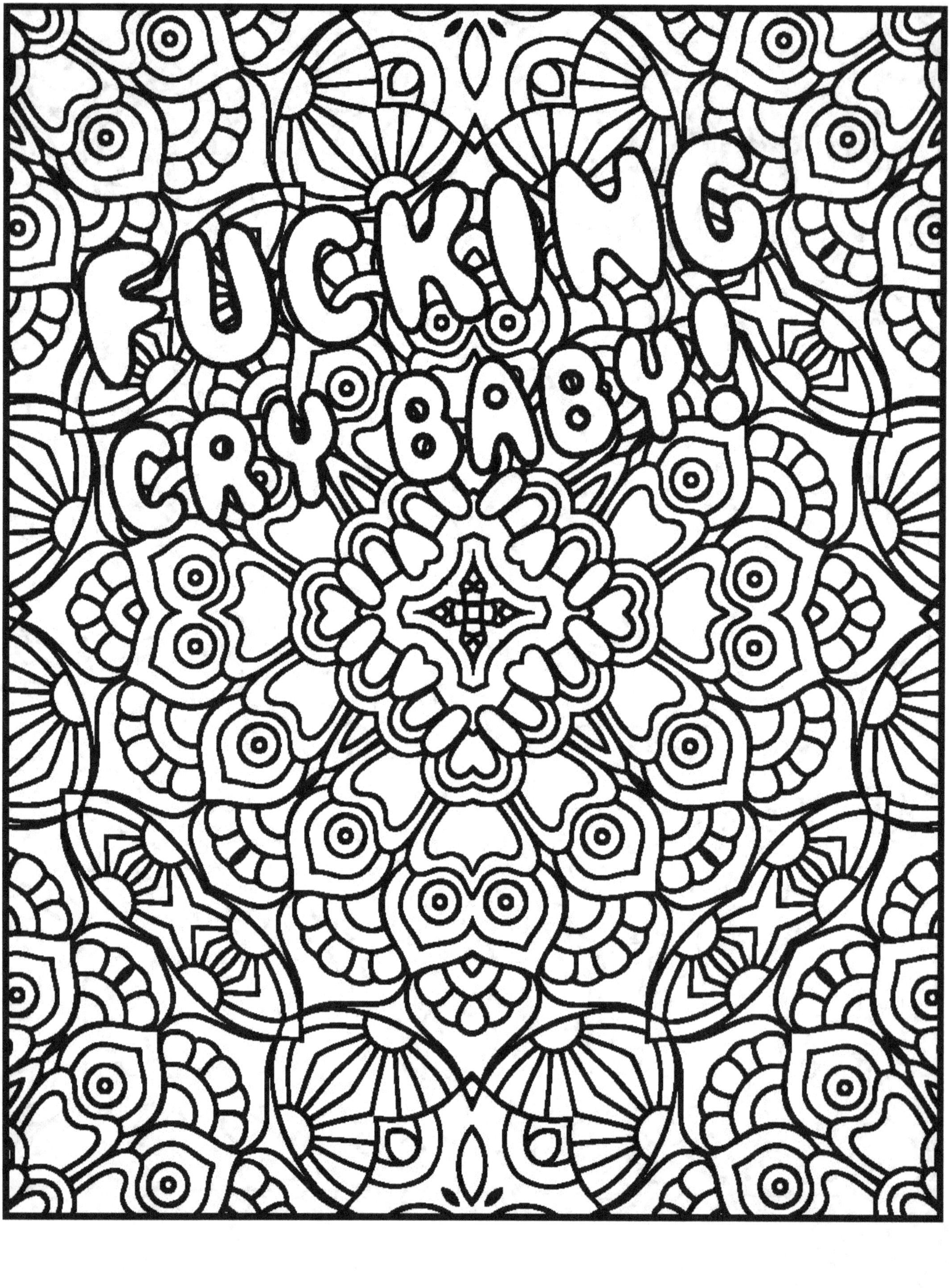
FUCKING
CRY BABY!

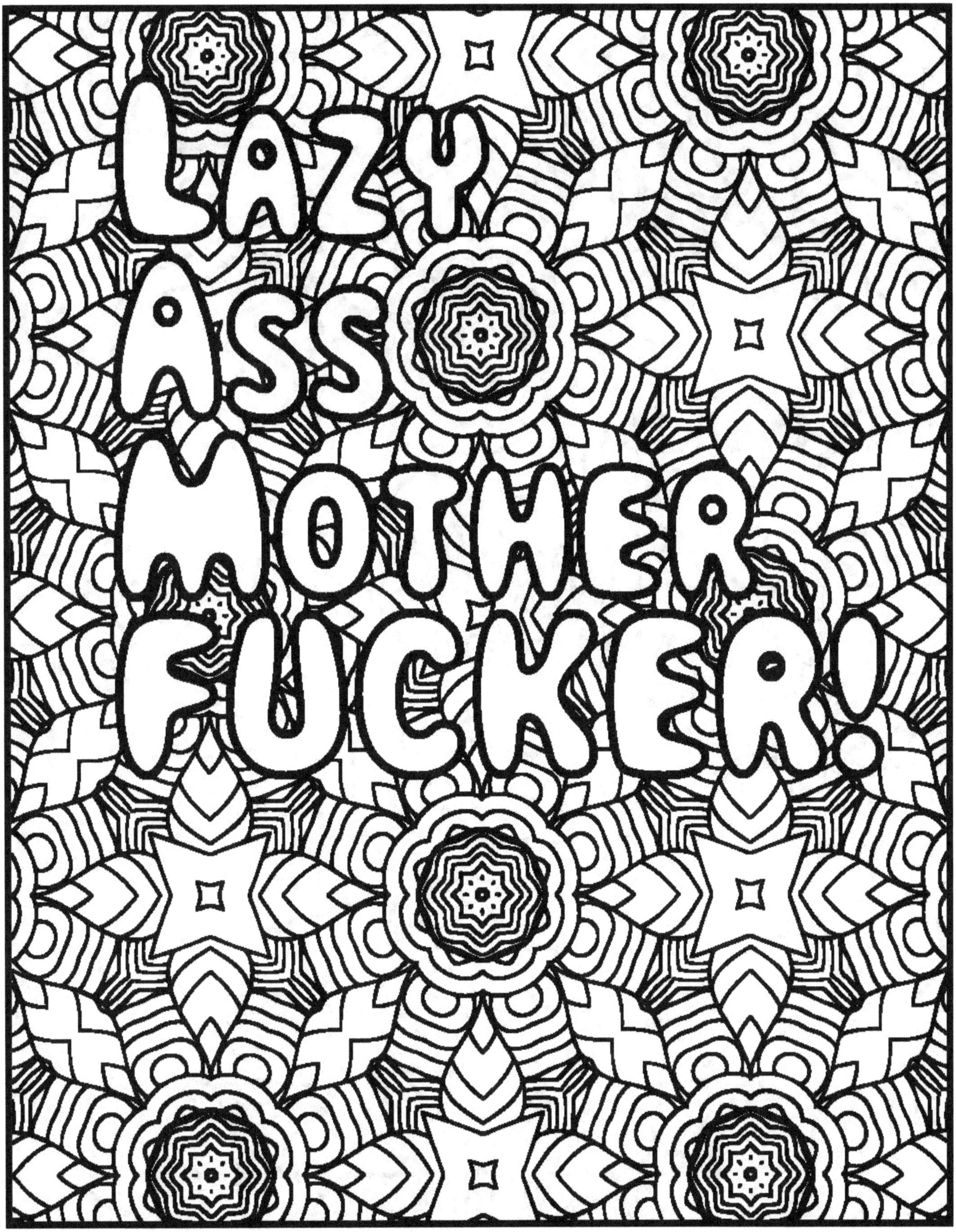
LAZY
ASS
MOTHER
FUCKER!

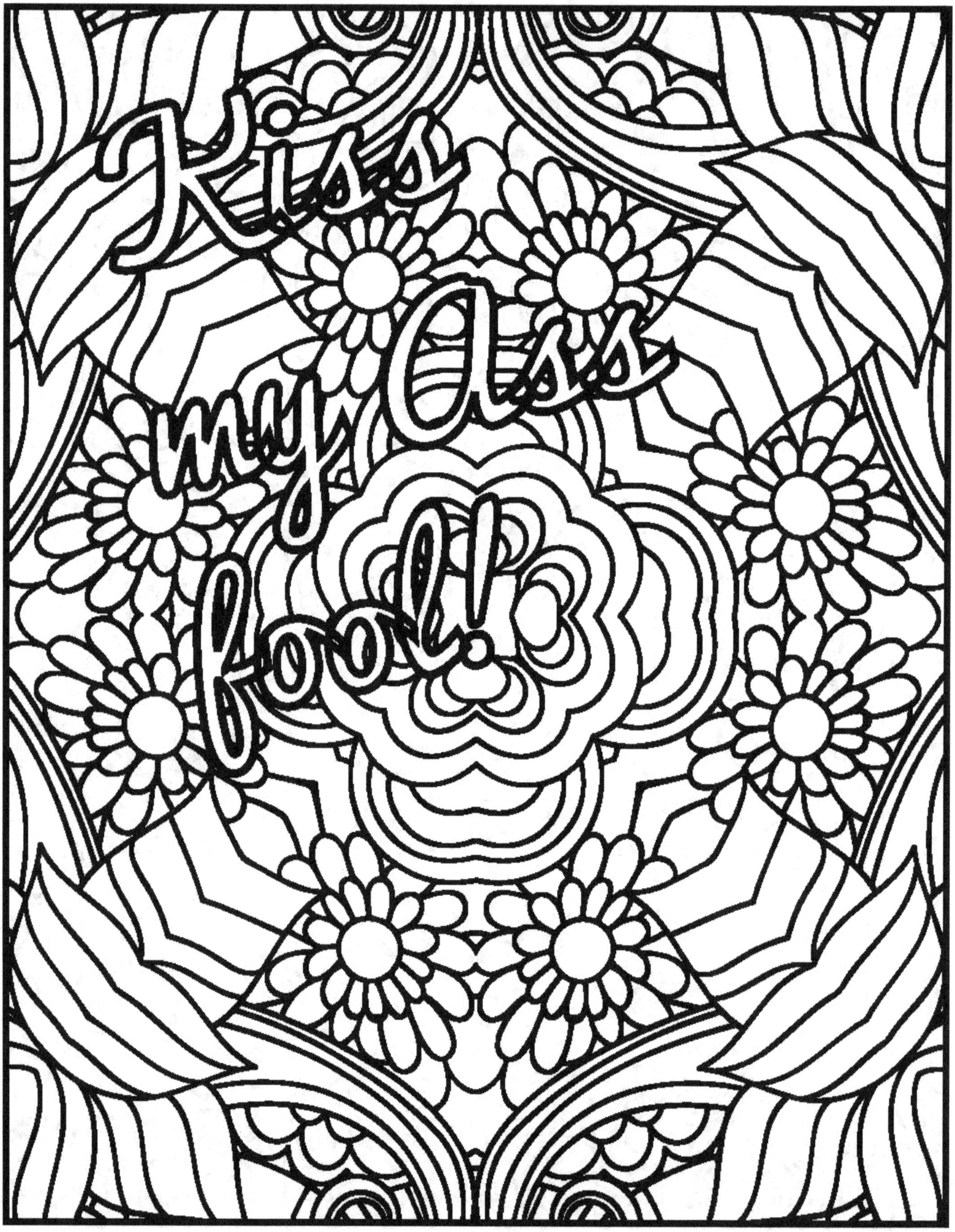
Kiss
my Ass
fool!

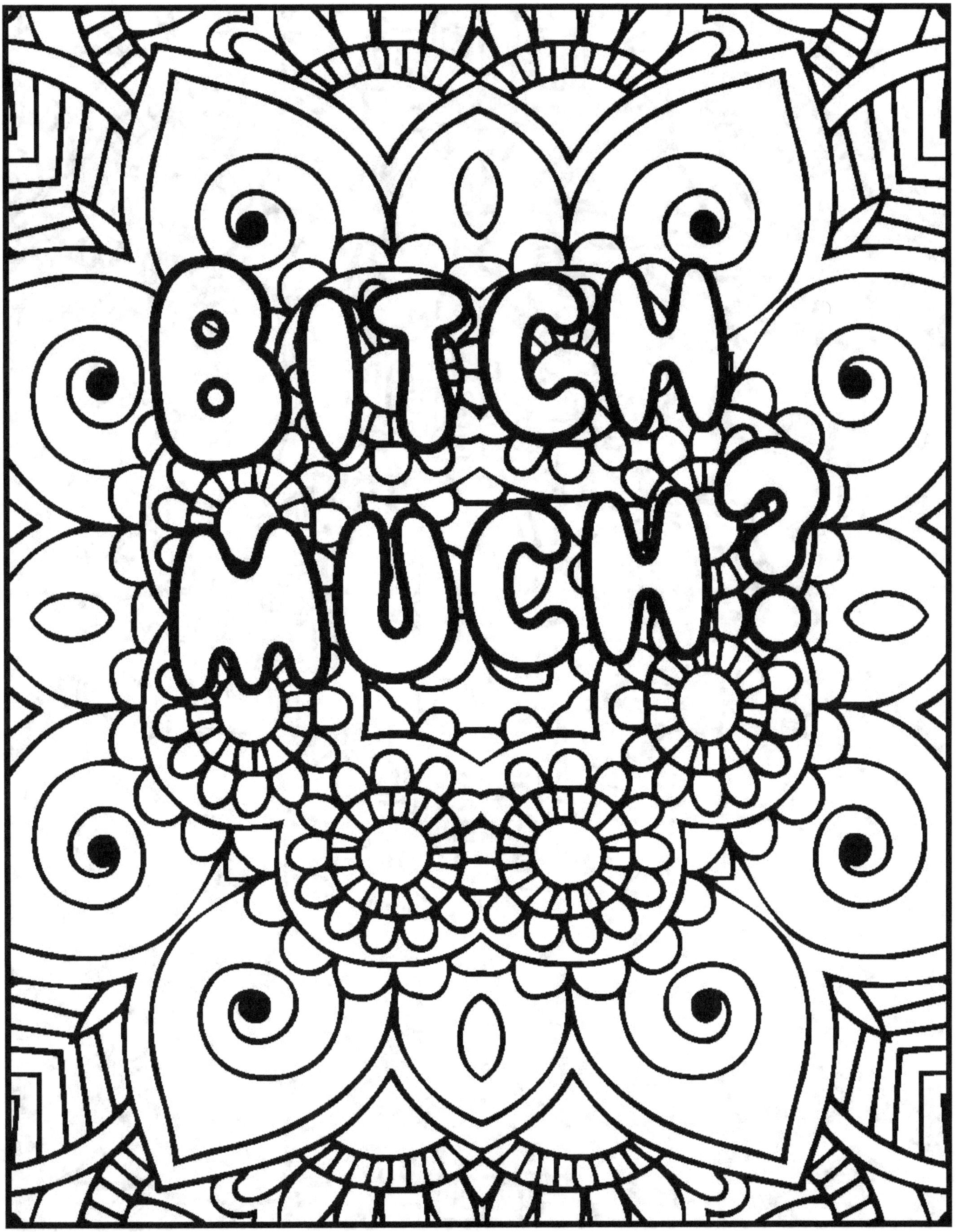
BITCH
MUCH?

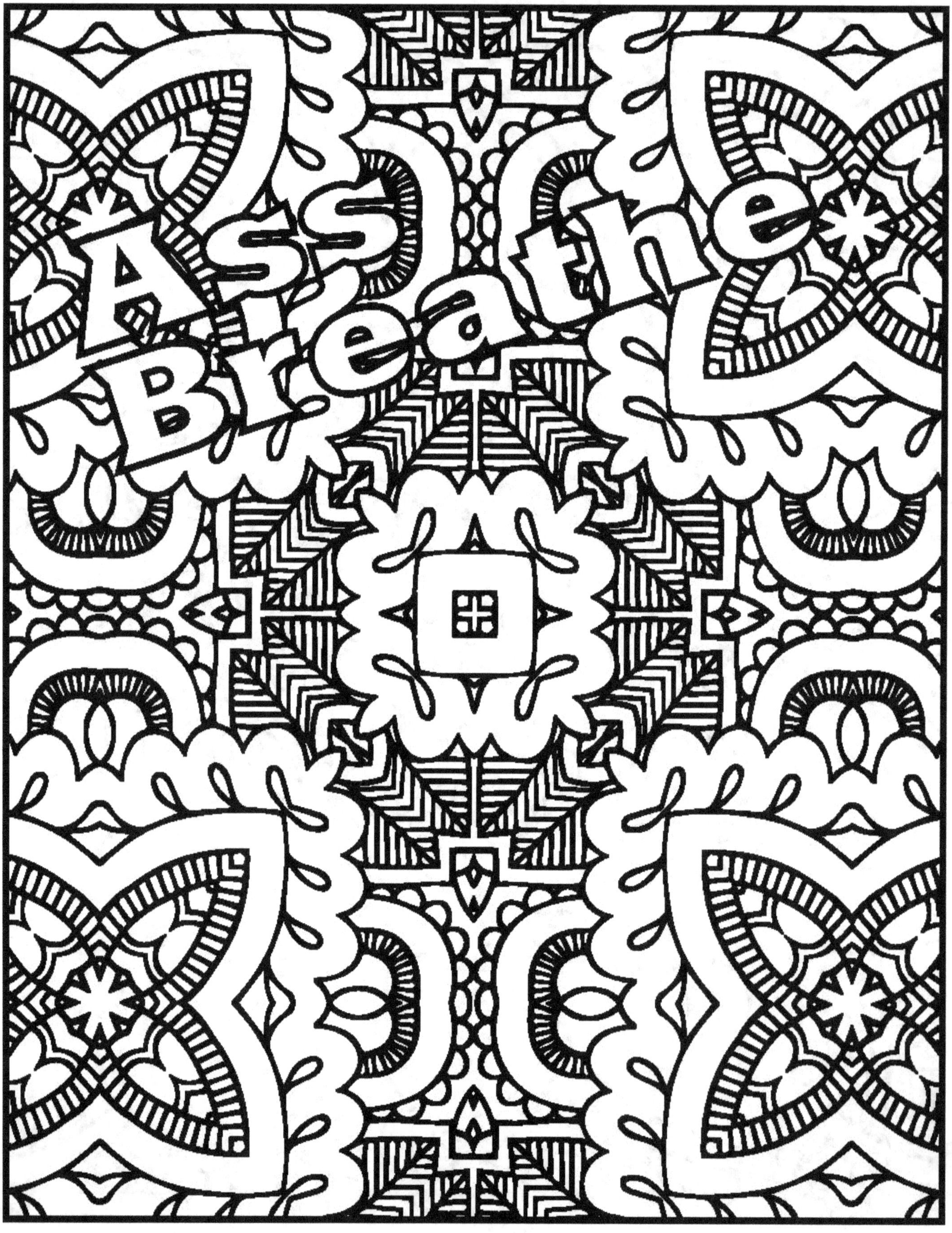
Ass
Breathe

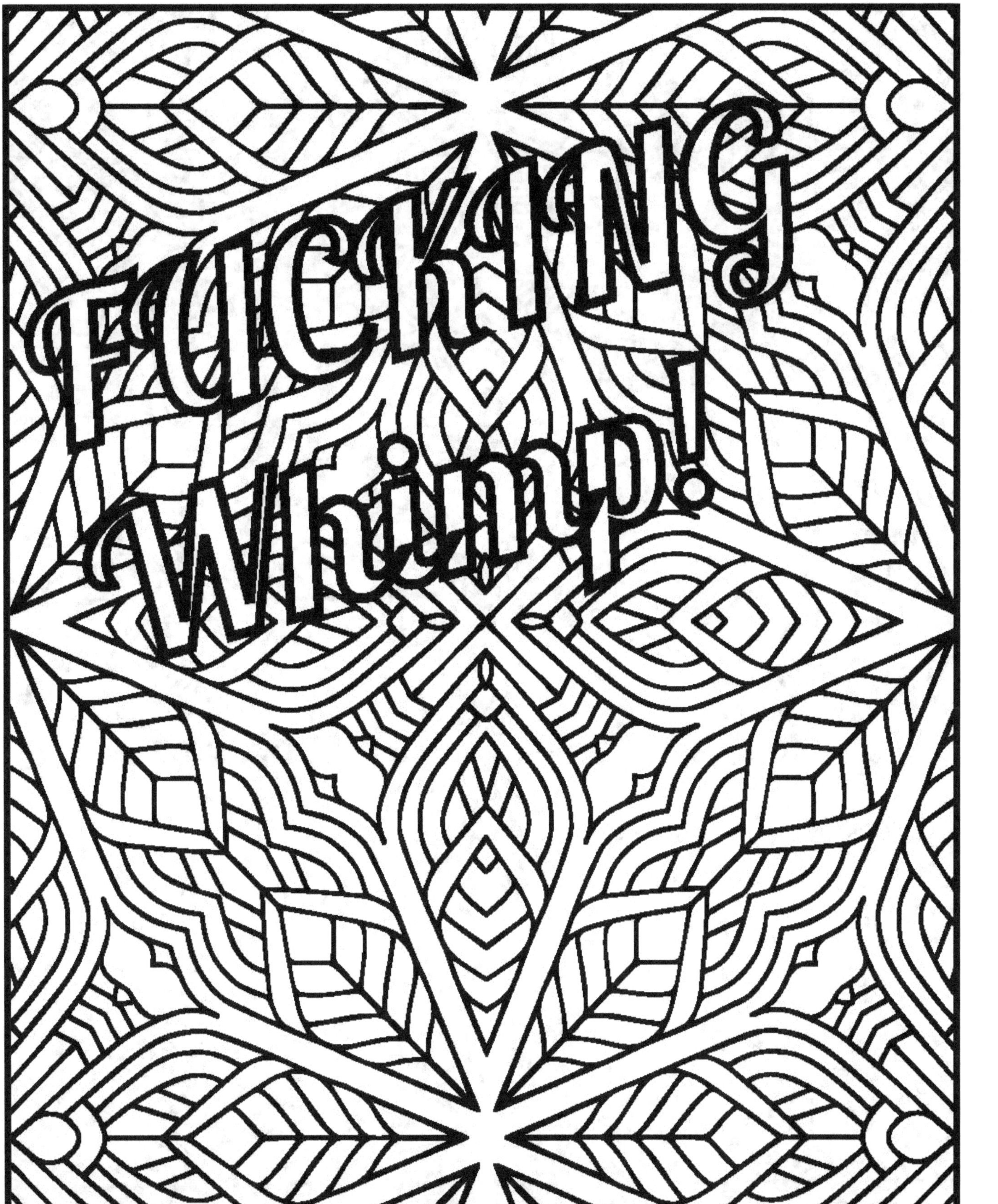
FUCKING
Whimp!

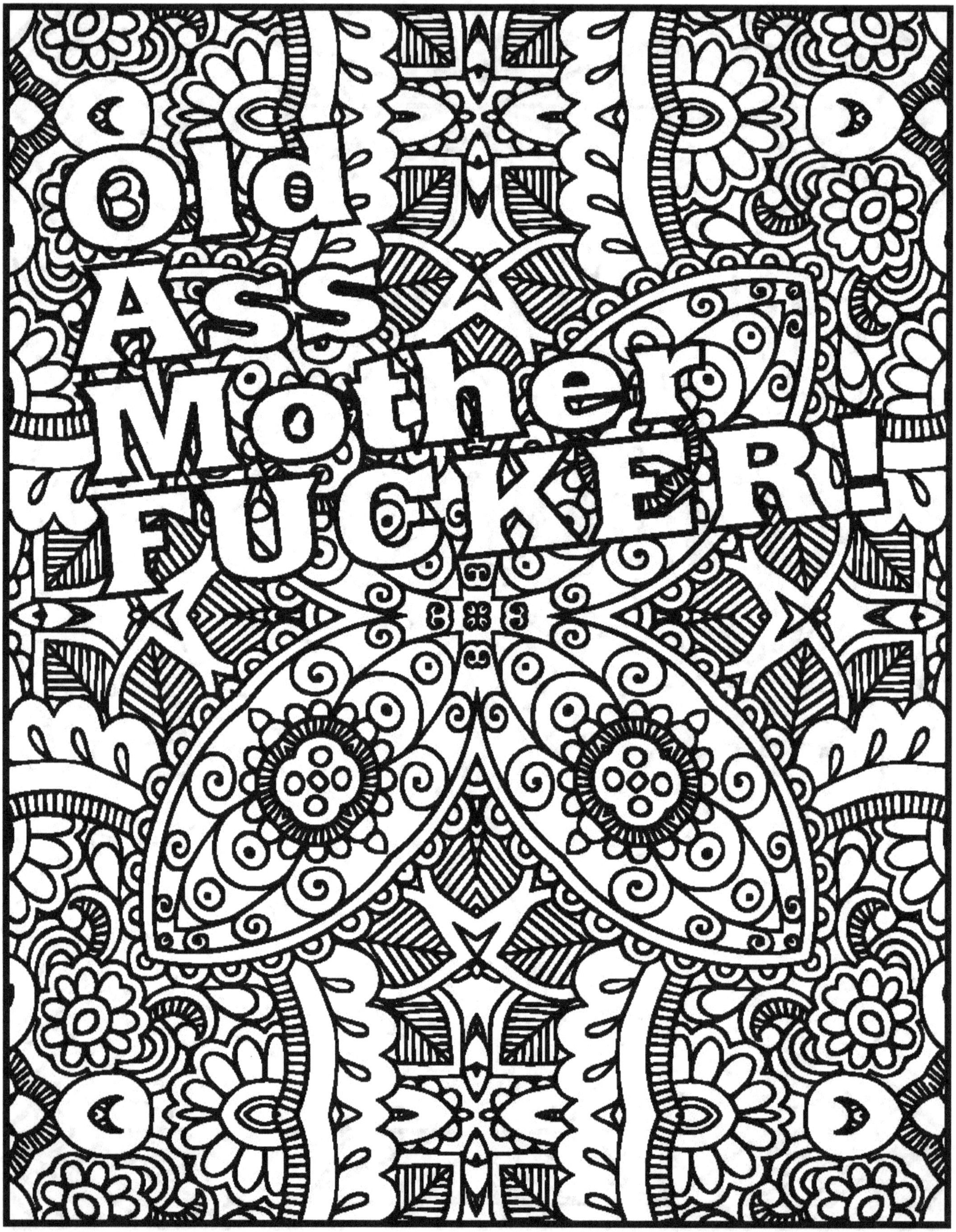
Old Ass Mother FUCKER!

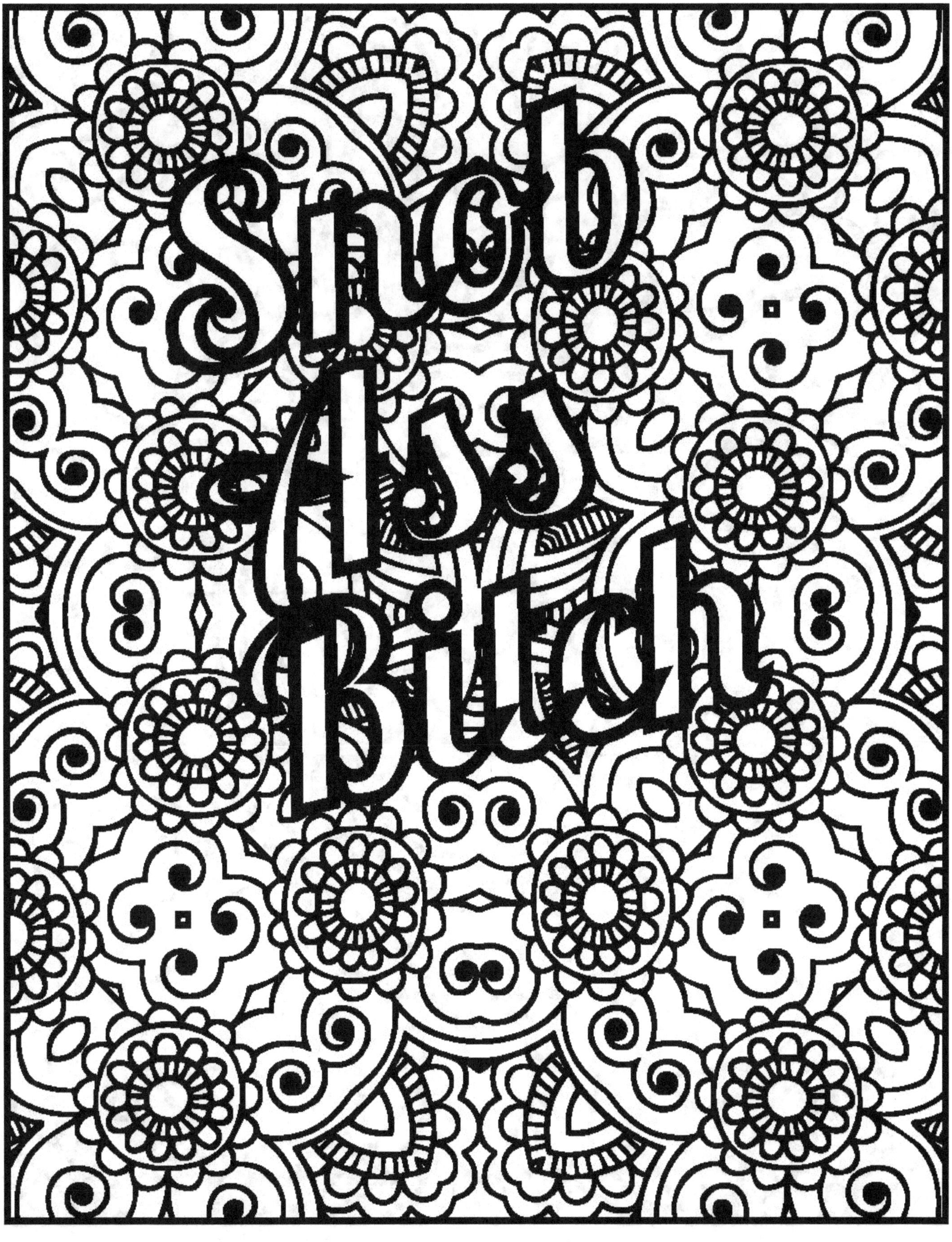
Snob
Ass
Bitch

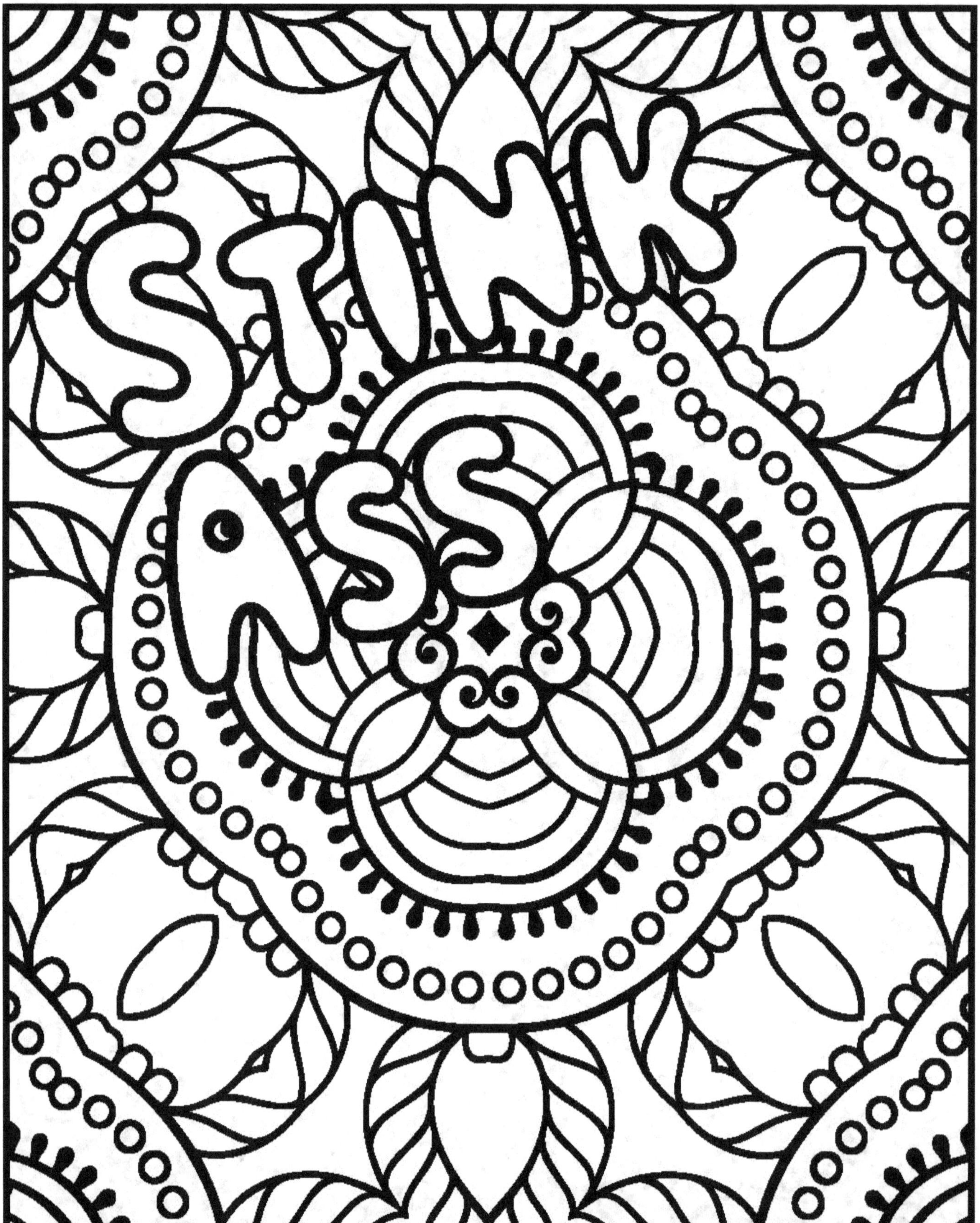
STINK
ASS

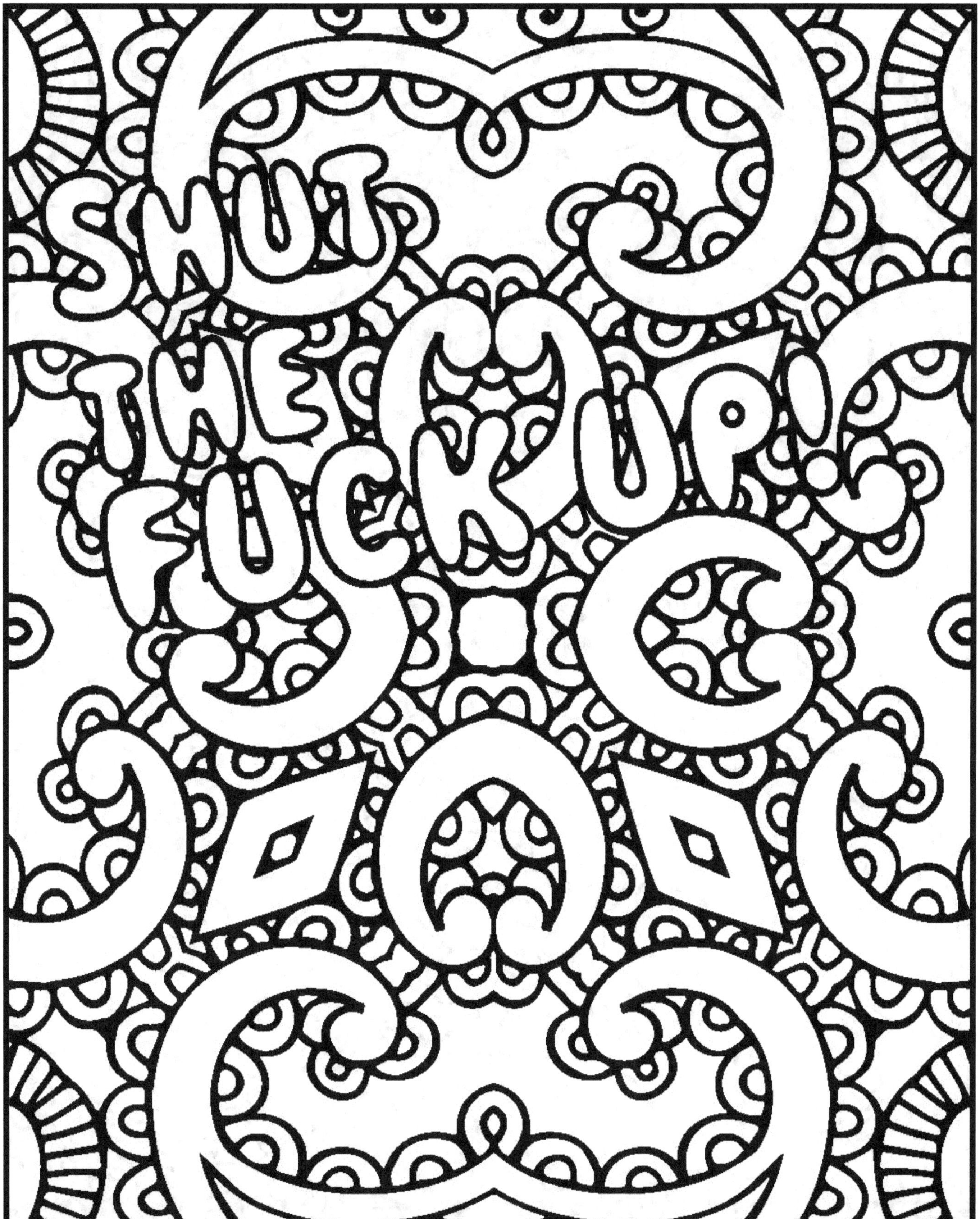
SHUT THE FUCK UP!

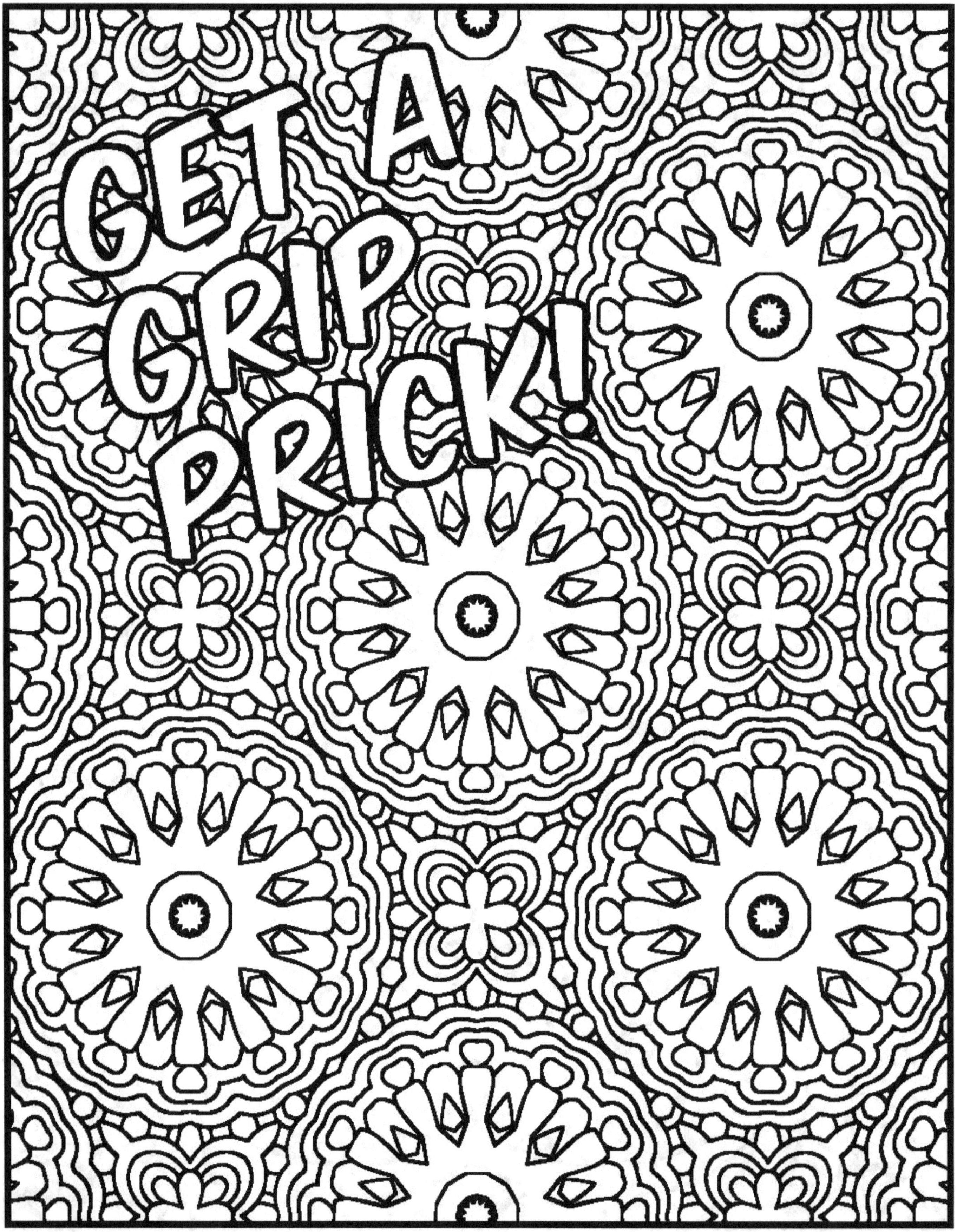
GET A
GRIP
PRICK!

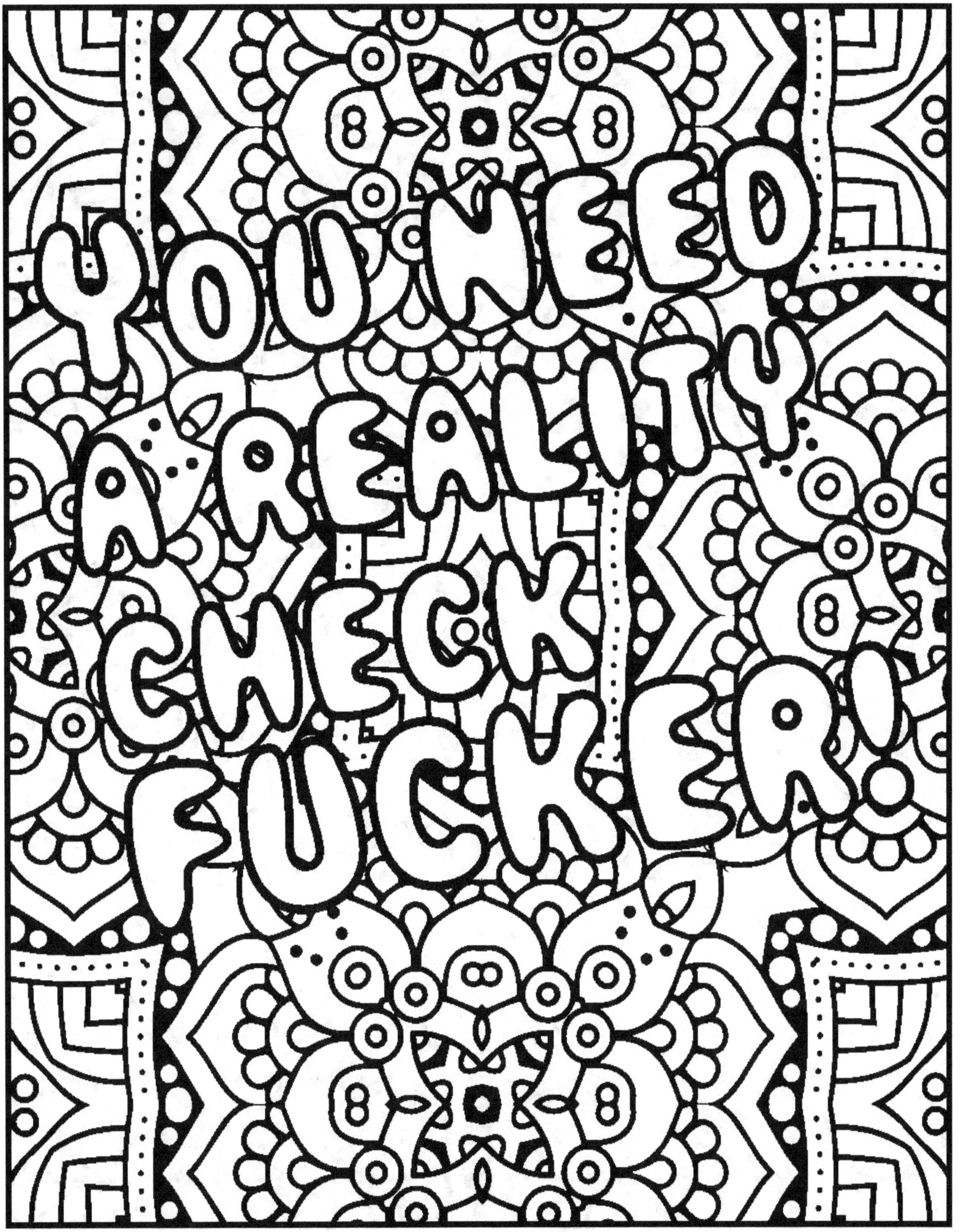
YOU NEED
A REALITY
CHECK
FUCKER!

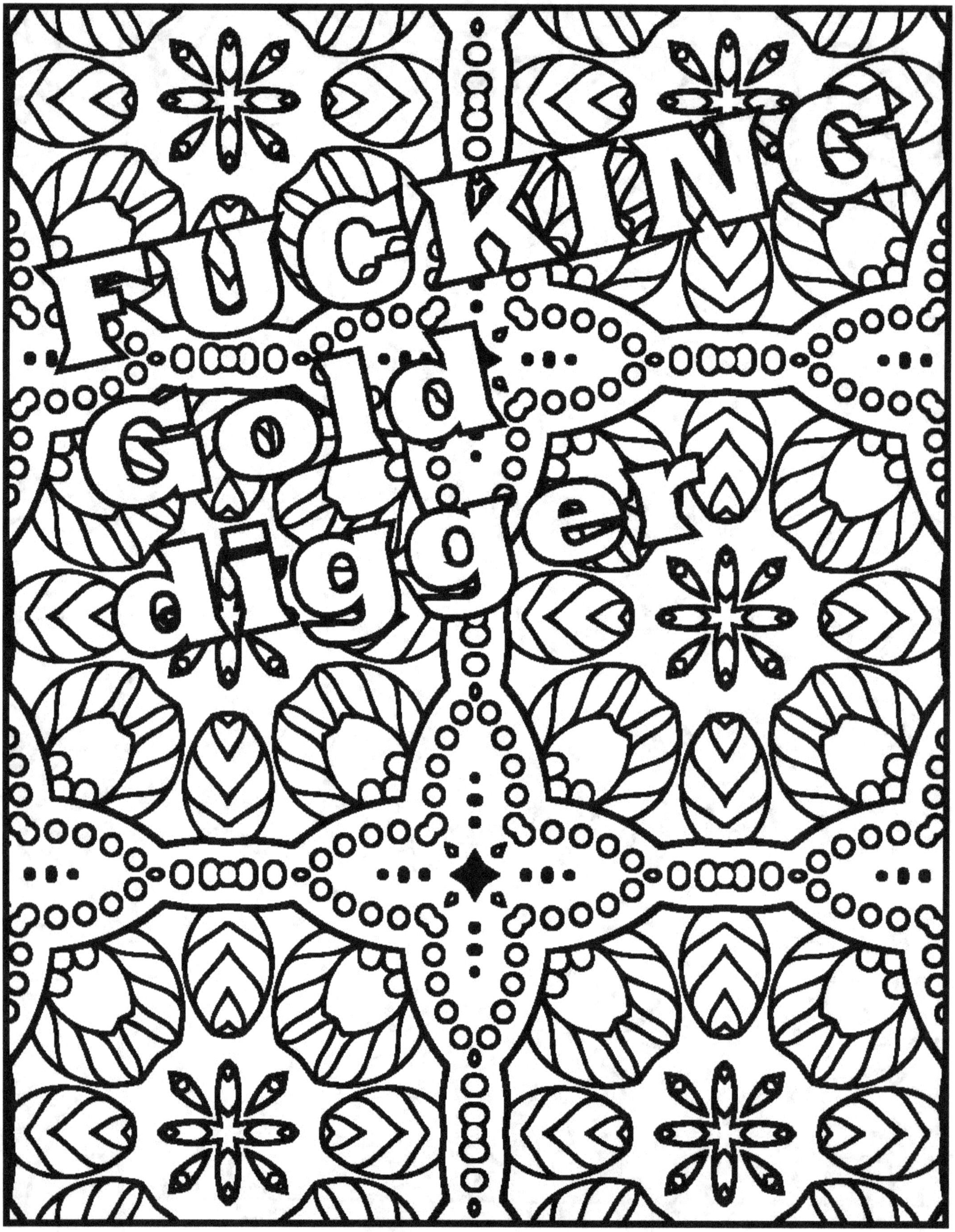
FUCKING
Gold
digger

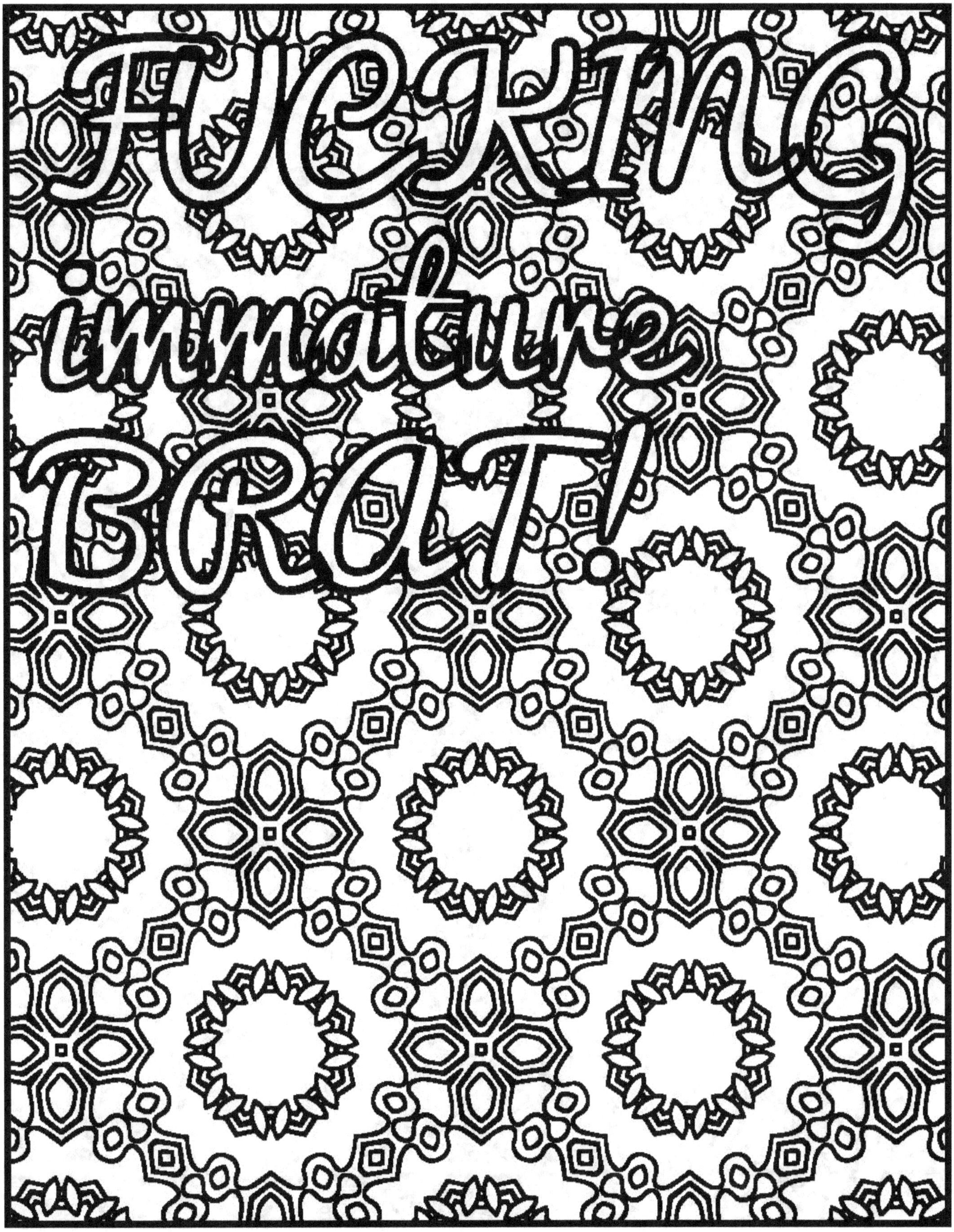
FUCKING
immature
BRAT!

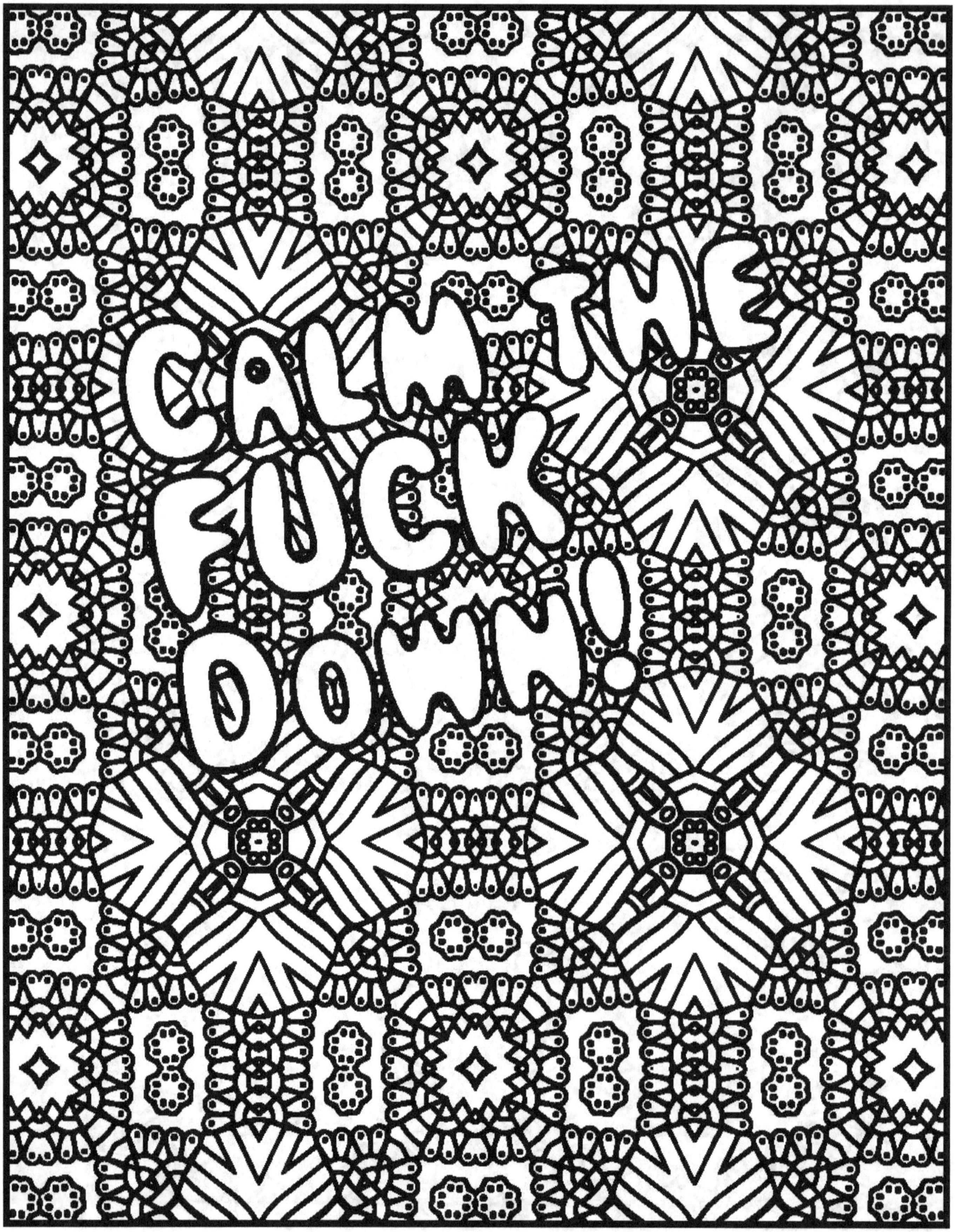
CALM THE
FUCK
DOWN!

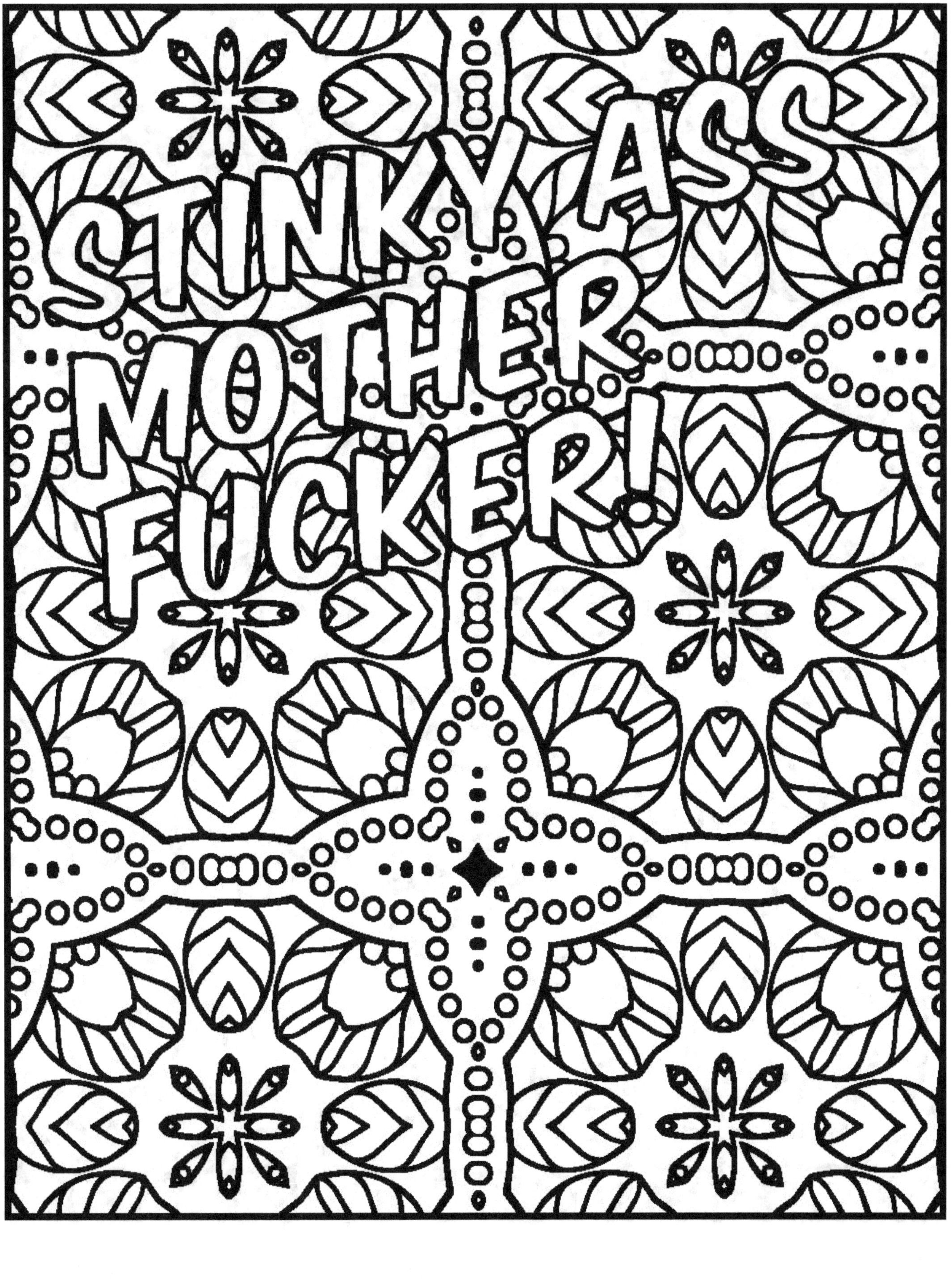
STINKY ASS
MOTHER
FUCKER!

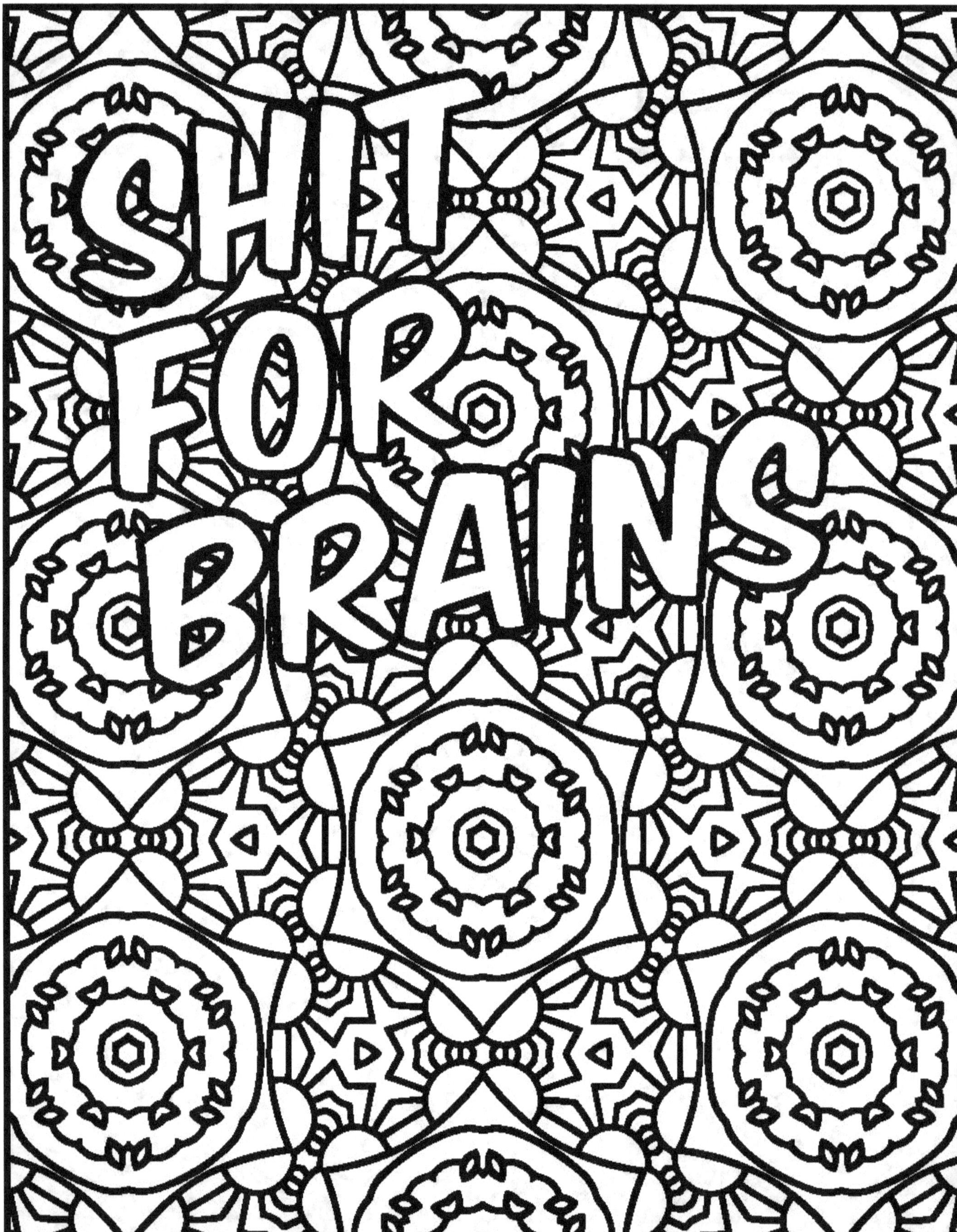
SHIT
FOR
BRAINS

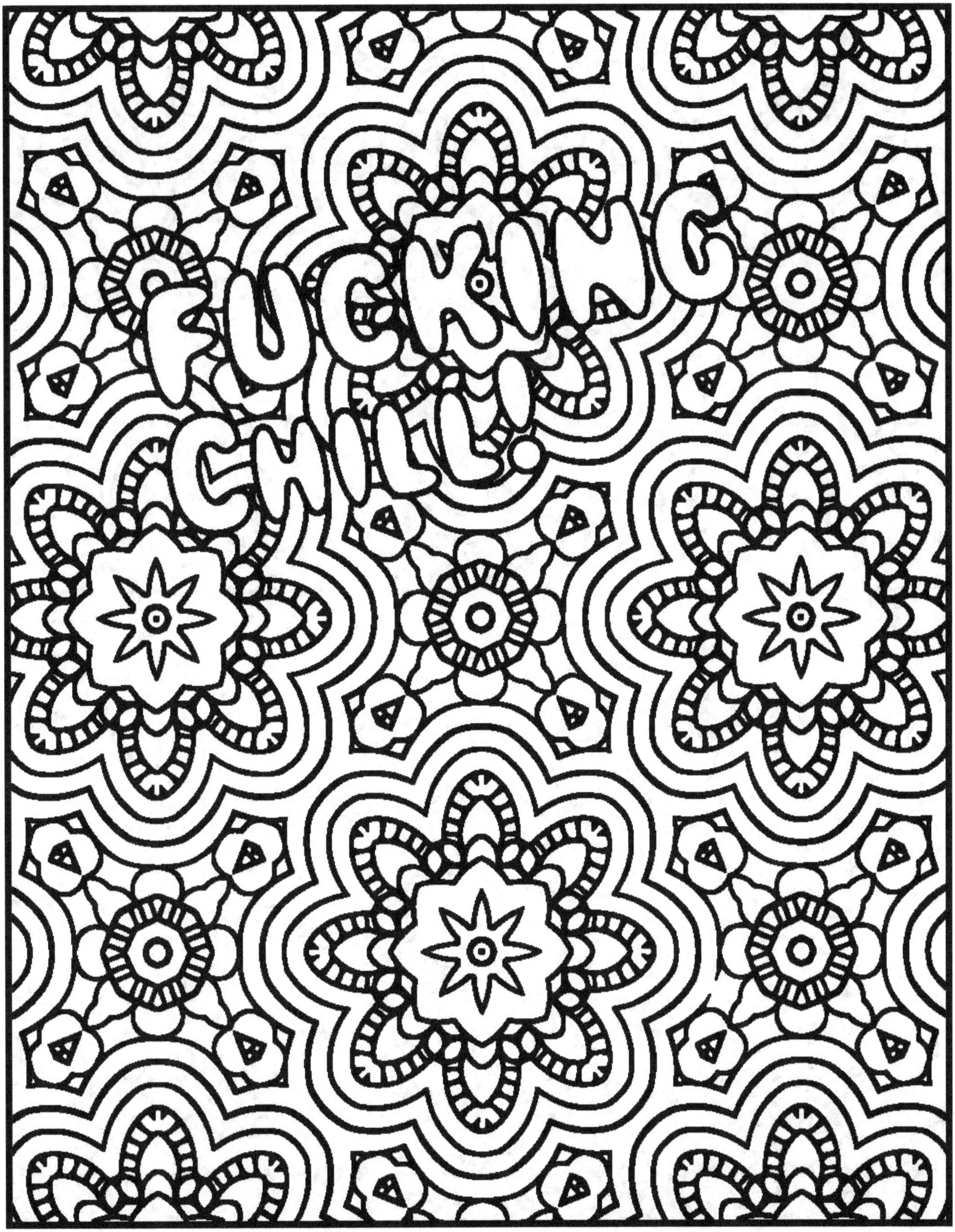
FUCKING
CHILL!

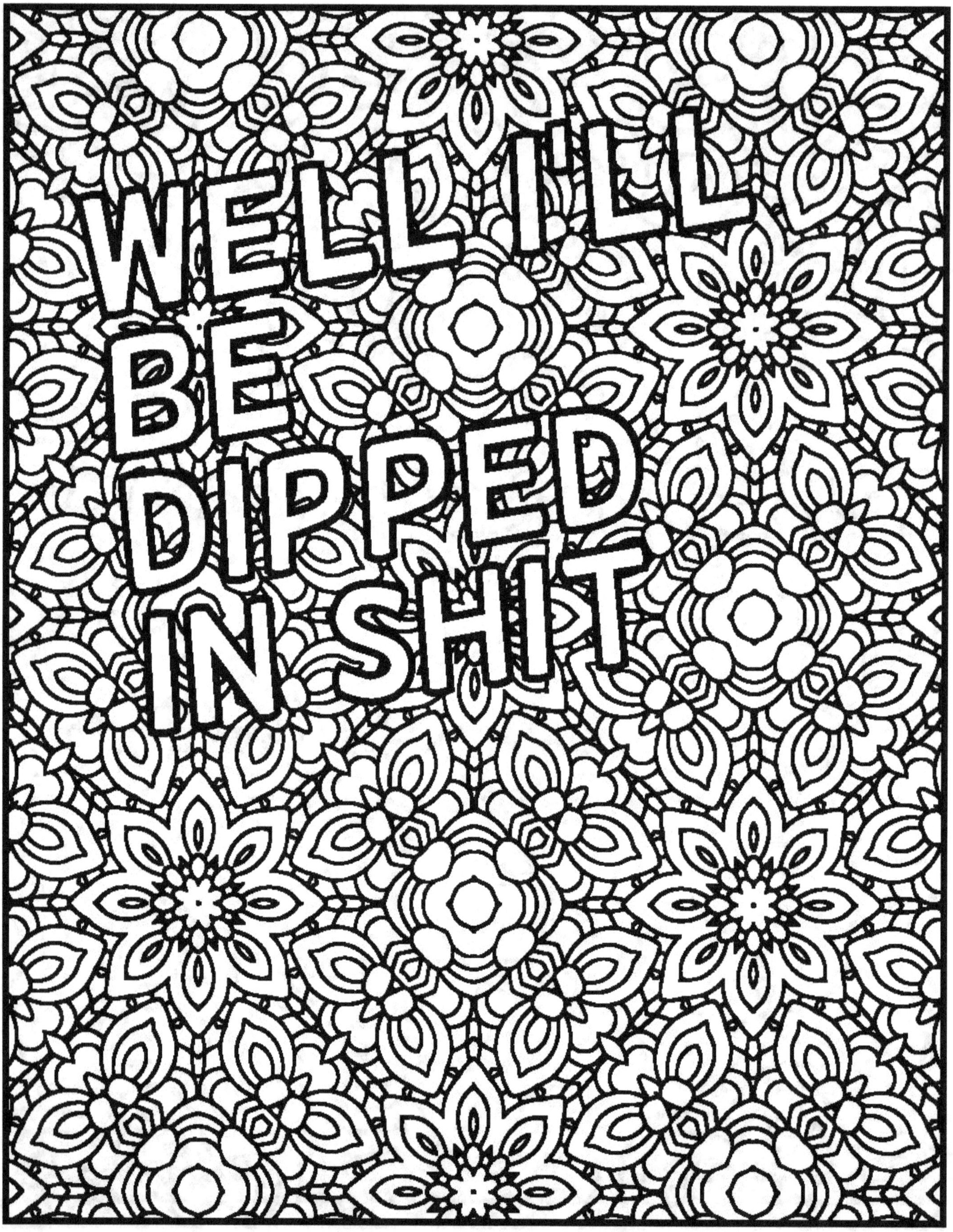
WELL I'LL
BE
DIPPED
IN SHIT

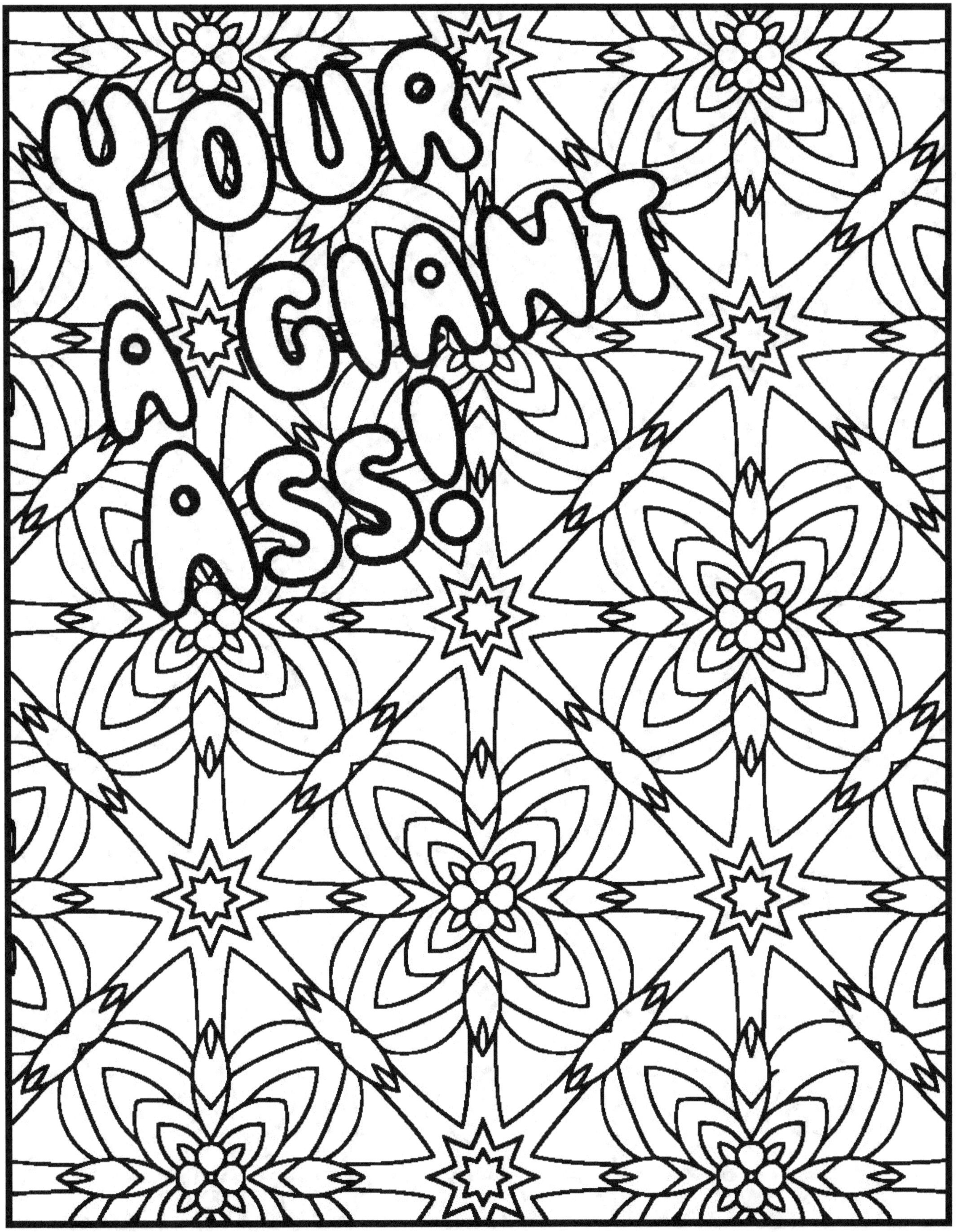
YOUR
A GIANT
ASS!

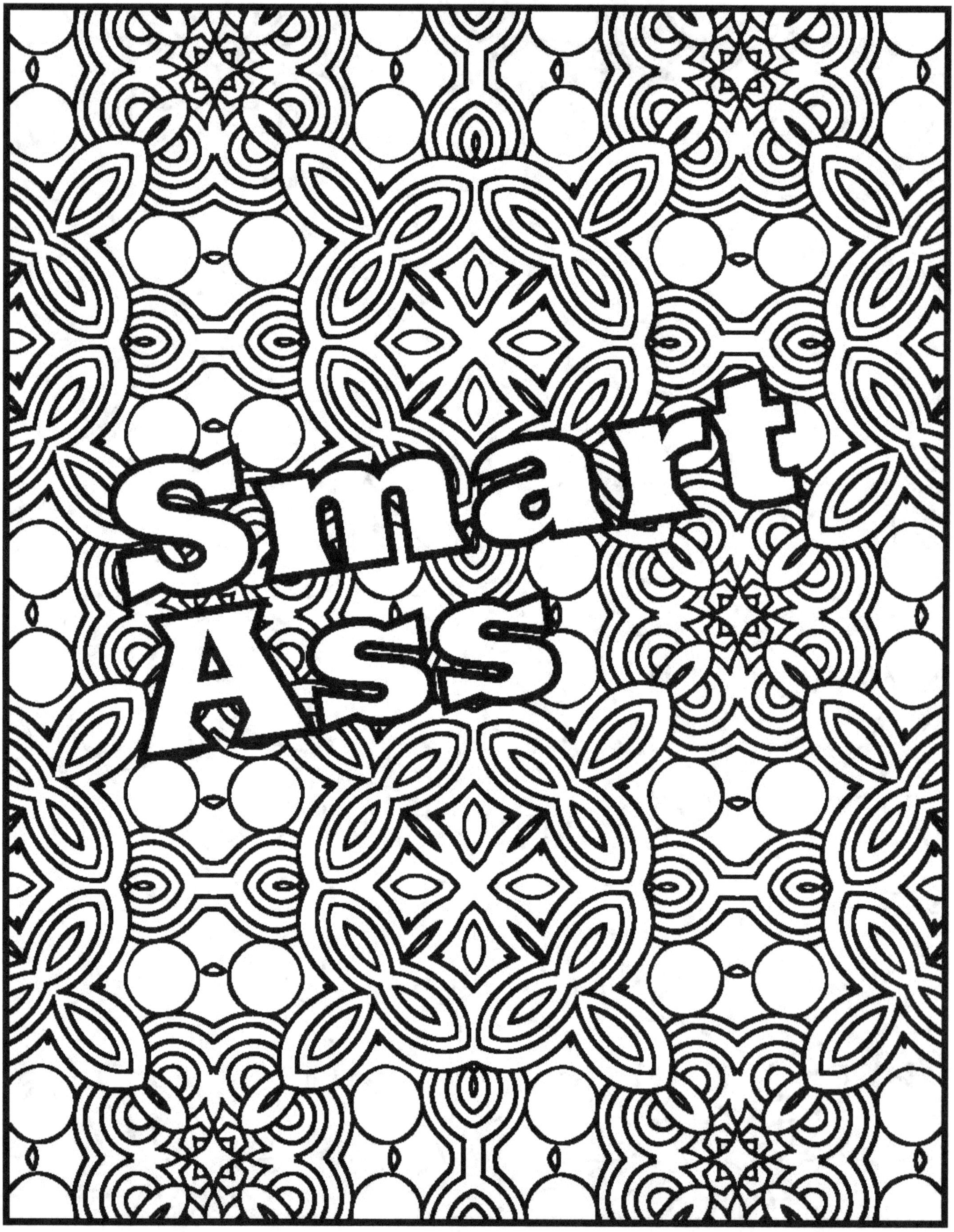
Smart
Ass

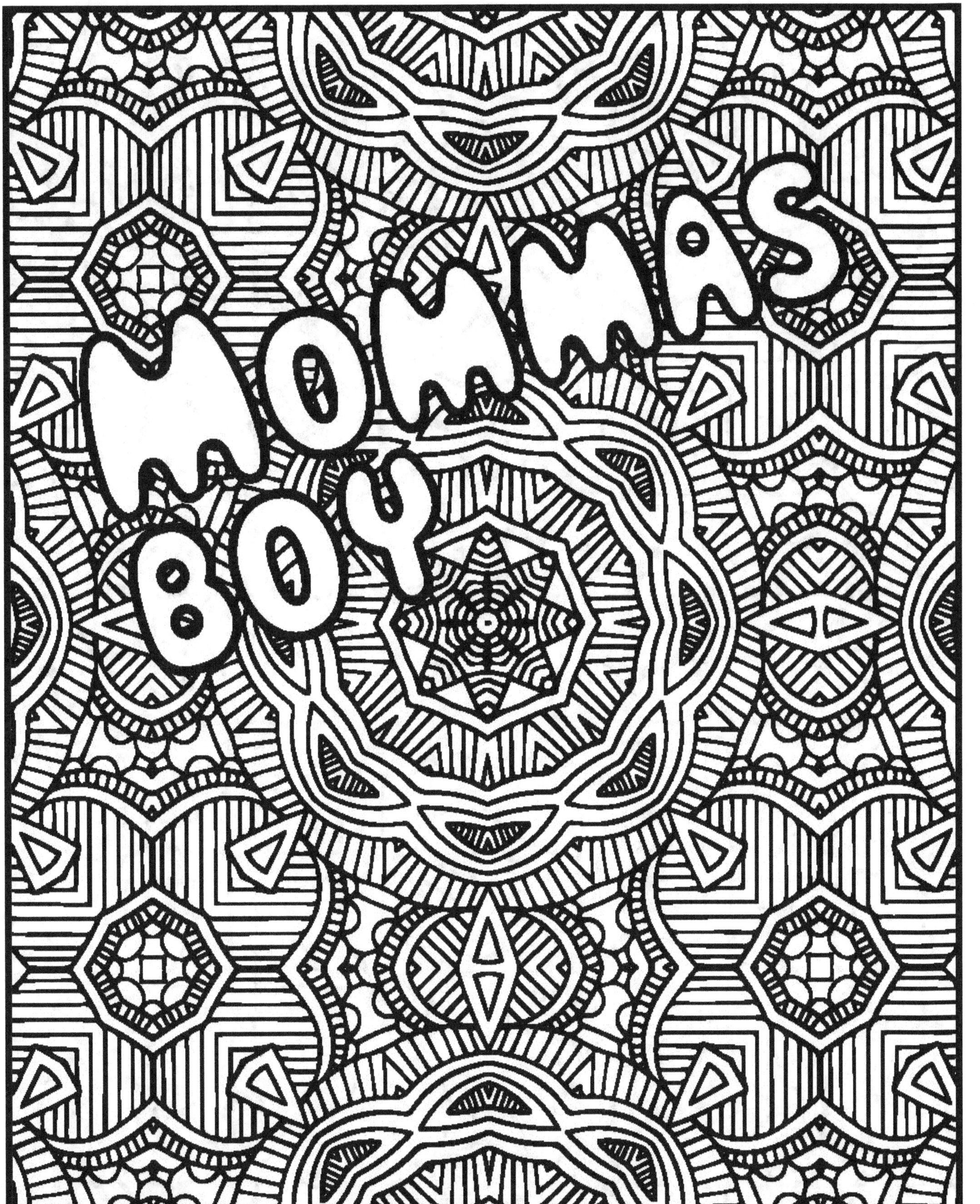
MOMMAS
BOY

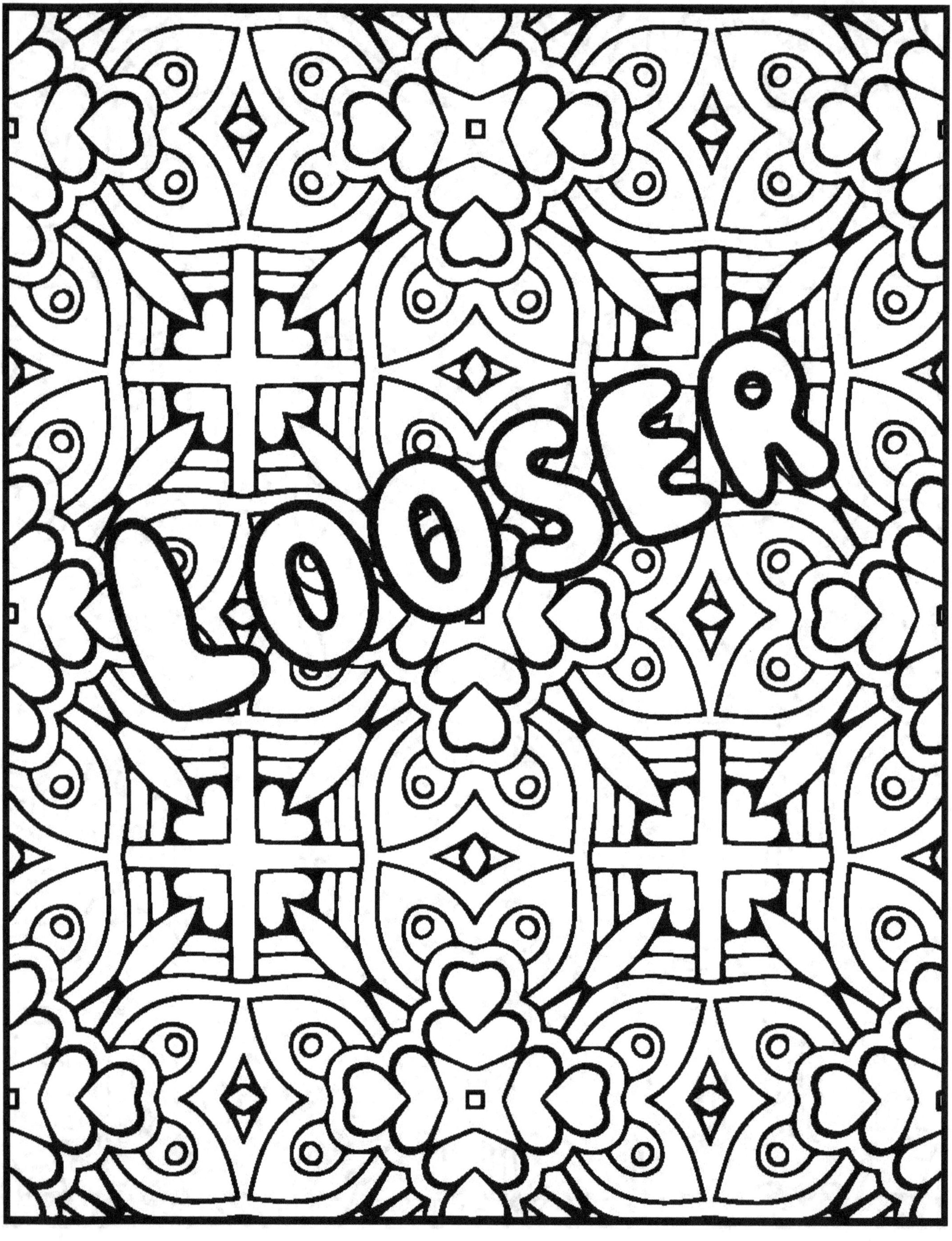
LOOSER

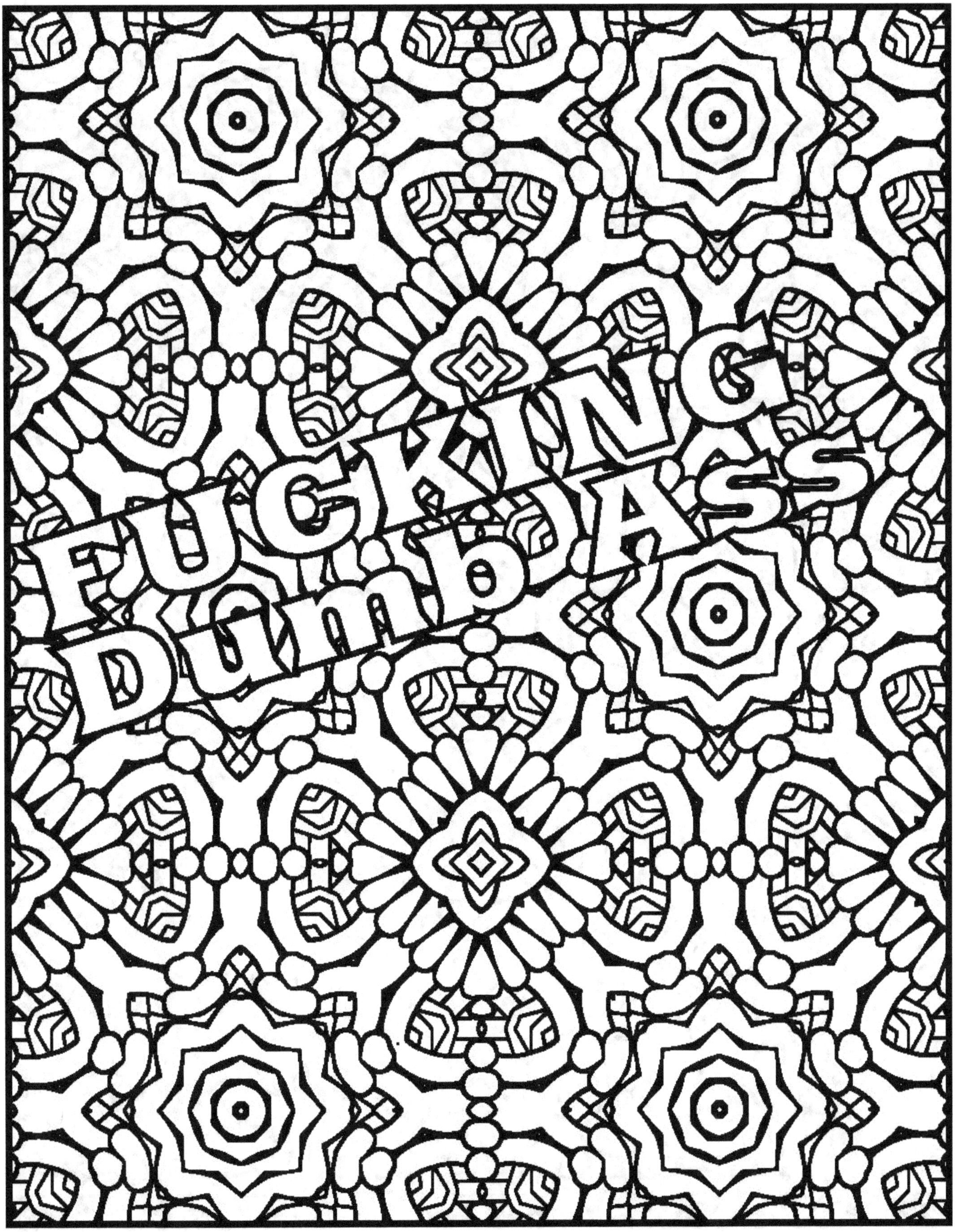
FUCKING
Dumb ASS

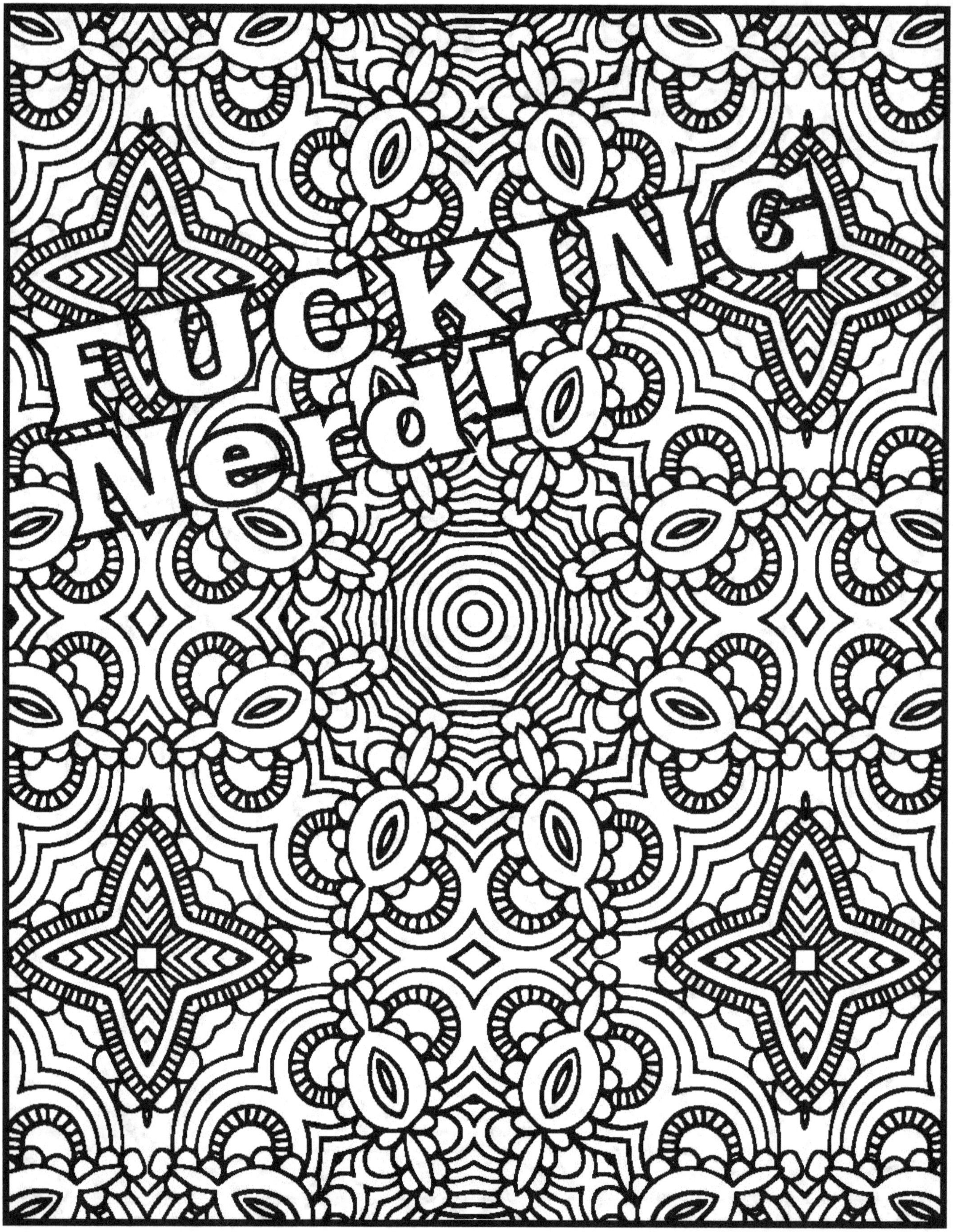
FUCKING
Nerd!

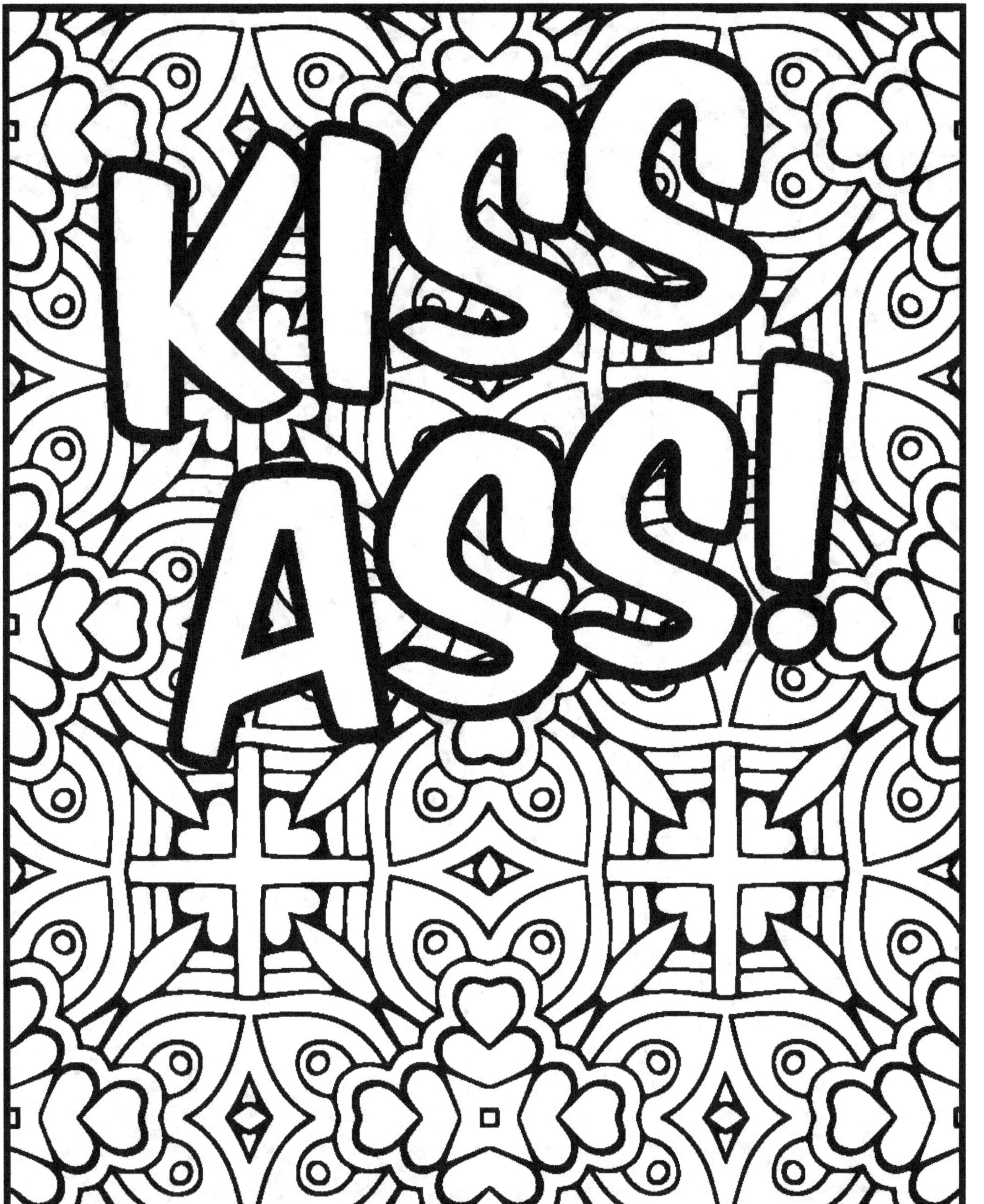
KISS
ASS!

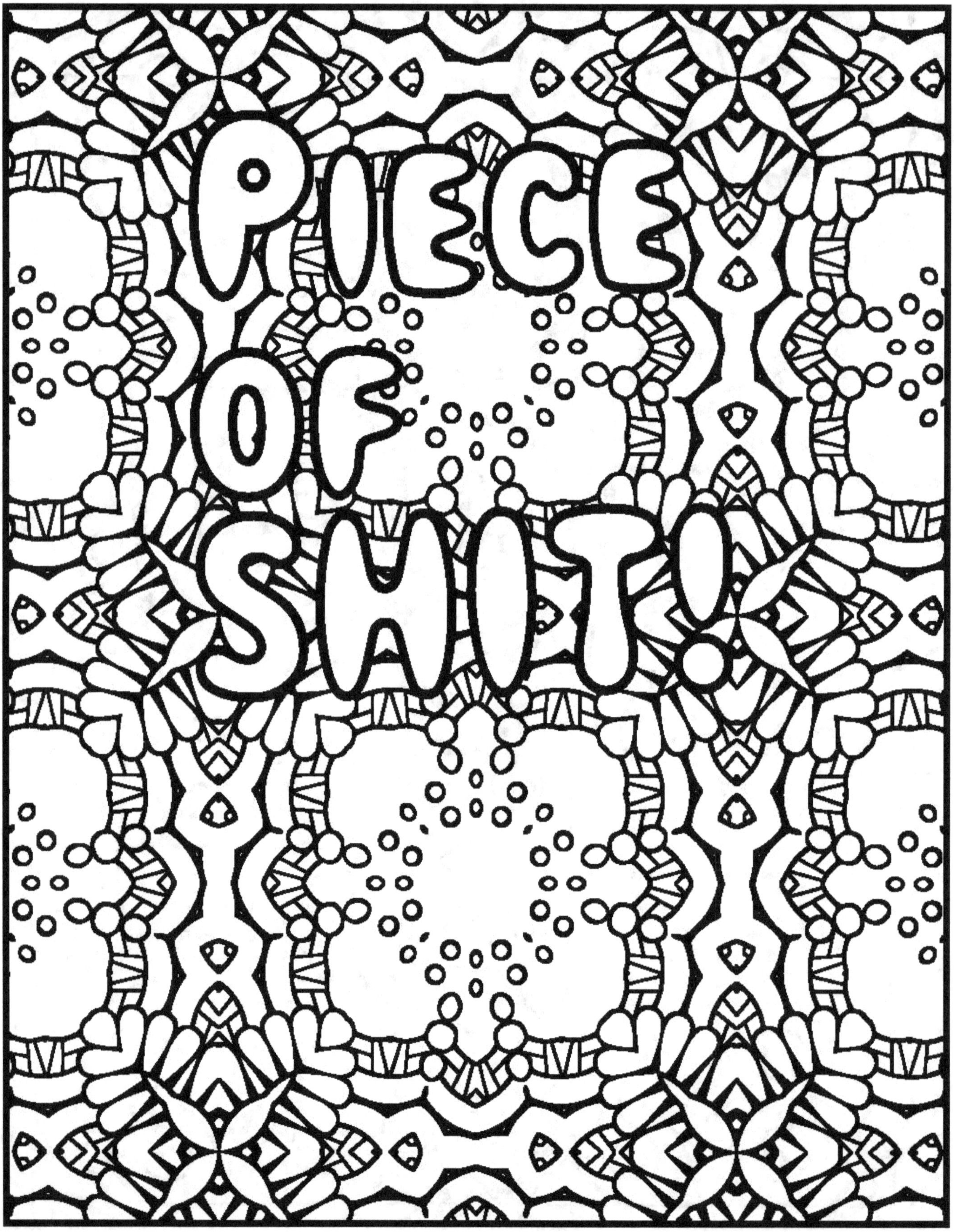
PIECE
OF
SHIT!

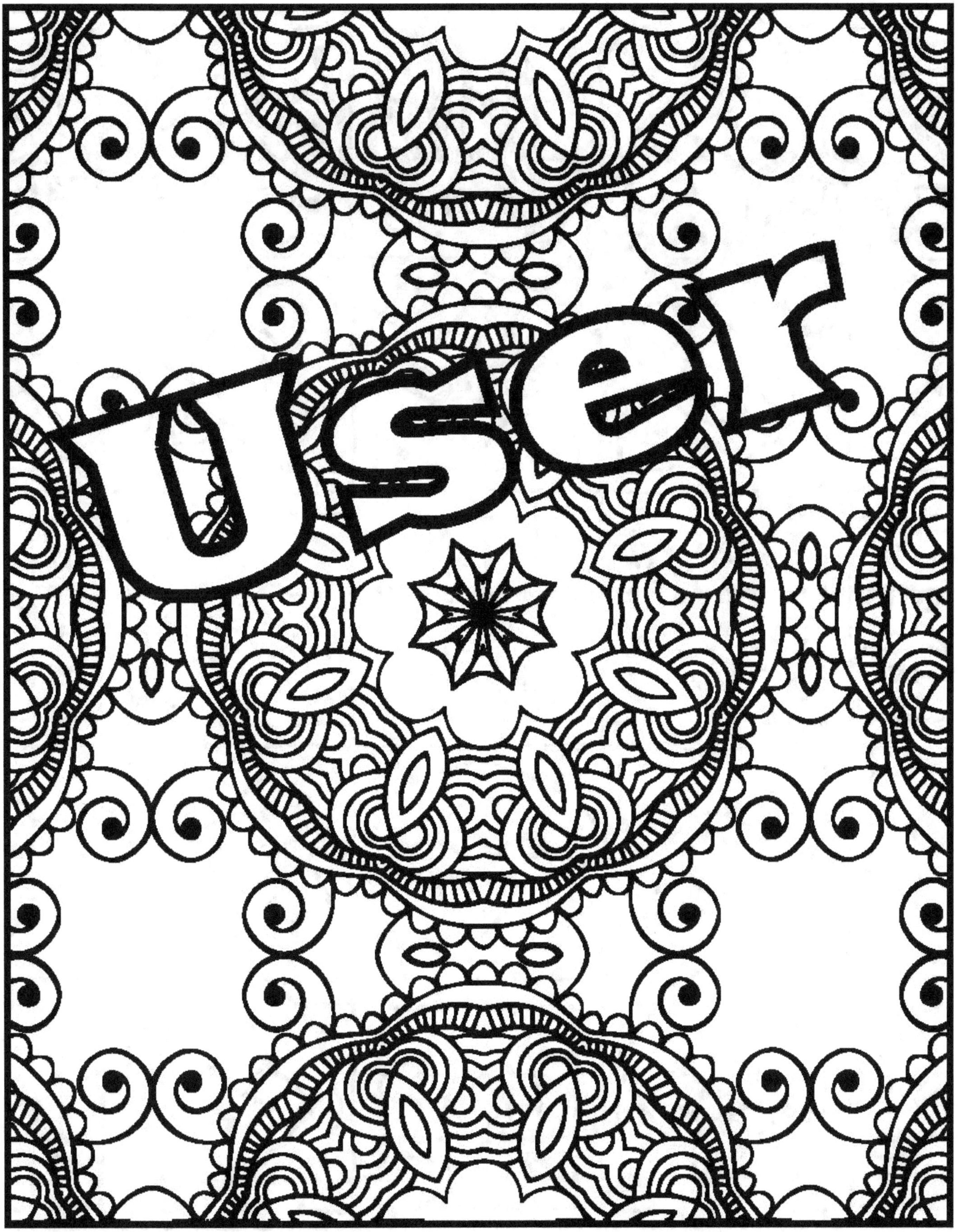
User

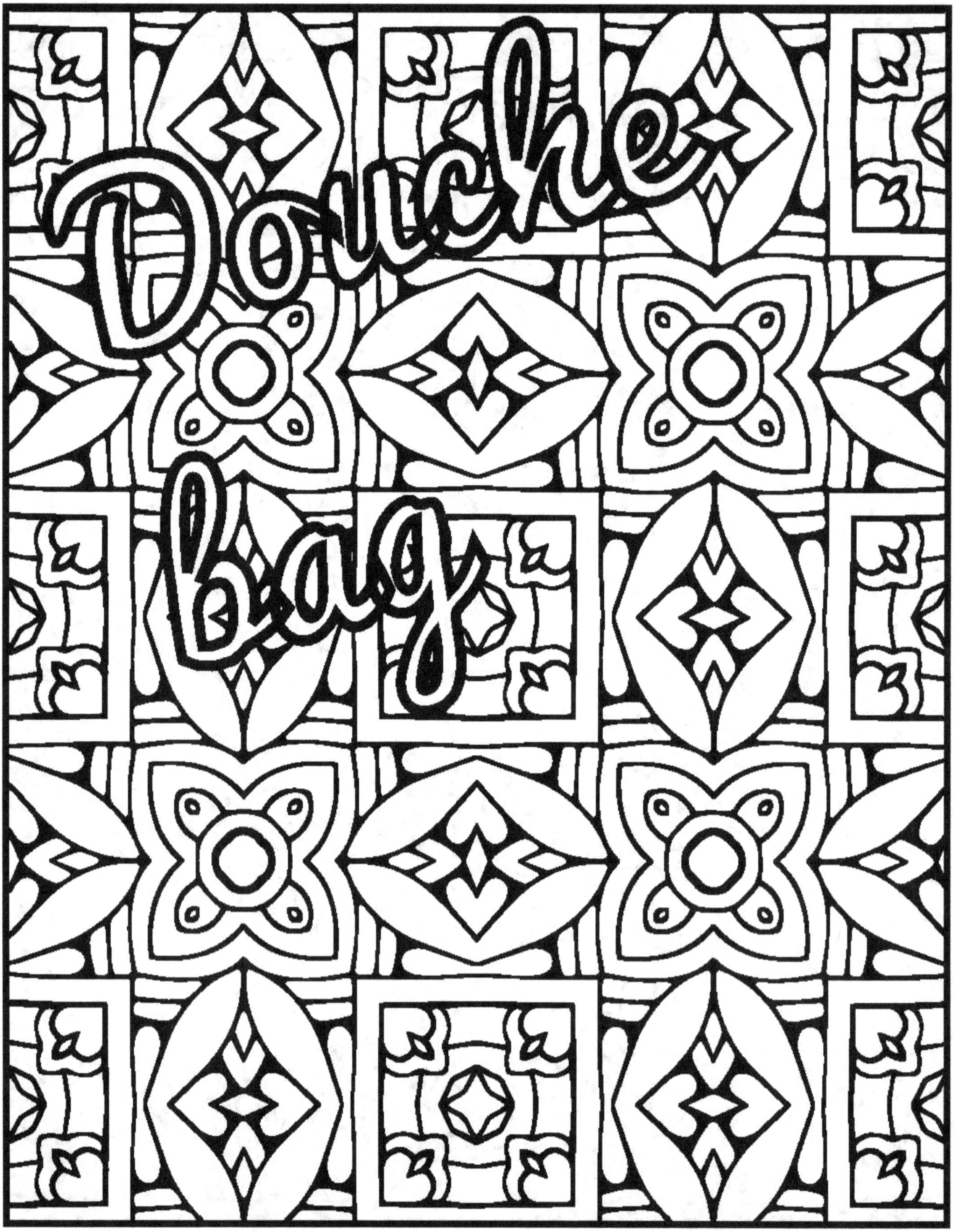
Douche
bag

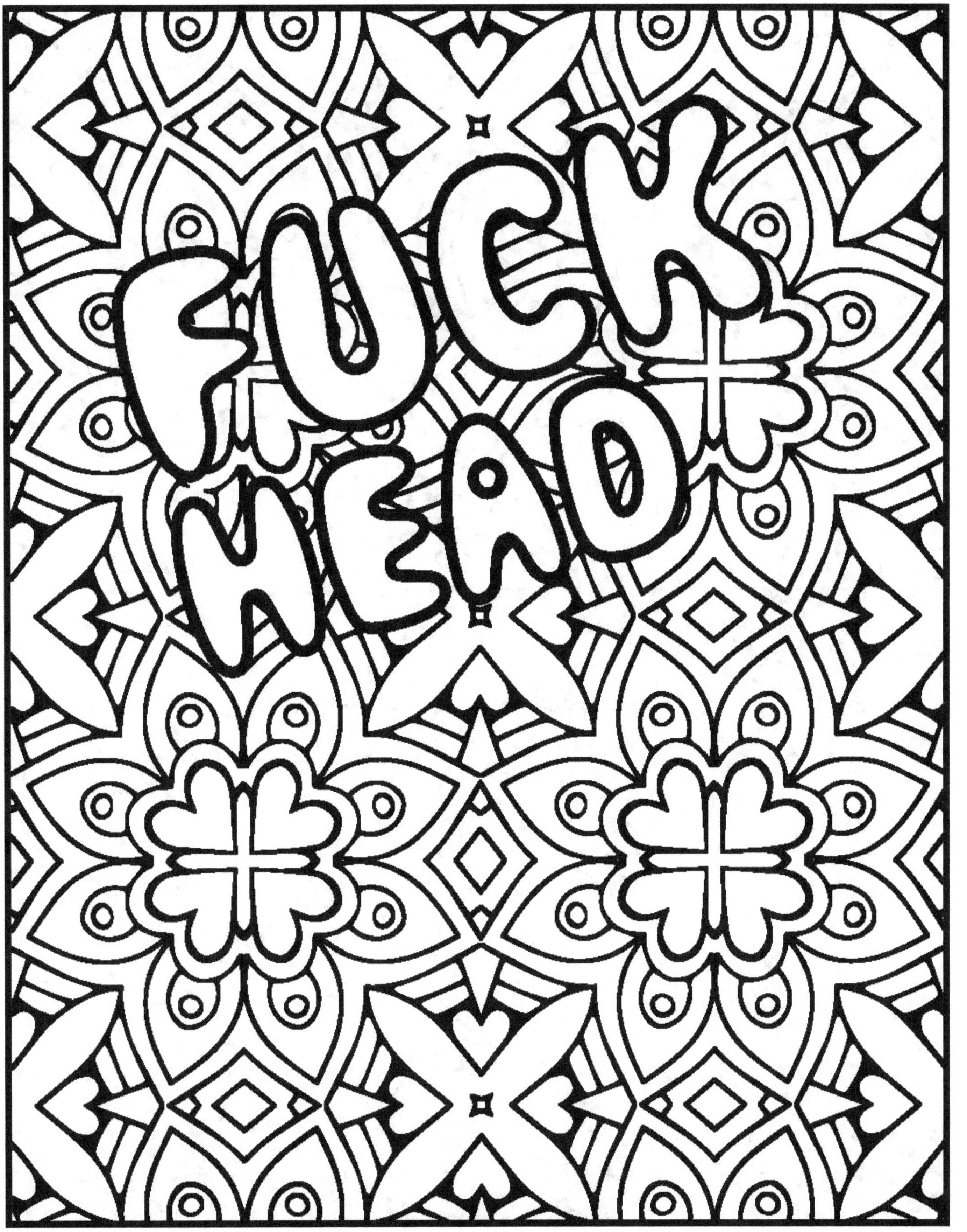
FUCK
HEAD

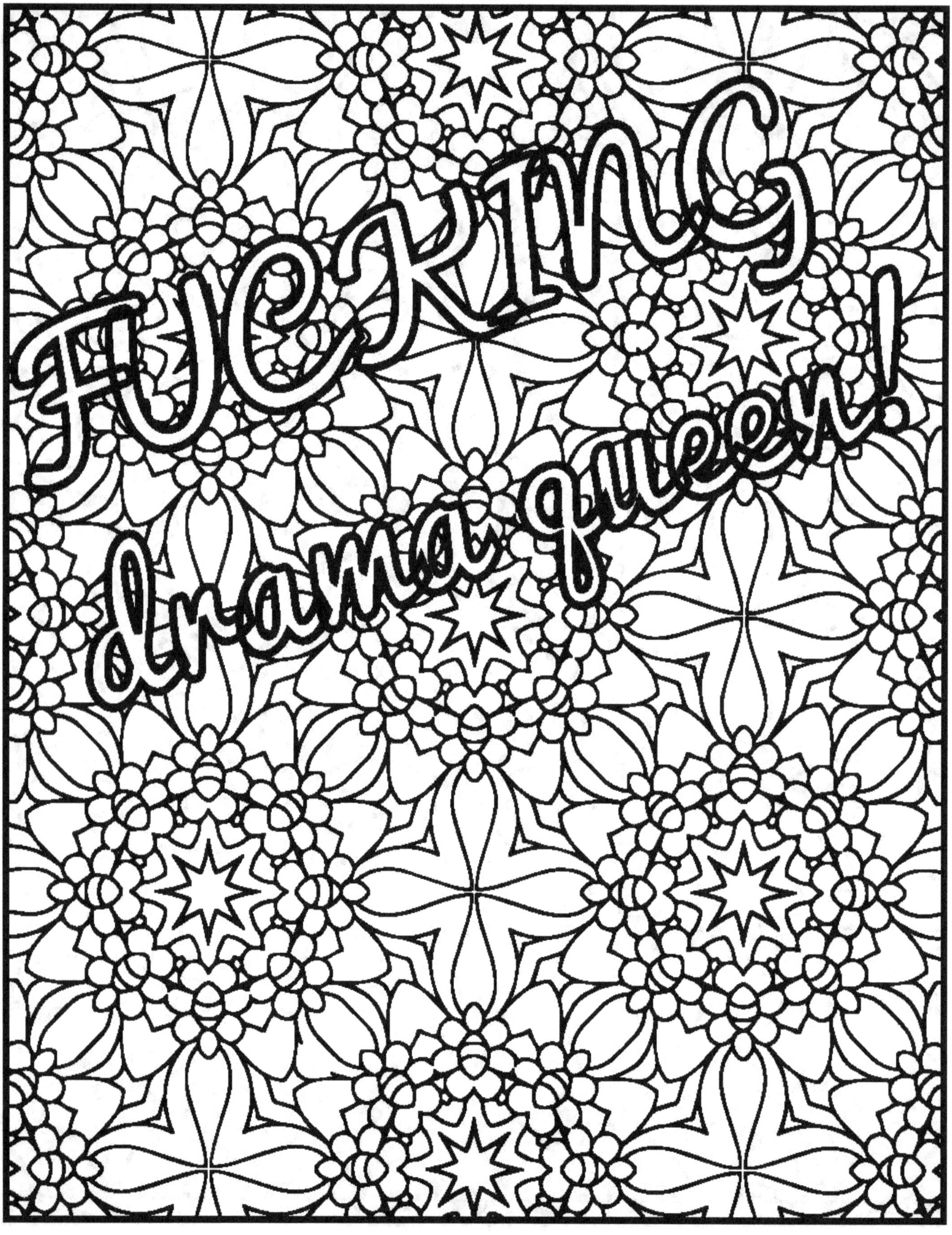
FUCKING
drama queen!

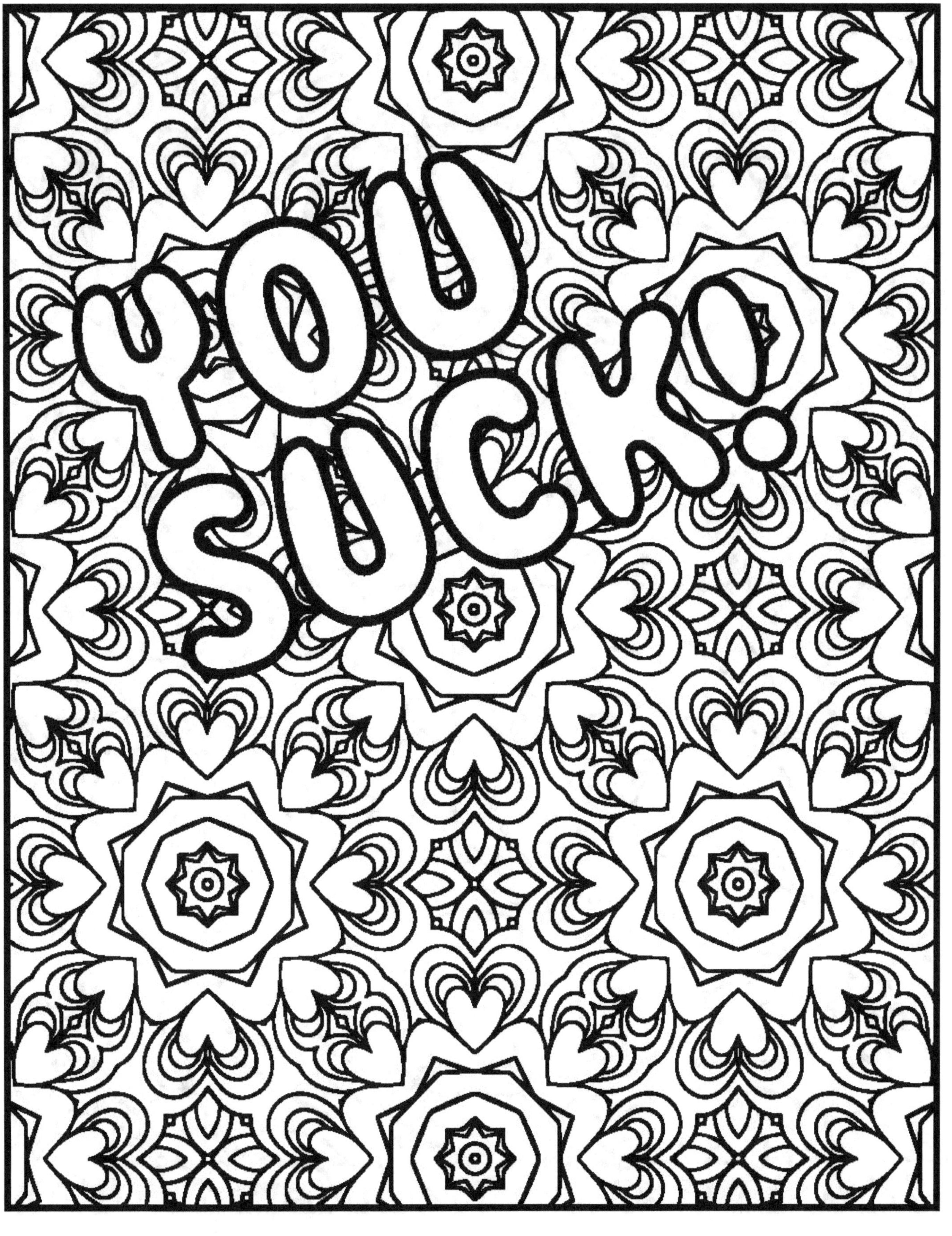
YOU
SUCK!

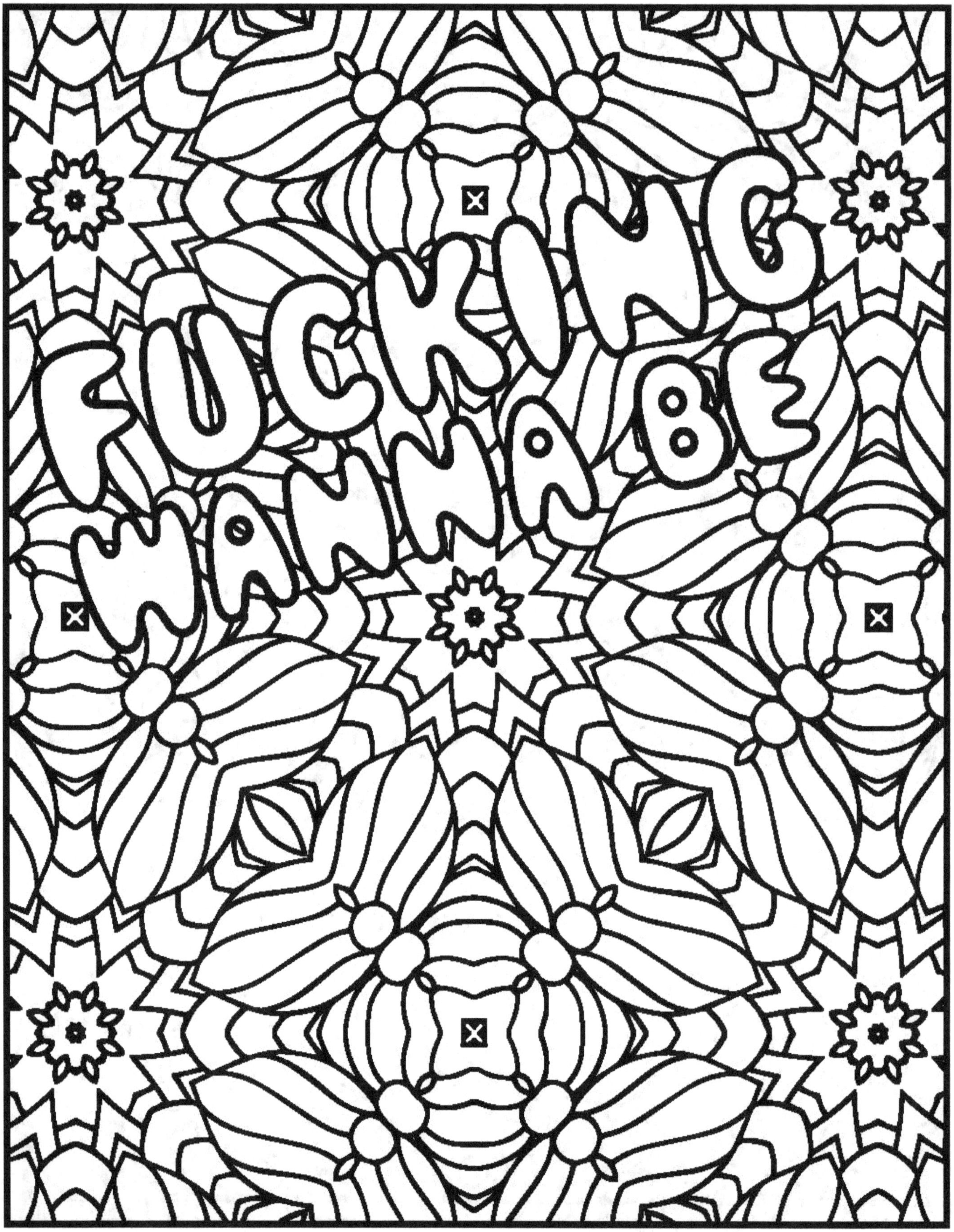
FUCKING
WANNABE

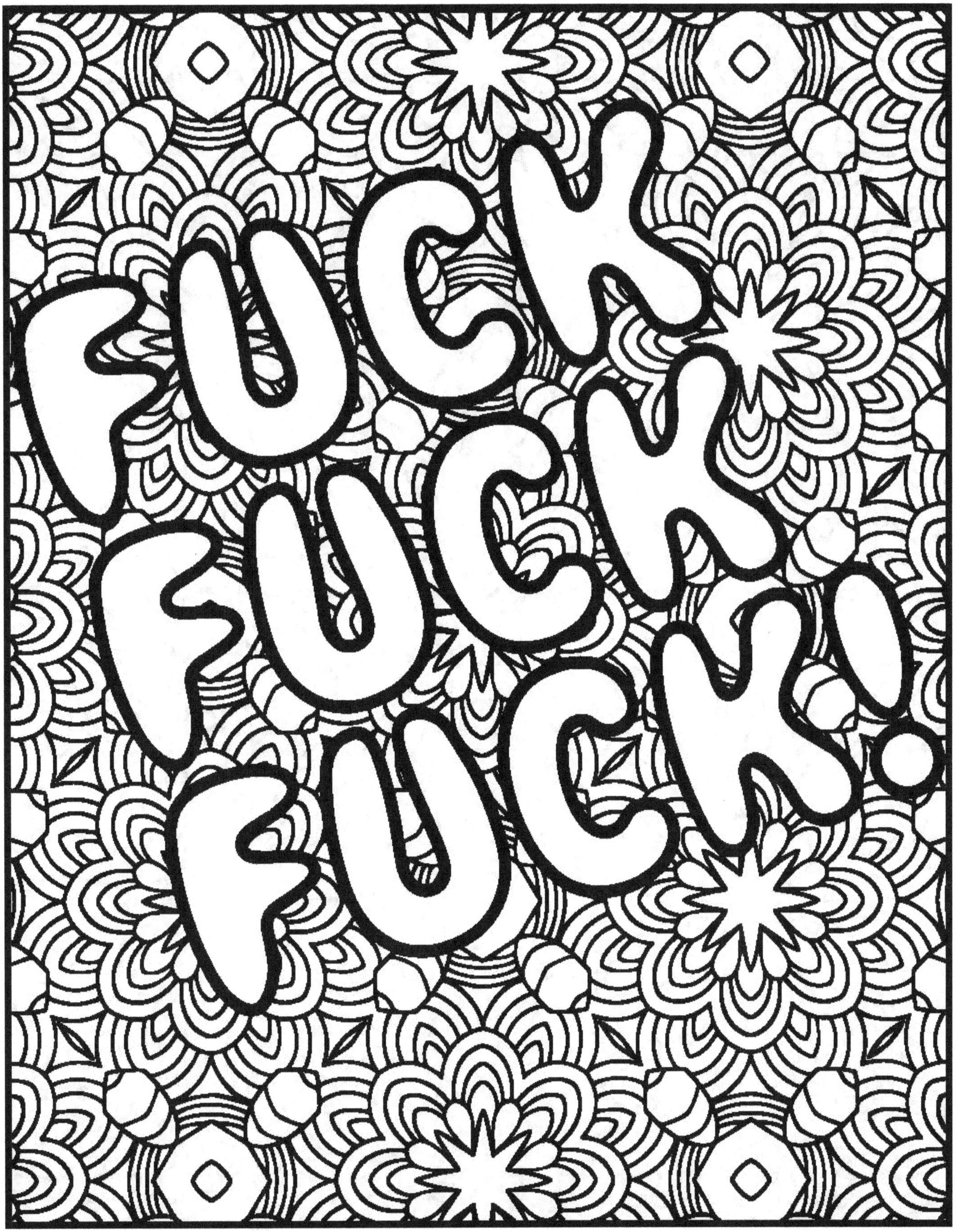
FUCK
FUCK
FUCK!!

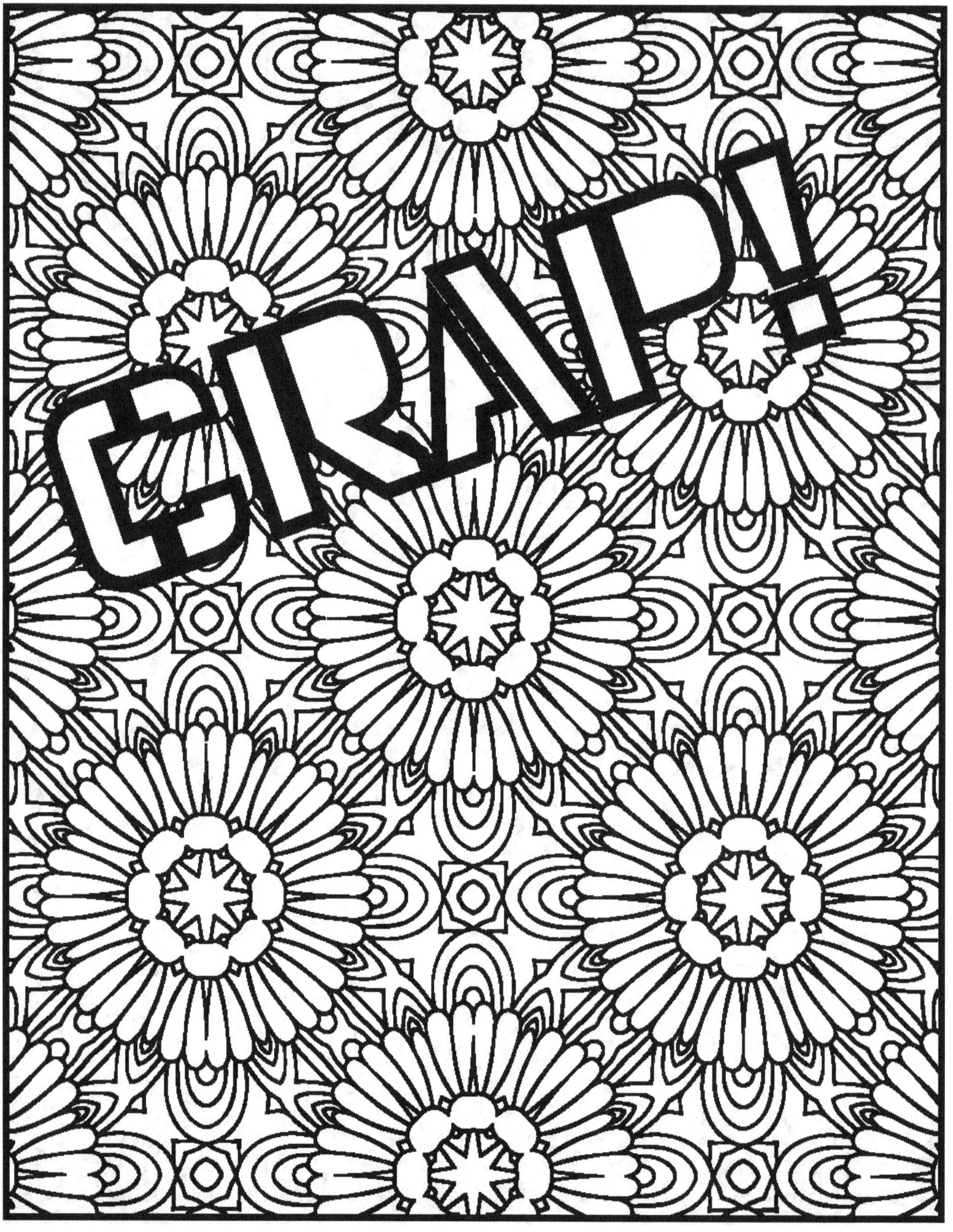
CRAP!

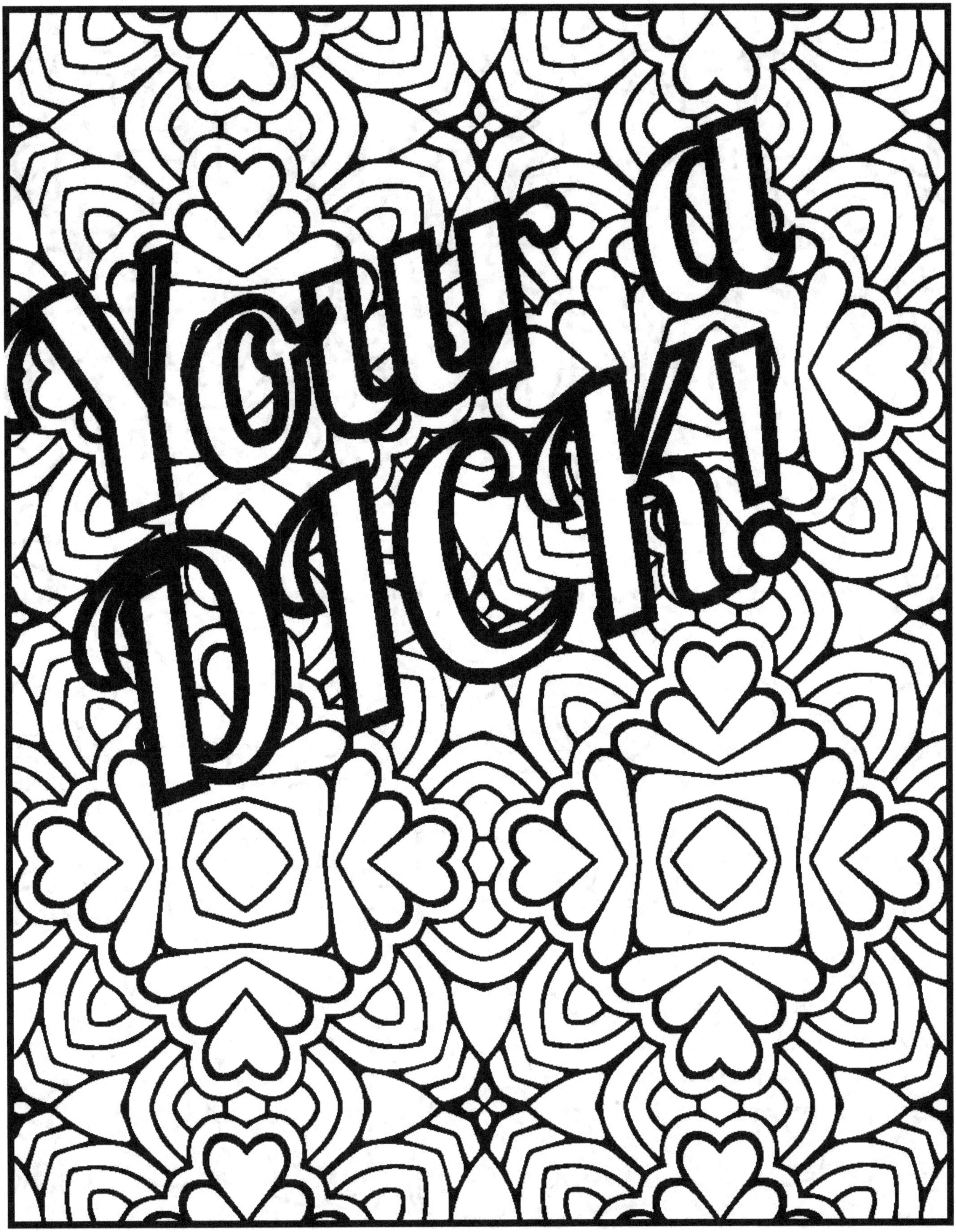
Your a
DICK!

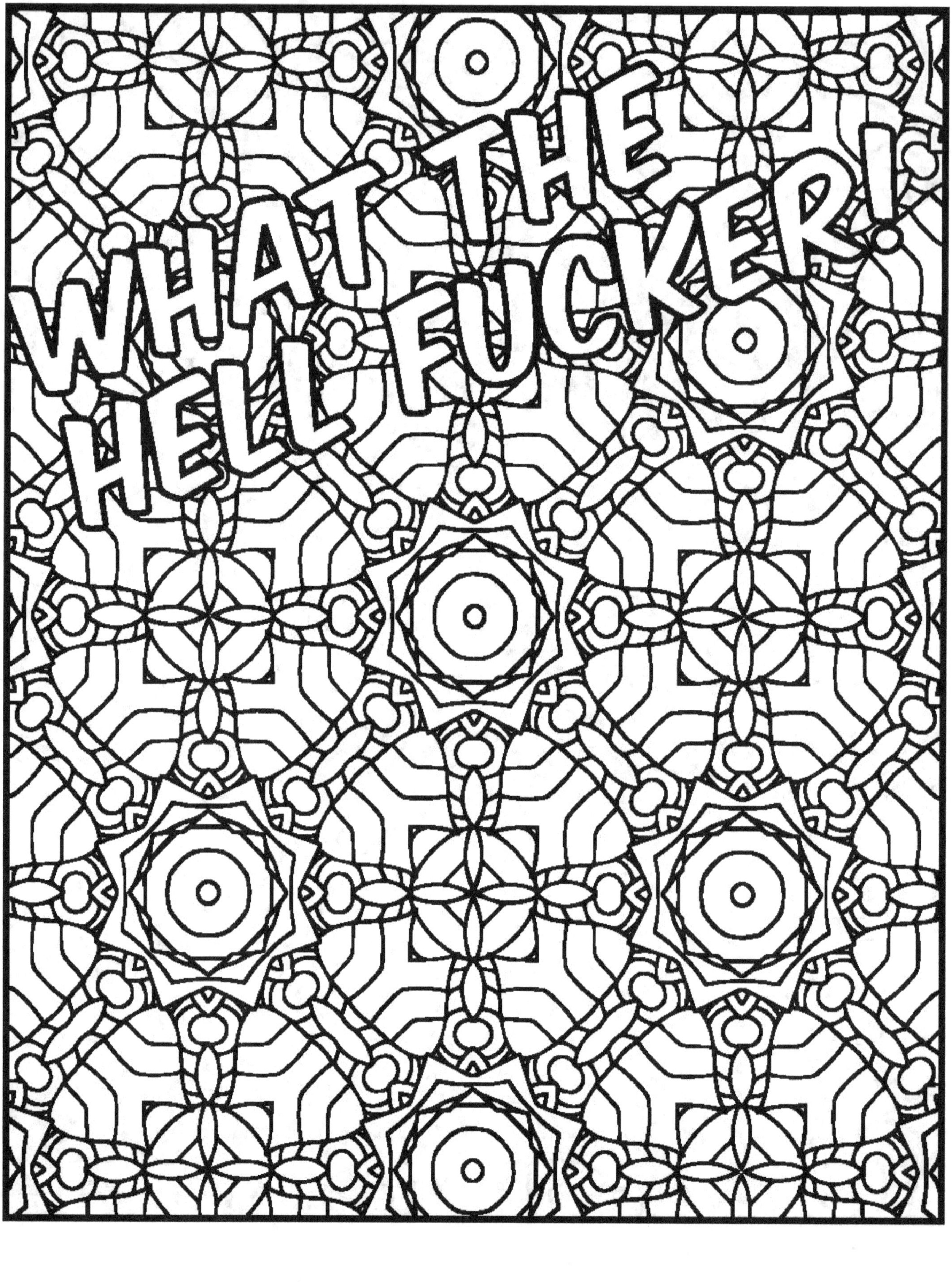
WHAT THE
HELL FUCKER!

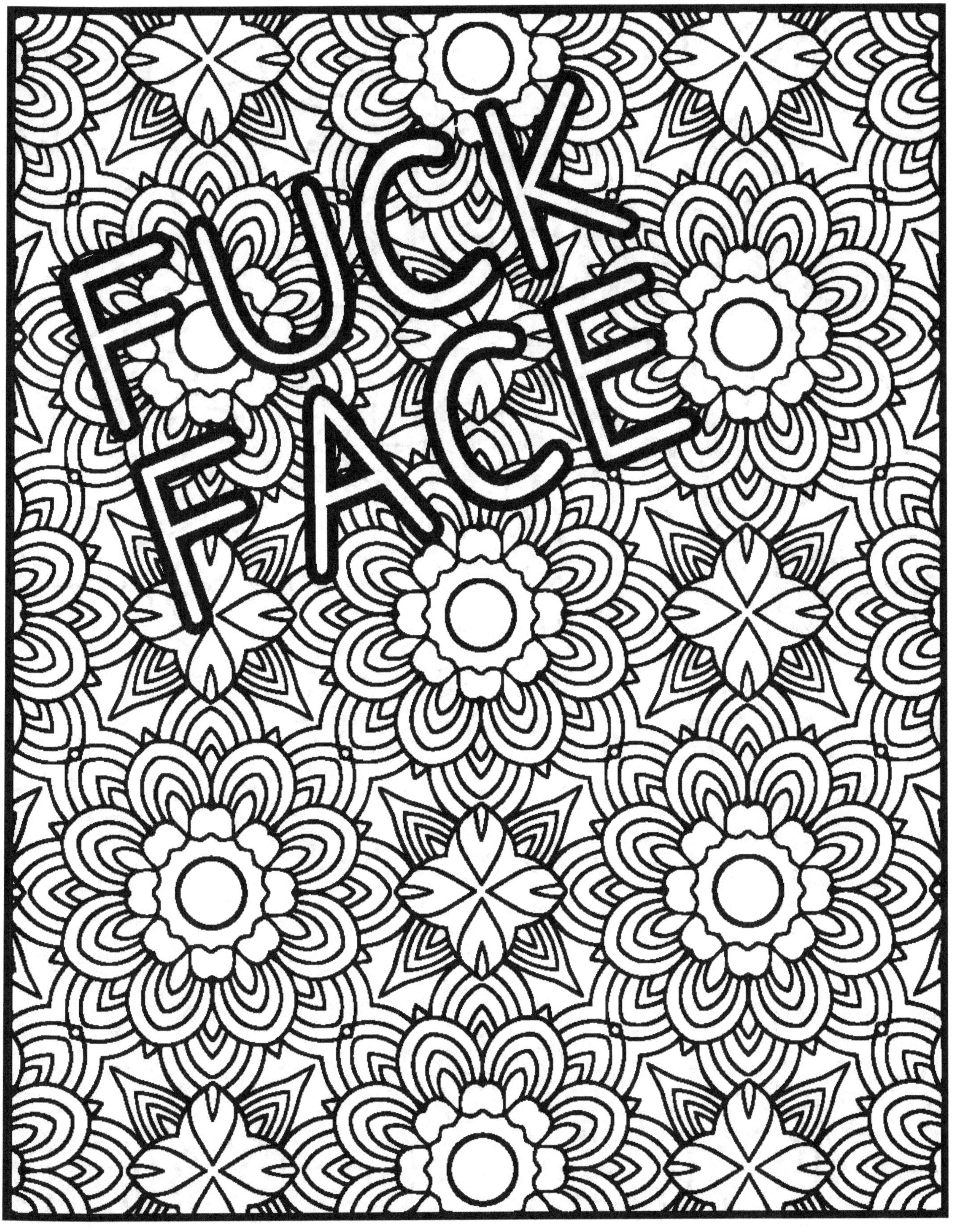
FUCK
FACE

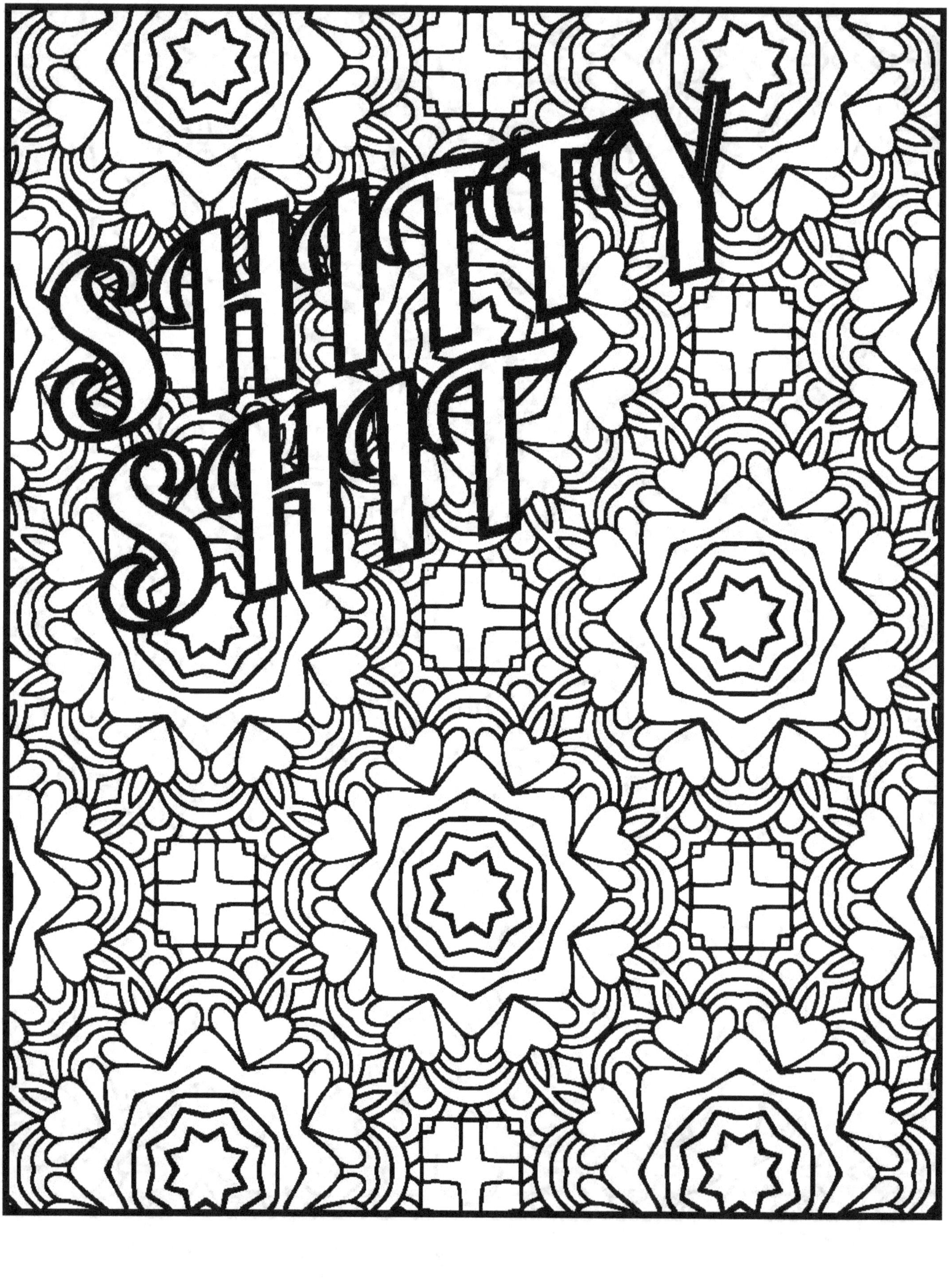
SHITTY
SHIT

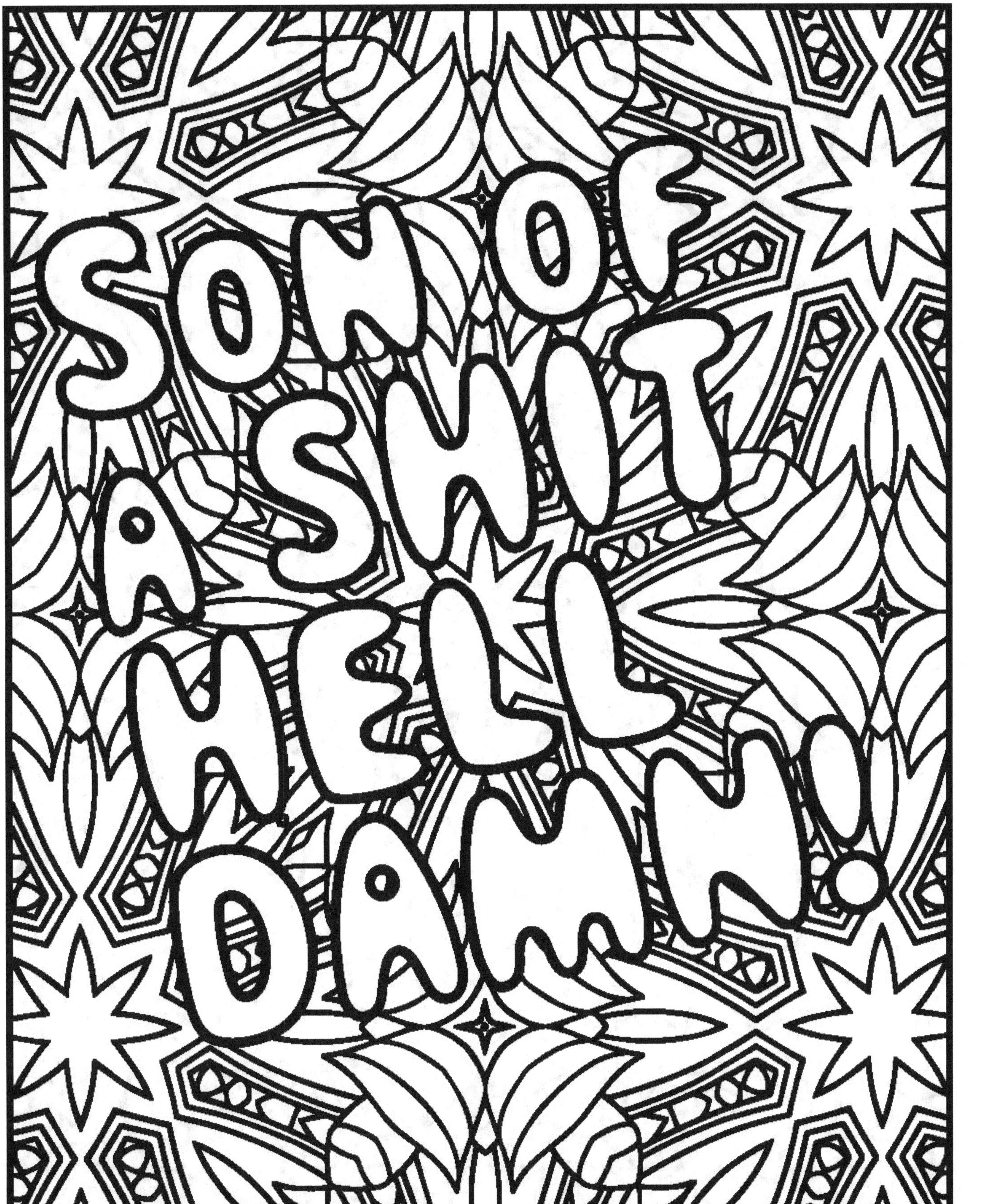
SON OF A SHIT HELL DAMN!!

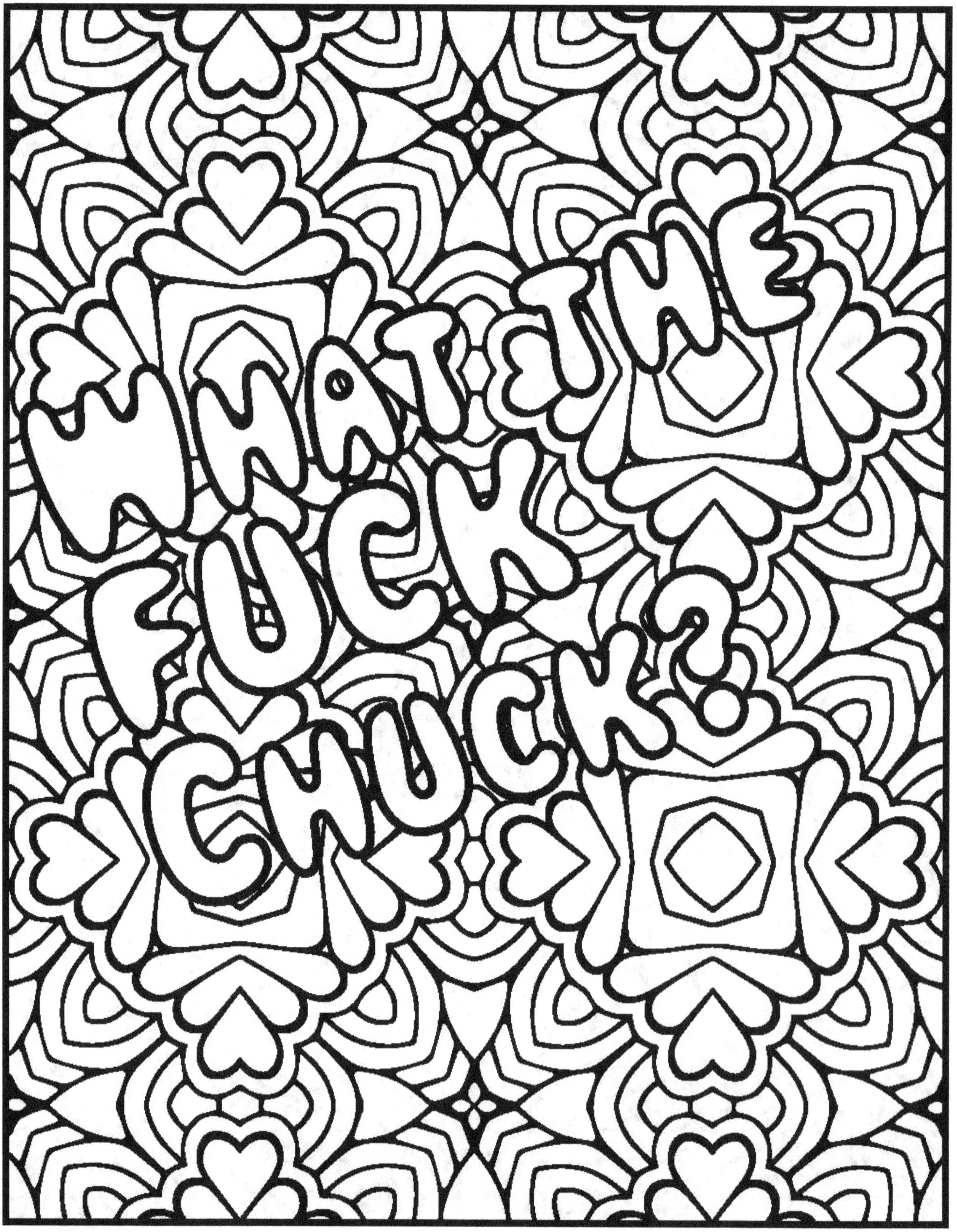
WHAT THE FUCK CHUCK?

www.ingramcontent.com/pod-product-compliance
Lightning Source LLC
Chambersburg PA
CBHW081520220526
45467CB00010B/2993
9798712401581